Uniquely Us

Relational joy is easily the most important factor in brain development. Joy is just as important for those with neurodiversity but the pathway to joy may be less flexible. When brains are misattuned, people become irritable and discouraged. Synchronicity matters! Dr. Holmes uses research and experience to provide the critical balancing factors that nurture a joyful and peaceful togetherness in neurodiverse couples and families.

Dr. E. James "Jim" Wilder, Ph.D, M.A.,
is a Neurotheologian and Life Model theoretician of Life Model Works; International speaker, author, and co-author of multiple books that intersect neuroscience and theology including but not limited to *Escaping Enemy Mode, Joy Starts Here,* and *The Other Half of Church.*

Uniquely Us is a must-read for clinicians, coaches, and those who live with love, and do life with someone who is Neurodivergent. Dr. Holmes and the contributing authors never whitewash the real struggle these couples face, including abuse, without losing hope that change can happen. The book is full of helpful research, best practices, and how-to's. My favorite part was the personal stories from the ND individuals who accepted their diagnosis and shared how they did their work to learn to become more loving and present people.

Leslie Vernick, MSW,
International speaker, relationship coach, and author of
The Emotionally Destructive Marriage and *How to Act Right When Your Spouse Acts Wrong.*

Dr. Stephanie Holmes, Dan, and contributing authors have crafted a masterfully edited text that not only conceptualizes the nature of autism but seeks to broaden perspective and create pathways of growth, knowledge, and healing for the self and couples. Research and techniques have traditionally centered around children and often present a singular self-focus of treatment, but the value of this text is the focus on adulthood and the marital realm, which makes this text a true gift to the world.

Dr. Kevin B. Hull, Ph.D., LMHC, RPT, CGP
is an Associate Professor and Faculty Advisor,
at the School of Behavioral Sciences at Liberty University.
He is the author of *Play Therapy & Asperger's Syndrome, Bridge Building,* and *Where There Is Despair, Hope.*

Dr. Stephanie and Rev. Dan Holmes are innovators in their pioneering work of understanding and bringing healing to NeuroDiverse Christian marriages. They bring a strong integration of neuroscience, Scripture, and practical wisdom to all of us. Their honesty about their own marriage journey is refreshing and brings hope. As a seasoned marriage therapist who has also worked with individuals on the autism spectrum (ASD Level 1) for the past 20 years, I have learned a great deal by reading this book. I immediately began applying their wisdom to the couples and individuals that I see in my clinical practice. Couples and clinicians alike will be blessed by this book.

Dr. W. Jesse Gill, Psy.D., Licensed Psychologist
is also the author of *Face to Face: Seven Keys to a Secure Marriage.*

Uniquely Us asks and answers critically important questions on the intersection of faith and neurodiverse marriages. It is not unusual for legalistic and rigid misunderstandings about Scripture to make a dysfunctional marriage even more difficult and for there to be harm as a result when it results in a spouse being deprived of effective tools to deal with the problems in a healthy way. This is magnified in neurodiverse Christian marriages where the AS/ND partner interprets Scriptures and teachings in an even more literal, black-and-white, inflexible, and rule-based way that increases the likelihood of abuse. I highly recommend this book to anyone who offers advice to ND/NT couples and to those who are in a neurodiverse marriage.

Karla Downing, M.A., LMFT
is the author of *10 Lifesaving Principles for Women in Difficult Marriages*
and founder of ChangeMyRelationship.com

Pastors and Christian mental health professionals are too often ill-prepared to provide counseling, spiritual care, and support to neurodiverse families who are coming to church in increasing numbers through the efforts of rapidly proliferating inclusion ministries. Dr. Stephanie Holmes and Rev. Dan Holmes have been uniquely positioned through their academic training, professional calling, and lived experience to serve as exceptional resources to the Christian community as we come alongside couples navigating the challenges of neurodiverse marriages. They blend practical wisdom with evidence-based practice to provide invaluable insight for Christians with autism and their spouses to thrive in their marriages while living out their faith.

Stephen Grcevich, M.D.
is President and Founder of Key Ministry, and author of
Mental Health and the Church: A Ministry Handbook for Including Children and Adults
with ADHD, Anxiety, Mood Disorders and Other Common Mental Health Conditions.

Dr. Stephanie Holmes and her husband Dan have been leading the way in the field of neurodiversity in marriage and family for years! This book is a "must-have" resource for all who provide counseling, coaching, or guidance to spouses and couples even if neurodiversity such as autism or ADHD has never been formally diagnosed. Clinicians and clergy have little to no education and training in understanding and recognizing neurodiversity and how marriages are impacted by partners' differences from one another. Differences in spoken and non-verbal language, how sensation is experienced and processed, how problems are solved, and the purpose of rules and routines are but a few of the relationship challenges that can be misinterpreted by clinicians and clergy. I have worked with countless partners and couples who have been unintentionally harmed by the guidance of providers who did not know about neurodiversity. This book provides paramount insight into the world of a neurodiverse couple!

Jodi Carlton, M.Ed.
Is the founder of the "YOUR Neurodiverse Relationship" podcast.
She uses her own neurodiverse family and relationship experiences
as a personal training ground for her understanding of neurodiversity
in relationships as well as recently becoming aware
of her own neurodivergence (ADHD).

Uniquely US

Gracefully Navigating the Maze of Neurodiverse Marriage

Autism • Marriage • Faith

REV. DR. STEPHANIE C. HOLMES
and REV. DAN HOLMES, MS

WITH CONTRIBUTING AUTHORS

NEW YORK

LONDON • NASHVILLE • MELBOURNE • VANCOUVER

Uniquely Us

Gracefully Navigating the Maze of Neurodiverse Marriage, Autism and Faith

Published in New York, New York, by Morgan James Publishing. Morgan James is a trademark of Morgan James, LLC. www.MorganJamesPublishing.com

Proudly distributed by Publishers Group West®

Morgan James BOGO™

A **FREE** ebook edition is available for you or a friend with the purchase of this print book.

CLEARLY SIGN YOUR NAME ABOVE

Instructions to claim your free ebook edition:
1. Visit MorganJamesBOGO.com
2. Sign your name CLEARLY in the space above
3. Complete the form and submit a photo of this entire page
4. You or your friend can download the ebook to your preferred device

ISBN 9781636985435 paperback
ISBN 9781636985442 ebook
Library of Congress Control Number:
2024941721

Cover Design by:
Callie Revell

Interior Design by:
Christopher Kirk
www.GFSstudio.com

Morgan James is a proud partner of Habitat for Humanity Peninsula and Greater Williamsburg. Partners in building since 2006.

Get involved today! Visit: www.morgan-james-publishing.com/giving-back

Acknowledgments & Dedication

First, we want to acknowledge and thank every participant in our 2023 survey and those who participated in the interview process to provide the research for both published academic articles and this book. We also want to thank individuals who sent in personal stories motivated by the hope of helping providers and pastors better understand and serve neurodiverse relationships.

Next, we thank each contributing author who was stretched to put their expertise and knowledge into a book chapter. We know this was a labor of love for the population we all serve or have served. An additional acknowledgment to Barbara Grant, who poured many hours into copy editing this book.

We are humbled and grateful for the endorsements of which not all could fit in the first few pages of this book. We appreciate your encouragement.

Our understanding of what was previously called Asperger's Syndrome, which led to our daughter being diagnosed at a young age, was greatly influenced, and shaped by the pioneering book on Asperger's Syndrome written by Dr. Tony Attwood. It is an honor that you wrote the foreword for us, Dr. Tony! Your pioneering research positively impacted our family!

Thank you MorganJames for believing in this book!

Finally, we are most thankful for our relationship with Jesus and the hope we have in Him for our future! Without a marriage centered and anchored in Jesus, we are not sure we would be where we are now, *Gracefully Navigating the Maze* of Our Neurodiverse Marriage!

$\mathcal{C}ontents$

Foreword

BY PROFESSOR TONY ATTWOOD

Autism has many qualities that can appeal to a potential partner. These include an intense passion for their interests, speaking their mind, being honest, and having a strong sense of social justice. There can also be technical or artistic abilities, good career prospects, and personality characteristics such as being kind and socially naive. Both partners may have shared interests, a sense of humour, and Christian values and recognise characteristics they are familiar with in a parent. This leads to a sense of familiarity and a natural ability to connect.

Some couples share autistic characteristics, if not a formal diagnosis, in terms of preferring solitary rather than social pursuits, preference for routines and consistency, intense interests and sensory sensitivity. They may have both experienced peer rejection at school and have a deep mutual empathy for each other's past social and emotional experiences. They feel more comfortable with someone who does not have great social expectations.

The early stages of dating may not indicate to either partner the long-term relationship issues associated with autism. The autistic partner may have initially camouflaged and suppressed their autistic characteristics to be more attractive to a non-autistic partner. They may have acquired a dating 'script' from watching romantic movies and created a 'mask' or artificial persona. However, eventually, the mask is removed, and it becomes apparent that the autistic partner has difficulty with the intuitive understanding of how to maintain a long-term relationship. Gradually, some of the characteristics of autism can cause distress and conflict in the relationship, such as difficulty reading social cues, expressing feelings, the frequency of social experiences, emotion regulation and repair, expression of love and affection, intimacy, communication, conflict management and household responsibilities.

In modern Western society, we have replaced the word husband or wife with the word partner. This reflects changing attitudes towards long-term relationships. There is an expectation of sharing the workload at home, doing domestic chores and caring for the children, and being each other's best friend regarding the disclosure of thoughts and feelings, reciprocal conversation, sharing experiences, and emotional support. Taking on the role of a best friend is not easy for an autistic partner to achieve due to their lifelong difficulties in making and maintaining friendships.

Conventional relationship counselling needs to be adapted to accommodate the profile of abilities and history of interpersonal experiences of an autistic partner. *Uniquely Us* explains the adaptations based on the authors' extensive relationship counselling expertise and contribution to the research literature. Their new book covers, in some depth, aspects of a neurodiverse relationship that may only be superficially explored in other publications, such as abuse in the relationship, neuroplasticity, Executive Function and religious beliefs. The latest theoretical models of autism are clearly explained and applied to aspects of everyday life for a neurodiverse couple and illustrated by quotations from partners whom the authors have interviewed. When reading *Uniquely Us,* there will be many 'light bulb' moments for both partners in a neurodiverse relationship and relationship counsellors.

Section 1

Research and Basic Understanding
of Adult Autism and
Neurodiverse Marriage

Introduction:
What is Neurodiversity?
What Autism Is and Is Not

REV. DR. STEPHANIE C. HOLMES

When my husband, Dan, and I attend conferences, whether as speakers, sponsors, or running a booth, we have found that many do not understand the term, "neurodiversity." At Christian-sponsored events, we have found that even fewer people understand what this means. It never fails that, at first, people will sidestep our booth or read the title and walk away. On the second day, a curious person will walk up when the room is quiet and ask, "I have been meaning to ask, what is neurodiversity?"

There are many thoughts and definitions about neurodiversity. Some are so broad that they include nearly half of what is in the current Diagnostic and Statistical Manual of Mental Disorders (*DSM-5*)[1]; however I like the definition presented by Harvard Health Publishing[2]: the authors stated that the word neurodiversity refers to types of brain neurology and wiring that are different from the typical population, and most often includes autism spectrum disorder (ASD), attention deficit hyperactivity disorder (ADHD), learning differences or disabilities and other developmental differences, difficulties, delays and divergencies[2]. Because the term "neurodiversity" can have a broader meaning, for this book we intend it to apply to autism (ASD) or ADHD.

The most inclusive way to view the autism spectrum is to include definitions of autism from previous diagnostic manuals, which may have featured terms like "Pervasive Disorders, Not Otherwise Specified" (PDDNOS), "High Functioning Autism" (HFA), "Asperger's Syndrome" (AS), "Rhett's Syndrome" or "Tourette's Syndrome"[3,4]. ASD is seen as a broad spectrum of developmental challenges that cause the individual to have challenges or differences socially, relationally, and behaviorally as well as sensory processing differences, restricted or repetitive behaviors, and various executive function challenges [1,5]. It is important to include these broader terms because in previous editions of the *DSM*, a clinician could not co-diagnose ADHD and autism, so they had to choose one or the other. PDDNOS was often a placeholder for autism or ADHD. When we work with adults who are neurodivergent, I encourage those diagnosed with ADHD or PDD-NOS before 2013 to consider if their neurodivergence could also include the autism spectrum.

In an interview with autism researcher Emily Rubin, Murphy[6] shared Rubin's definition of autism: She sees it as a neurological difference that makes it difficult for the person to predict the actions of others, as well as one that compromises their ability to cope with social expectations and to emotionally regulate or make transitions in less predictable environments. Autism researchers observe that individuals on the autism spectrum struggle with Theory of Mind (ToM), recognizing emotions, and executive function (which includes organizing, planning, prioritizing, mental flexibility, self-awareness, evaluating social impact, and accessing working memory). Stitcher[7] cites research describing ToM as the inability to understand the intentions and thoughts of others as well as understanding that others can have different perspectives. This can include the inability or misreading of non-verbal communication, such as facial expressions, gestures, or inflections in tone. This may cause the autistic individual to miss aspects or nuances of social communication. When people think of autism, they often recall the movie *Rain Man* and envision emotional dysregulation (sometimes referred to as meltdowns), strict adherence to routines, and passionate "special" interests that are not age-appropriate.

The current *DSM-5*[1] describes autism as a spectrum with severity levels ranging from 1 to 3. Level 1 is associated with what was previously called Asperger's Syndrome in the *DSM-IV*[3,4] or high functioning autism (HFA). The two broadest categories of diagnostic criteria for ASD are listed as social communication differences and difficulties, and repetitive behaviors or routines. Autism Level 1 means the person requires little to some support in these areas. Autism Level 2 requires moderate to substantial support, and Autism Level 3 requires very substantial support. Most individuals who have been seen as counseling or coaching clients by the contributing authors of this book would fall into Autism Level 1;

most would not have required support in school, so unless there were substantial behavior issues that disrupted their individual learning or the classroom, they likely would not have been diagnosed. In my practice, some clients are Level 2, but this level of severity was not discovered until the individual had challenges maintaining a job, or they married and then struggled to share in the emotional and relational load of daily family life.

Because autism is categorized as a *developmental* delay or disorder, many incorrectly believe this is a childhood diagnosis, and that somehow the individual may grow out of it, or their brain development may simply catch up. When I was in graduate school in the 1990s (shortly after the *DSM-IV* was released), the professor predicted that we would rarely see someone with Asperger's come to counseling, and we would certainly not encounter anyone on the spectrum who was married with children, because autistic people simply prefer to live in solitude. When I talk with colleagues who were in graduate school at the same time or earlier than I, we discuss another feature of the older *DSMs*, referred to as the GAF (Global Assessment of Functioning). This is how the GAF was given: in a diagnostic interview, the clinician would give a GAF score of 1 to 100 based on their subjective opinion of how much the disorder or mental health issue affected the person's day-to-day life. The GAF score was comprised of the initial interview with the client, a review of their medical records, and a self-assessment of their ability to function (provided by the client). That was it: a self-assessment of functioning and the clinician's view of how much the suspected diagnosis impaired the individual's daily life. Seldom did this include information given about the client's marriage or consider input from others who lived with the client and observed their daily functioning. To many clinicians, being able to have a job or career meant the person did not have a GAF low enough to receive a diagnosis. So even if the clinician observed autism spectrum traits, if they believed the individual's life was not severely impacted, they probably did not make an autism diagnosis. This is still one of the most common reasons adults on the autism spectrum give for not receiving a diagnosis: they are thought to be successful at a career and too intelligent.

It is important to add to this autism discussion that autism and intelligence are two different issues. One's intelligence, whether the IQ score is low or high, is not a determinant of an autism diagnosis. When someone receives an autism diagnosis and a full psychological evaluation is conducted, the clinician may note whether scores of any IQ tests showed cognitive impairment or perhaps giftedness or exceptional intelligence. However, impaired cognitive function or low IQ is a separate and compounding or co-occurring issue distinct from autism.

Finally, it is important to understand that autism is not a spiritual issue. It is a neurological wiring difference which will be discussed further in later chapters. A lady named

Jane (who was advising someone married to a man on the autism spectrum) made the following (unfortunate) comment in a blog:

> *Autism is caused by a spirit, and it can be cast out through prayer and fasting (KJV). The NIV leaves out fasting but that is important. This has been effective with children with autism...I don't know a lot about adults with level 1 Asperger's/autism. There is often other unrepentant sin coupled with autism, so deliverance of commanding the spirit to come out - naming it by name - pornography, lust, and pride, etc., works. Most of the spirits were cast out through commanding them by name in Jesus Christ's name. Some, like autism, only come out through prayer and fasting. Autism is not who the person is and it is (a) stealing, killing (sickness), and destroying the person who has it and those who are affected by it.*

Jane is not the only Christian who has called autism a demon, sickness, or spirit. In September of 2023, an article titled, "Pastor resigns from Stoutland School Board amidst backlash from autism comments made in a sermon," by Michael Hoffman[8], quotes the pastor as saying, "Well, either the devil has attacked them [children with autism], he's brought this infirmity upon them, he's got them, or God doesn't like them that much. My God doesn't make junk! How about we cast that demon out and then treat the problem?" The pastor is reported to have said in the follow-up that people got confused by what he was talking about when he referred to junk, so he added "Autism is born from a demonic spirit. By junk, I meant, autism, that condition, the illness, the neurodivergence." Comments and ignorance about autism in the Christian community lead to stigma and shame, and many whom I have worked with in Christian communities have stated they are not comfortable being open and upfront about their autism identification or marriage struggles because of misunderstandings and ignorance about autism in the Christian community at large. As we broaden the discussion on autism in marriage, we will distinguish autism spectrum behaviors and traits from character flaws, sin, and spiritual growth issues.

How to use this book depends on who you are as a reader. If you suspect you are autistic or are currently married to an autistic person in a neurodiverse marriage, the vision of this book is to guide you in finding the next steps to get appropriate help. The book will explain and discuss common challenges in neurodiverse marriage through examples, stories, research, and professional and lived experience. If you are a pastor, lay counselor, chaplain, biblical counselor, therapist, coach, or clinician who works in marriage ministry or marriage therapy, we want to broaden your view of autism and neurodiverse marriage to educate and equip you to better serve your couples.

We hope to offer ideas for effective strategies when ministering to neurodiverse couples, so you can more effectively help them move from surviving to a healthy, fulfilling Christian marriage. We invite you to lay down biases and what you previously thought about autism and to broaden your perspective on adult autism and the additional complexities and nuances that faith and autism present to a neurodiverse couple.

Each author in this book is a professing Christian who has direct lived experience as a spouse, parent, or grandparent of someone on the spectrum, or who themselves are neurodivergent. Each author has professional experience and is autism-aware and trained in how to work with ASD/ADHD individuals and neurodiverse marriages and families. Their insights, informed by a combination of lived and professional experience, along with their Christian faith, are what make this book the first of its kind. We want you to know that you are not alone as you begin to discover the intricacies of neurodiverse marriage, and we want to give you hope that, though these marriages may be challenging and complex, with proper identification and help they can be healthy and dynamic! Conversely, without proper identification and support, these marriages may perpetuate trauma and abuse, which is why this topic is so important to us and to our contributing authors.

Chapter One
Navigating the Maze of Adult Autism Identification and Acceptance: Finding the "Lost Generation"

REV. DR. STEPHANIE C. HOLMES & REV. DAN HOLMES, MS

As you read in the Introduction, both the diagnostic criteria and the understanding of autism have changed substantially over the past 50 years. However, while some are concerned autism is being over-diagnosed, we are concerned it is being missed by clinicians and counselors who lack training in the assessment and diagnosis of adults on the autism spectrum as well as other neurodivergences. We are most concerned about how autism and neurodiversity are viewed and misunderstood in Christian faith-based circles.

The heart of this book is not only to advocate for a better understanding and identification of autism in adults, but for clinicians, clergy, coaches, and chaplains who do marriage work to understand autism or neurodiversity in marital relationships. More and more couples are coming to an awareness that they are in a neurodiverse relationship (that is, one where at least one partner/spouse is neurodivergent). For this book, we will refer more to "neurodivergent" as the general term for someone on the *autism spectrum*, unless otherwise specified. Much research before this last year refers to the spouse who is not on the spectrum as "neuro-typical" (NT), but many are finding the NT spouse may have a neurodivergence of their own, and hence, *non-autistic* (NA) is another shorthand way to express the neurological differences between the two spouses.

A common trend that diagnostic professionals have observed is that when a child, grandchild or someone in the family gets an autism diagnosis, it provides clarity to others in the genetic line or family tree who may also have some degree of autism in their neuro-profile. As research and knowledge about autism deepen, diagnostic criteria and understanding of what it means to be on the spectrum will evolve. When many adults were children, their Autism Level 1 traits (previously designated as Asperger's Syndrome/AS or high functioning autism/HFA) may easily have been missed, and so, these adults are not finding out about their spectrum profile or neurodiversity until much later in life, if at all. While Hans Asperger is now considered a controversial figure in the field of autism (due to his possible political affiliations), his work in the 1940s continues to be important in understanding the breadth and depth represented by the autism spectrum.

For research I (Stephanie) published in an academic journal[1], I looked at the potential impact of an AS/ND adult not having a diagnosis and how that affected their marital dynamics. As previously stated, researchers note that autism is a lifelong neurodevelopmental issue with persistent challenges in social communication and reciprocal social interactions.[1,2,3,4,5]

Researchers have argued that the changes in criteria, untrained clinicians, and stereotypes of autism have kept many from getting a diagnosis.[6] While clinicians and diagnosticians are generally becoming more aware of the autism spectrum, many remain divided on identifying autism in adults (especially women) – they are often untrained in diagnosing adult autism or still hold to common myths and stereotypes associated with autism. Despite the confusion, prevalence rates for autism have been steadily rising. Dr. Martha Herbert, a pediatric neurologist with the Harvard Research School of Medicine, conducted research before the release of the current *Diagnostic and Statistical Manual of Mental Disorders (DSM-5)*, and she found that changes from the 1980 *(DSM-III)* to the 1994 *(DSM-IV)* diagnostic criteria only accounted for 400% of the 1200% increase in diagnoses. That leaves a staggering 800% increase which is still not yet fully understood.[7] Research also investigated incidence rates, and a 2019 study[8] (which consisted of 2.1 million participants in a five-country cohort) reported the heritability rate of ASD to be about 80%.[8] Current research is focused on identifying genetic markers associated with autism as well as possible environmental factors.

The now obvious greater prevalence of autism is important because when I (Stephanie) was in graduate school in the 1990s, I was told by a professor that I would "never see someone with Asperger's in therapy" and "that people with Asperger's prefer to be alone and would seldom marry". (This is ironic because I, as well as the contributing authors to this book, now work mostly with autistic adults and neurodiverse relationships.) Though I was introduced to Asperger's Syndrome in school, I did not begin to fully understand it until I read Dr. Tony Attwood's book, *Asperger's Syndrome: A Guide for Parents and Professionals* (1998),[2] which has since been updated and re-released as: *The Complete Guide to Asperger's Syndrome (Autism Spectrum Disorder).*[3] Attwood's 1998 work was one of the first comprehensive guides to understanding the breadth of the autism spectrum. These two books not only shaped my foundation and understanding of AS/ND, but they were vital for better understanding my daughter and husband (that history is detailed in our book: *Embracing the Autism Spectrum: Finding Hope & Joy in the NeuroDiverse Family Journey*). I wonder how many budding clinicians, counselors, and doctors were given the same misinformation in school as I was about the autism spectrum. And how many have done additional due diligence to understand the autism spectrum beyond a perfunctory "diagnostic" class? I began researching autism because of a personal need; anecdotally, I find that many who are licensed or credentialed to diagnose autism in children have not done further study or broadened their understanding of *adult* autism. This lack of diagnostic training and understanding leads to confusion and even trauma in AS/ND adults and their marriages across the globe.

The current autism prevalence rate reported by the Center for Disease Control and Prevention (CDC) at the time of this publication is 1 in 36 American children,[9] while the World Health Organization reports a worldwide rate of autism in children to be 1 in 100.[10] With these rates in mind, and a possible 80% hereditary rate of autism occurring without intellectual or cognitive impairment, could AS/ND adults have been missed as children when diagnosis criteria was changing? Lai and Baron-Cohen[11] coined the phrase "the lost generation" to describe those who were missed before HFA and Asperger's were added to the diagnostic lexicon of the 1994 *DSM-IV.* Adults in their 40s and over are said to be the ones most often missed or misdiagnosed.[12] My research agreed with previous findings: 86% of those in the study were only diagnosed over the age of 30.[1]

As more and more couples seek help for their complex marriages (which turn out to be neurodiverse relationships), it is becoming obvious that there are not enough trained marriage helpers to give adequate neurodiverse relationship care and support.[13,14] Those who are neurodiverse *Christian* couples (NDCCs) find it even more difficult to find marriage counselors who are faith-based *and* trained in neurodiverse relationships.[5] Current diagnostic criteria and research indicate that those on the autism spectrum struggle to initiate, develop, cultivate, and maintain their long-term relationships.[15] Frequently, it is the non-autistic (NA/NT) partner who is less satisfied by the marriage and reports being in greatest distress; they are often the ones who take the lead in finding a resource or support for the marriage.[5,15] The autistic or neurodivergent (AS/ND) partner typically reports higher marital satisfaction.[5,16] Most studies that are written look at the impact of marriage on the NA/NT spouse.[17] A recent study I published[5] examined marriage through the perspective of AS/ND spouses and the challenges these adults face when seeking an autism evaluation.

Diagnostic changes and lack of proper assessment are usually the first barriers autistic adults encounter in the maze of identification. In the 1940s, Hans Asperger's research led him to find a broader phenotype or perspective on autism than his fellow researcher Leo Kanner.[18,19,20] Lai and Baron-Cohen[11] stated that they believe the biggest gap in locating the 'lost generation' existed in the time between the 1980 *(DSM-III)* and 1994 *(DSM-IV)* manuals. The 1980s manual was based more on the research of Kanner, while the 1994 manual included the research and "syndrome" that would bear the name of Hans Asperger. When he was studying this "autism phenotype," Asperger referred to his patients as "little professors" because he observed his patients consuming knowledge and intellectualizing emotions: they were challenged in expressing or articulating their own emotions as well as identifying and understanding the emotions of others in social interactions. In addition to these observations, Asperger noted that "the little professors" had challenges in social interactions, reading social cues, giving empathetic responses, and interacting with peers, but that they could talk at great length on topics of their passionate or particular interest.[21] In 1997, researchers Volkmar and Klin[22] compared what was at the time *six different* sets of clinical criteria for identifying this "higher functioning" form of autism. It is no wonder that clinicians today struggle to properly assess and diagnose AS, as many researchers still do not agree on the core criteria of the autism spectrum. Volkmar and Klin[21] also noted that there was disagreement about the need for an AS sensory profile. Brown and Dunn[23] report there are several sensory profiles in autism, which are often missed by many diagnosing professionals. (More on this in a later chapter.)

In addition to the challenges of getting a proper diagnosis due to ignorance and a lack of training, things like stereotypes, stigma, and "hyper-spiritualizing" lengthen this identification maze by adding unnecessary twists and turns.

In addition to the challenges of getting a proper diagnosis due to ignorance and a lack of training, things like stereotypes, stigma, and "hyper-spiritualizing" lengthen this identification maze by adding unnecessary twists and turns. Many who diagnose and assess autism end up missing adults on the spectrum because they are used to working with children or they do not understand and observe the adult's masking or compensatory strategies. These have often been acquired over the lifetime of coping.[13,24,25] In addition to this confusion, the lack of studies into adult autism contributes to a poor understanding of autism or neurodiversity in marital relationships. While there are podcasts, books, and blogs on neurodiverse marriage, *research* on autism/neurodiversity in marriage is still scant.[26] No wonder navigating a neurodiverse marriage can feel like an unending maze with no end or solution in sight. If professionals and clinicians are confused and unaware, what must this be like for the neurodiverse couple who is navigating the maze blindly?

In the little research that exists about neurodiverse couples, very few studies focus on the perspective of the autistic or neurodivergent adult. Strunz and his fellow researchers[16] recruited 229 autistic adults for a study on relationship satisfaction. Their research demonstrated that those on the spectrum showed higher satisfaction if married or in a relationship with someone else on the spectrum (or neurodivergent). "Satisfaction" was defined by autistic adults as having similar sensory profiles, social needs and similar shared interests. This resulted in lower relational stress for the AS/NDs than for those in a relationship with an NA/NT partner. The 2016 study reported that 65% of autistic adults had fears and anxiety about not being able to fulfill a partner's expectations; 50% reported not understanding how to maintain a romantic relationship after the pursuit of the partner, and 28% reported the physical nature of relationships was rated as "unpleasant-to-painful" for them.

Because there is little research in the field regarding the AS/ND perspective, I (Stephanie) conducted exploratory and phenomenological research to examine this.[1] *Exploratory* refers to research that offers a new lens or perspective or provides additional research on a relatively unknown topic. *Phenomenological* research uses the words and experiences of study participants to understand the topic more deeply. Data is typically gathered through surveys, questionnaires, and personal interviews. In my study, we used a 38-question survey designed by a team of neurotypical and neurodivergent individuals, which was then examined by a clinician on the spectrum to assess for bias or harm. Questions from the survey that we will explore here include:

Q. 10: Were there any other diagnoses you received prior to the diagnosis or identification of the autism spectrum?

Q. 12: At what age was the autism identification made in your life?

Q. 16: How would you rate your satisfaction with your relationship?

Q. 30: Did anyone who worked with you as a marriage helper, or anyone you mentioned autism/neurodiversity say anything dismissive or disregard autism?

For the broader 38-question survey, we had a total of 322 participants who completed the entire survey. Of those 322 participants, 108 identified or reported they were on the autism spectrum. The research was limited in its examination of the female autistic perspective, as only a few AS/ND participants were female. For the first level of data analysis, themes were coded from the answers and simple percentages were used to analyze participants' responses; for the second level of the analysis, 20 couples were interviewed, and their responses were transcribed and examined for patterns or themes.

First, I wanted to look at the participants' average *age* at diagnosis, to see if my results supported the findings of the "lost generation" (diagnosed older than age 40).

Age of Individual at Diagnosis/Identification of the Autism Spectrum*

Age	N: 108	% (rounded)
40-49	47	42
30-39	17	16
60-69	17	16
50-59	13	12
19-29	9	9
6-10	2	2
11-18	2	2
1-5	1	1
70-79	0	0

*322 participants answered and were allowed to give multiple reasons from the larger survey population.

As the table reveals, 77% of the participants were identified on the spectrum at age 40 or older; and 86% of the individuals were identified over the age of 30. The greatest interval of identification was in the 40-49 age demographic. Many were diagnosed under the Asperger's Syndrome criteria (before the 2013 *DSM-5*). Notations of individuals who self-identified indicated that the diagnosing clinician stated that they were uncertain of an autism classification under *DSM-5* criteria, since they saw traits of autism but could not give an official diagnosis because they were unable to establish a childhood history, and/ or the individual was too "high functioning" or "successful". Thirty-one of the 108 had self-identified using an online measure such as the Autism-Spectrum Quotient.[27]

Below are participant quotes taken from the research article,[1] which was published in 2023 in the *Global Journal of Intellectual & Developmental Disabilities*. Participant 1, a male from the Southeast region of the United States (US), identified as a person of color and stated that due to trauma in his childhood, he believes the autism was missed earlier in life. He stated, "There is additional stigma of autism for people of color." Participant 4, also from the Southeast, said, "Getting the diagnosis [later in life] can challenge your identity, and you really have to understand your identity… is not your diagnosis." Participant 4 had been diagnosed with ADHD during the *DSM-4* era, when guidelines stipulated that an individual could be diagnosed as having either AS or ADHD, but not both. It was not until much later when this person was also diagnosed with ASD, that he and his partner understood the communication challenges they had been facing daily. Participant 5 from Australia stated that they had mixed feelings about finding out the diagnosis later in life. On the one hand, it explained many of the difficulties he had had over his lifetime, but on the other, he was distressed about the negative impact his unknown diagnosis had created on his marriage and family, as well as his missed opportunities for support. Participant 15 from the US Midwest described his reaction to having a later-in-life diagnosis in this way:

> *I see it as potentially a negative and here's the reason. When you say someone has autism, you think of the person that can't function or can't speak who only looks down or has no eye contact with flittering hands. So, I saw it as a negative. The earlier you find out the better.*

Of the 23 adults interviewed on their initial reaction to discovering autism later in life, 9 adults indicated they saw this diagnosis in a negative light, 3 had mixed or no emotions about the identification, and 11 found the diagnosis to be positive, bringing a sense of relief and understanding about their differences. Three of those who had a negative view wished they and their spouse did *not* know, saying that learning of the diagnosis brought hopelessness in their marital dynamics ever improving. The second barrier in the maze of identification can be an *acceptance* of the diagnosis by both spouses: one or the other may experience anger, defensiveness, denial or deep grief.

Anecdotally, Dan spoke on our podcast series, *Just the Guys*, and the AS/ND "guys" had this to share about their diagnosis journey: There are different responses to finding out you are neurodiverse or on the spectrum later in life.

Outside of the Maze: Dan's Insights and Hindsight Learning and Other Diagnosis Journeys

There are as many views of an ASD diagnosis as there are people. I know my own view, and those of a handful of people I have talked with. That means I don't know everyone's experience, nor will I claim to. We are still all people, so there are some commonalities: we are all affected by the same set of major emotions, and we all experience a set of reactions to our diagnosis which may or may not be overt.

In my case, the diagnosis was a non-event. I went to the evaluation without expectation of what that would be like, but I did expect the outcome. Almost a decade earlier my eldest daughter was diagnosed with Asperger's. We had lived with it in her, and we had seen similar behaviors, speech, and reasoning in me. Over the course of those 10 years, I knew what was going on. This was getting a name for what I already knew.

It didn't change my opinion of myself, nor did it change the opinion of those in my immediate family.

What did I think about it? Did it cause me grief or anger or … whichever? No. It didn't change my opinion of myself, nor did it change the opinion of those in my immediate family. Did I broadcast it to the world? No, I didn't do that either, but I also don't tell the world much of anything so that isn't an indicator of anything, anyway.

I was, and still am, very selective about what I disclose to whom. Two reasons: the first is practical. I don't talk much, and I figure mentioning I am on the autism spectrum would require more explanation than I would want to give. Second, there needs to be a reason. I have spoken at conferences. We have a book and a podcast. This isn't a secret, but it is something I talk about on purpose: how does the other party benefit from me telling my story? If I am in conversation and the topic comes up, *and* if I perceive the other person would get value from me talking about this, then I might speak about it. I won't inject it into a conversation simply because the topic came up. It needs to be valuable (purely a subjective and in-the-moment judgment call) to the receiver. It needs to be useable in some way: supportive, encouraging, hopeful, … and so on.

If I viewed it as a non-event, something that just is, others see it as a positive or a negative. Those who see it in a positive light believe it has revealed something that had been hidden, and that it explains their behaviors, relationships, thinking patterns, and emotions. To them, this was an 'a-ha' – the fear that they continually do things that are negatively impacting themselves and those around them, but will forever be a mystery, is now gone. There is an explanation, and therefore, there is relief. That doesn't make the coming days any easier, but it does provide a path. With a known cause, a plan to inculcate a set of correcting measures can be created and executed. This doesn't make autism go away; it provides a way to grow into who you want to be for you and those around you.

For those who see it as a negative, there are a few things I have noticed. One of them is that it is a "cause": If there wasn't AS in their life, then by extension, the way things are right now – and *they* – would be better. It is thought of as a medical condition or being 'too short,' an 'if only' pattern of thinking. Another view is that it is an assault on who they are: "I can't be autistic because I am too ___." Whatever the blank is, from smart to successful, or even too many friends, it can't be *me*. It runs counter to a self-narrative, and therefore can't be true, and so sometimes isn't accepted. The final one I will mention is how the diagnosed person is perceived by themselves or others: it is a 'less than' mentality. Before the diagnosis and after the diagnosis is perhaps like two different people, and the latter one isn't as good as the first.

Most of us spent the first 18 years of our life in school. Some of us continued for 4 or more years into college. In many cases, 20% of our lifetime is spent in formal school-ing. We are simultaneously growing mentally, physically, spiritually, and socially during those years. We are also generally unaware, at the moment, that those four aspects of our being are maturing. When we get to adulthood and recognize we aren't as mature as we thought we were, we irrationally put on the learning brakes. Our self-image collides with reality, and we purposefully halt some of those aspects of learning (and perhaps cloak it in spirituality). We have learned through our vocation and have likely become very good at whatever role we play. The job was learning in its purest form. It was natural and provided a sense of accomplishment. However, when an autism diagnosis presents a new need to learn and grow, we may no longer want to. Even though that growth is of benefit to our family life and possibly even our job.

If this is where you are, ask yourself, 'Why?' What harm, not hurt, can come from growing through your autism? What don't you want to consider? Are you concerned about what you might have to give up? Have you considered what you might gain? Think about your favorite food. Did you ever order it at a restaurant, or make it for yourself before you knew what it was or that it even existed? That is what this is like. You may have to give up something, but what you receive in return is much richer than you know how to ask for and is certainly worth whatever you choose to put down.

Genuine self-improvement is a life of self-mastery. It is an amalgam of self-control and self-discipline. Self-control so that you temper your desires, and self-discipline so that you engage in the benefits of the difficult. It takes both to grow healthily, but in doing so you become a better person and a better person to be around. It enhances all forms of your relationships. I encourage you to embrace this mindset if you don't already have it. I am not suggesting you accept it blindly. I am asking if you would 'taste and see.' Be genuine in your efforts to improve and be honest with your circumstances, changes, and the timeline required to reap the rewards. Our marriage needed over a decade for us to repent, repair, and build trust and safety, in order to be where we are now. I didn't know it could be this rich. It is. I invite you to join me. You can. It takes both of you; it isn't easy, but it is certainly worth it.

Excerpts below are taken from a *Just the Guys* podcast on later-in-life diagnosis. The three questions being answered in each's responses were about 1) their autism diagnosis journey, 2) advice for those who are resistant to being tested or assessed, and 3) how their spouse reacted.

Mark's Diagnosis Journey:

I was not open because of years ago getting diagnosed with ADD and I thought, "There's no way." And to find out that I was so completely wrong in my thinking. When this came along, I was more open to it. The acceptance of the tenants of it and the fact that I have it. What does that mean? I started getting counseling and it made all the difference in the world. Acceptance for me was pretty easy because of a past experience where I was completely wrong in my thinking. I was not very self-aware but did find I thought I was smarter than those around me. For me, it was I know I'm smart, I am a West Point graduate, why can I not figure out this marriage and relationship thing? That was as far as I got in that.

Ok, what would you say to guys out there who are sort of on the fence or resistant to acceptance or even diagnosis, to encourage them in that? What would you say? For me, this has been something that's just been in my brain, going over and over so much because I know several guys who I guarantee you would get a [positive] diagnosis, but they are adamant, no way, I'm not doing it. That's not me. Ok, alright, you've got to let them walk their own path. For me, this is one of those things that I'd really like to get a good handle on for how to help somebody, help the guys. Elon Musk, on "Saturday Night Live" saying he was AS, but helps that cultural thing, but individuals is where I see most of the trouble.

My wife, a counselor friend of hers said, "You know, Mark might be on the spectrum. But don't tell it." My wife immediately came home and said, "I think you're on the spectrum." She was accepting of it. We both went to learn together, and she accepted it. In fact, she just ran right to me and said, "Let's figure this out."

Perry's Diagnosis Journey:

I had people use the term autistic around me several times because of shows like Big Bang Theory: "Oh, Perry is a lot like Sheldon." Or other characters that were in the media at that point. I'd been kind of denying it, saying those two people are way wackier and funnier to be around than I am. But of course, that's the characterization of that type of personality that makes it into the media. I think I had heard the echoes of the diagnosis long enough that when I finally read that book and started to get in the head of someone who was expressing those thoughts and trying to make those connections, that bit of acceptance came. And then, at the time, I think it was before the DSM-5 change between Asperger's and the diagnosis of autism in general. There's this little bit of community and identity based around the term Asperger and so being an "Aspie" was an immediate, you automatically get some of the traits that are with that. Some of that identity piece was easier to pick up because I could easily classify within a group of people who were similarly quirky and had defined traits that were well-known in aspects of media. For me, it opened up the discovery process. It was like, alright, here's the name that I can put to this. Now, let me investigate all the different paths that this can take me, as far as what the implications are and how to have a great life as somebody who fits that label, if we want to use that term.

Yeah, I guess it comes down to if somebody's resistant, you have to get to a deeper question of where does the resistance come from? What are they afraid of acknowledging? What is the implication on either side of the diagnosis? If you get the diagnosis, does the world end or does it give you potentially a clear path to start to solve problems? If you come out on the other side and you try to take the test and you don't get the diagnosis, what does that mean? Trying to see it as a decision branch and then say what are the implications on each side? What is the next step on either side of that? It's not something that we should go "Well, no that's never me." If you're resistant to take the test because you believe, "No, it's never me," then it means that there's a core fear inside of you that if you take it, you're going to find out that it is you.

For us, it was weird. My wife was also an autism specialist in her capacity as a speech-language therapist. She had definitely known a lot of the traits that were there and had even joked about it. Her coworkers were also always pointing at me, going, "He's probably on the spectrum." When it got confirmed, it was kind of like – oh, yeah, and a celebration of that puzzle piece being solved. Then, also a little bit of mourning because she knew the struggle that comes with it as well and some of the things that are naturally going to be hard, that she couldn't just say, "Oh that's a personality quirk." No, it's not a personality quirk that you can just will yourself to overcome or change a habit, it is a brain-wiring thing. Yeah, there are bridges for lots of the natural things that are there, but connecting at certain levels is something that – you almost have to redefine what that looks like sometimes. There was a little bit of mourning along with the catharsis of knowing what was going on.

(Please check out the chapter references to find out more about Perry's podcast and books on cyber security and digital folklore).[31,32,33]

Clay's Diagnosis Journey:

It was cathartic for me to solve the puzzle… as Perry said, solving the puzzle because I was in midlife and had similar struggles as Dan. I [had] a lot of friends in school and college and law school, but always felt like I struggled to fit in. I went out into the working world and practiced law and did consulting work for 20 years. I was fairly successful and had a lot of business contacts. My career achievements were solid, not spectacular, but I was doing very well. As far as my perception of the outside world, I was sitting there thinking, "If all that's the case, [what] is this anxiety and depression that I'm going through, that have me in the middle of a suicidal and emotional breakdown?" God, in his gracious way, swooped in at the right time and put a book in front of me called 'Human' by an Australian named Warren Mayocchi. It was a biography of a guy like me, who was diagnosed midlife, and it was a carbon copy of my life, as if someone on the other side of the globe wrote my biography sight unseen. At that point, I realized this answered all the questions that puzzled me… it answers all of them. ADHD didn't answer all the questions. Depression or anxiety or PTSD was even one diagnosis I had. None of those answered all the questions. Asperger's answered all the questions. But that still wasn't good enough for me. My biggest fear was that I was wrong and this wasn't the answer, so I was absolutely compelled to seek out and get a diagnosis, which I received in December of 2015. That was cathartic for sure. But then after a while, I realized something more ominous: that everything that I thought I knew about myself, I wasn't so sure about anymore. It's kind of for me, the year or two after the diagnosis was more of a grieving process, that I was mourning the loss of my former self.

For those resistant, I think an easier way to do it than seeking out a psychiatric profes-sional is to maybe point to some online tests. (Dr. Stephanie notes that if you choose to do an online test, have your spouse present and be open to a different opinion, as online tests do require self-awareness, which can be a problem for those on the autism spectrum.) I found those were pretty useful and not too intrusive. Perhaps one thing to emphasize is that you don't have to tell anybody if you don't want to, and you probably shouldn't (unless you have deter-mined it is safe to do so). At least in my opinion. But that might answer some questions that are repeatedly tripping you up. I know that it was so much with me figuring out the marriage thing, although I did a terrible job of that. I just remember when I was in the working world, wondering why I did just as good if not better work than anyone else, but always found myself on the losing end of office politics. Sometimes in rather terrible ways that cost me a job or three. You're right. Seeking the diagnosis has got to be [one's] own personal decision, but there's ways short of that (like the online tests) that I think are really helpful to at least get to a point to where you realize that it's not the end of the world if you get diagnosed. It's really kind of the end of the beginning.

My wife was confused mostly because she didn't understand much about Asperger's and autism, so it was kind of a learning experience for both of us together, and it was by no means easy. But yeah, we got the diagnosis, and she sat down with psychologist and they had extensive interviews as part of the diagnosis process. We really had to learn together once we realized; I realized that every man on my side of the family going back at least 4 generations, now I see they were all obviously on the spectrum, and possibly my mother. We're looking down at our little one, gosh he really does fight to watch the water go down the drain for long, long, long periods of time and so, that's the saving grace of the entire episode, was getting ahead on a child's Asperger's at such an early age… that we then work[ed] on it, and working with him and learning how to raise him to be the best little guy he can be and avoid situations that we know will be troublesome for him.

(Please check out the chapter references to see two books authored by Clay about an autistic's perspective in corporate America and his book for business owners). [34,35]

Co-Occurring Issues

The next part of the maze which makes getting an autism identification more challeng-ing is navigating the co-occurring conditions or presenting features that are similar to some other diagnoses. The table below shows data collected in my 2023 study[1] and indicates how co-occurring issues can mask or confuse the full understanding of an autism diagnosis.

Diagnosis Given Prior to the Autism
Diagnosis/Identification of the Autism Spectrum

	N: 108	% (rounded)
No Other Diagnosis Received	61	56
Depressive Disorders	31	28
ADD/ADHD	27	25
Anxiety Disorders (OCD, GAD)	23	21
Trauma Related Diagnosis	12	11
Social Phobia/Social Anxiety	8	7
Learning Disorder/ Learning Challenges	7	6
Personality Disorder	4	4
Sensory Integration Disorder	3	3
ODD/PDA/Conduct Disorder	1	1

Participants were able to choose more than one from a list of diagnoses.

As you notice, the percentages do not add up to 100%. This is because participants were allowed to choose as many diagnoses as possible that were given to them before the autism identification. Co-occurring issues are common with autism spectrum, as Dr. Matthew Fisher pointed out in a podcast interview with me:[28]

> *Often the symptoms that are causing the most concern for the individual or family are what gets looked at first. What can be treated or helped with medication? When there is relief, it is not uncommon to stop looking for root causes, but to bring symptom relief.*

Fisher, a psychiatrist, explained that it is often "concerning behaviors" that lead to a child getting a diagnosis, and if those behaviors are observable or severe enough to impact functioning, the child may receive multiple diagnoses. Not all on the spectrum have outward dysregulation; they may have internal anxiety which may not be a problem at school or work, so it doesn't trigger alarm or concern. When someone is struggling with executive function deficits or memory or task completion, the presentation may look more like ADHD. If someone is more anxious or rigid, this may look more like an anxiety disorder. Repetitive behaviors or routines could be taken for obsessive-compulsive disorder (OCD).

The above table indicates that for those in our study, depression, ADHD, and anxiety disorders were the first diagnoses received. What is unknown and was not asked about in the survey is if these were known to be current, co-occurring conditions. Co-occurring issues can greatly change the presentation of autism from person to person. In a podcast interview, Dr. Tony Attwood said, "Rarely is autism, autism pure. Meaning that there is no other diagnosis present." Dr. Attwood, I, and contributing authors advocate and remind the reader that autism is not a mental health condition but is classified as a neurodevelopmental *disorder* in the *DSM-5*. We see this as more of a neurological *difference* or *diversity*.

All participants in the study (either ND/AS or NA/NT) shared reasons they were given that they or their spouse could not possibly be on the autism spectrum. The next table indicates what the diagnosing clinician's reasons were for this:

Reasons Given by Professionals that Were Autism Unaware Dismissing Autism Spectrum:
The Professional or Counselor said, "You (or your spouse) cannot have Autism/Asperger's Because..."

	N	%
No remarks were made about autism	168	53
They/you have a friend(s) or appear social	68	21
They/you are successful at work	64	20
They/you are too smart/intelligent	64	20
They/you maintain eye contact well	57	18
Gave a reason from their experience of work or other stereotype around autism	49	15
The professional or counselor did not believe in labels or believes "everyone is somewhere on the spectrum"	44	13
They/you are too well liked	42	13
Their/your interests or passion is a normal interest in insinuated the interest itself must be weird, not useful, or atypical	39	12
They/you got married. Autistic people prefer to be alone	34	10
They/you are not clumsy, in fact even athletic	24	7
A feature was mentioned indicating they did not look autistic	5	2

In open-ended questions and comments allowed at the end of the survey (which asked for further clarification of the diagnostic process), many stated that the professional they worked with was not specifically autism-aware or trained to assess autism in adults. In my private practice, I have read dozens of full psychological evaluations (provided by clients), where every single criterion of autism has been observed or commented upon by the evaluator, and still, the client did not receive an autism diagnosis! The most common evaluator comments I have read are "they are too successful at work," or "they show too high of intelligence." After the survey, 20 couples were interviewed using a semi-structured questionnaire. All but 1 of these couples identified as belonging to the Christian faith, and the couple who stated they were not faith-based did say they grew up in "religious homes". For the 19 Christian couples interviewed (who went to Christian counselors or clergy for help), the most frequent comments offered by marriage helpers or clergy included, "all marriages have struggles," "that is just a man thing," and "these are common male-to-female communication issues." Strategies given to improve their marriages revolved around "praying more," "go[ing] out on more dates," "hav[ing] more sex," and to the women, "you simply need to submit more [and] obey your husband" to reduce conflict. Not only was this advice not helpful, but it was also dismissive, demeaning, and blaming; it often enabled unhealthy behaviors and exacerbated issues. (Later in the book, we will look more closely at Christian teachings on marriage that can complicate the neurodiverse relationship.) Before offering some suggestions for navigating this maze of diagnosis and acceptance, it helps to ask: how does *not* having a diagnosis impact the NA/NT spouse?

Printed with permission, blogger Mary Gable (pseudonym) explains her story:

The count is two to one: Two couple's counselors have said my spouse is on the spectrum. One has disagreed but affirmed he struggles to express empathy. [Dr. Stephanie's note, that she was one of the 2 who confirmed the identification. The one who denied was online, spent a few hours with the individual and couple, and did not allow the spouse's observations to be considered in the assessment].

I'd hoped this last go-round would cement the truth I've worked to understand for ten years. Golly… Pause with me as I soak that in. Ten. Whole. Years. It's been over a decade since I entered that bookstore. Passing time while waiting to pick up my children, I meandered through the self-help aisle; opened a book on autism; and read a list of traits that described my spouse. Later at home, I introduced him to the idea, hoping only to better bridge our communication divide.

Within weeks, we met a church member who said he was a licensed counselor. Not long into our conversation, my spouse said, "He thinks I'm on the spectrum." From there, the counselor stated that he works with people on the spectrum. So, once home, we talked about it and decided to see him. After several months of work, the therapist agreed with my hunch that my spouse is on the spectrum. So, I tried to adjust, accept, and do better.

Before continuing with our story, I just want to emphasize that at this point, we'd worked with the therapist of his choice. One he sought out. I hadn't had the guts to pursue validation. He took the first step.

About four years later, I hit a new low. I found an email from a friend I rarely hear from with the name of a local counselor who specializes in neurodiverse couple's therapy. After working with the second professional locally in person for several months, again I heard, "Yes, he's on the spectrum."

*But since my spouse's assessment was done through therapy work, his children balked. They felt that the therapists who'd assessed us as we worked to reconcile conflict weren't trustworthy. So, five years later, as tension built, my spouse reached out to a third counselor and the "he said/ she said" debate began again. So, before I offered my thoughts in our latest first-couple-session, I asked the counselor how they assessed for Autism online given such divided perspectives. The professional encouraged trust in the process, and I obliged. I shared story after story, during our four or five sessions—and then asked the same question again when the therapist asked if we had questions as our last online assessment appointment ended. Again, it was implied I should trust the process. Thus, a week later, I sat dumbfounded when the therapist asserted that based on **my spouse's answers,** he was not on the spectrum.*

It's not so much that my spouse may not be on the spectrum, but that by asserting he isn't, without affirming my experiences as his wife, he left me to carry a heavy load. Again, that may not be a fair statement. But for now, I have no energy to defend, explain, or prove myself anymore. Because there's a good chance that if the therapist doesn't believe my husband is on the spectrum, he carries concern about labels I'm not willing to face. And since my husband's family members have asserted that very thing, it's a bit too much for me to address right now.

Fortunately, during the years I operated under the diagnosis of a neurodiverse marriage, I learned that one of the most important aspects of survival centers on my relationship with God. A dear friend told me just this morning, "We often want to believe our homes should be safe places. But in truth, the only reliable place of safety is deep within us; where our soul connects with the God of love."

Faced with the sea of doubt, I can honestly state that day by day, God has shown up, affirming his deep, abiding love for me right now… today… smack in the middle of this unwanted dead end.

While his family may disagree, I'm confident that my pursuit of a diagnosis was only to help our marriage. **Not to undermine my husband**. From God's perspective, neuro-typical or not, we are all one under the cross, in need of the Savior's love and mercy. Equal. Broken. But different for sure. I'd simply hoped that by understanding that difference, we would be empowered to communicate more effectively and love more devotedly.

So, what do I do now? I lean ever more onto the same cross I've been leaning on all my life. I trust my reputation to the One who made me. I take long walks. I huddle under my weighted blanket. Then, I get back up; believe in my experiences and a God who loves me; and use the techniques I've learned, regardless of the diagnosis. Detached and determined, I speak love in my home. Is this easy? Not. At. All. But it's possible due to the grace of God.

Navigating the Maze of Identification and Acceptance of Autism/ Neurodiversity:

Step 1: Finding the right provider, clinician, or evaluator with expertise and training in identifying autism in adults is the first part of navigating this neurodiverse marriage maze. Part of your work as a neurodiverse couple is *Education* which encompasses knowing how your differing neuro-profiles impact your marriage and shape your expectations. Often, clients ask if a formal diagnosis is needed. The answer to that question depends on the 'Why' of getting a diagnosis. A more comprehensive answer is given on my (Dr. Stephanie's) YouTube channel (https://www.youtube.com/@dr.stephaniec. holmes3536), but for many who work with neurodiverse couples, self-identification may be adequate to begin your marriage work. A formal diagnosis is often needed or required if the individual is asking for accommodations or modifications in school, the workplace or if making a disability claim. There are different ways of getting an assessment or evaluation, but the most important tip in navigating this maze is making sure the chosen assessor is qualified beyond just having a degree or licensure. Ask the professional in a consultation about their experience diagnosing autistic *adults*, what instruments or tests they use, and what training (beyond their degree) they have had towards understanding and identifying adult autism. In my assessments, I (Dr. Stephanie) insist that the spouse be present, or I have questions that are directed to the spouse. The assessment I use (the MIGDAS-2) allows for additional input beyond the self-report of the one being evaluated. As autism can impact self-awareness (and adults on the spectrum may have learned compensatory strategies), additional objective input is better for a more thorough assessment. A full psychological evaluation can be quite expensive and often does provide valuable information, but requesting a full psychological evaluation does not always mean that *autism* is being assessed. If getting a psych evaluation, I advise that you specifically ask that autism be assessed, especially if it is suspected. Sometimes neurodiversity is not the only challenge of the relationship. If either partner has a personality disorder or mental health issue, this makes the couple's work very challenging. You may find you have several providers on this journey, each helping you work with different issues. Some conditions can be treated or improved with medication; targeted medication can help in managing issues that are beyond the scope of the neurodiverse marriage.

Step 2: Identification, assessment, or diagnosis is only Step 1 in the maze. The next step can be much more challenging to navigate: both spouses must accept the neurodiversity differences between the couple and work to understand the lived experience of the other. As you read, different people have different experiences being diagnosed later in life, but without acceptance, you may find yourself stuck in the maze. I (Stephanie) differentiate between cognitive acceptance and true, committed acceptance. Cognitive acceptance sounds like this, "Well, I (or they) seem to fit the profile." In reality, both spouses need to commit and accept that the neurodiversity will require changing some expectations, working through some past pain, and grieving losses. Ideally, each person must do their work while navigating the maze of neurodiverse marriage as a *team*. Though each can only control the choices they make individually, it will take *teamwork* to find marital satisfaction and fulfillment for *both* spouses. There are two extremes presented in some books about neurodiverse relationships. Extreme #1 might look like this: Because there is an autism diagnosis, the AS/ND person gets a pass on changing or trying to meet the needs of the NA/NT spouse. The approach is more disability-focused, lowering all expectations on the neurodivergent spouse and insisting the non-autistic spouse adjust, modify, and accommodate, all the while laying down their personal needs and relationship dreams. Extreme #2 usually has to do with trying to "neuro-typicalize" the autistic spouse. This approach gives the non-autistic spouse the pass and insists if the AS/ND spouse works hard enough, they can be more 'neuro-typical.' Neither approach works. Both spouses will have different journeys, goals, and personal work, each changing some behaviors and expectations. Coming together as a team will help you navigate your way to a new sense of 'who we are as a couple'. This is also where mainstream Christian self-help marriage books can be problematic, as they do not consider neurological development and other mental health challenges in the advice they give.

Step 3 involves working on the "double empathy problem." As I stated in the 2023 research article:

> It is important to note that while differences in the theory of mind are noted as a diagnostic criterion; research indicates between an autistic and non-autistic partner there is a double empathy problem,[1,29] and autistic-to-autistic communication is highly effective.[1,30] Some researchers challenge if the issue alone exists with the autistic person, as double empathy refers to the challenges that exist when people with different experiences or neurotypes are interacting with each other; each person may struggle to empathize with the other. Differences in language, use of language, or comprehension can exacerbate the double empathy problem.[1,29] Crompton et al.[30] studied communication between autistics, non-autistics, and mixed neurotypes. Their findings indicated that autistic-to-autistic communication was as effective as non-autistic-to-non-autistic communication, but when mixed neurotypes are communicating less information is shared and communication is less effective.[1]

Step 4: Keep educating yourselves. You can find more insights from me (Dr. Stephanie) on my YouTube channel, which features topics such as: *"What do we need? Assessment, Evaluation?"* or *"What can I do if my spouse will not accept the identification or diagnosis?"* More on *"Double Empathy"* and insights from our experience (Dan and Stephanie) as we discuss our neurodiverse Christian marriage as professionals and lived experience. If you are ready to pursue more education, we offer a beginner's self-study course: *"AS-NT or Neurodiverse Couples Struggling to Connect"* as well as the *NeuroDiverse Christian Couples podcast* available on Mental Health New Radio and other podcast outlets.

Step 5: Are both partners/spouses ready for marriage work? See Appendix A for 10 Things to Consider before starting marriage work.

Chapter Two
Navigating the Maze of Expectations and Challenges of Mutual Marital Satisfaction: Satisfaction from the Perspective of the Neurodivergent or Autistic Spouse

REV. DR. STEPHANIE C. HOLMES AND REV. DAN HOLMES, MS

I n my practice, I (Dr. Stephanie) often use metaphors to help neurodiverse couples understand the journey of navigating marital satisfaction. I compare the identification of being a neurodiverse couple to stepping onto a "game board." A familiar analogy I use is the children's game "Chutes and Ladders." Some days, couples discover tools and skills that propel them forward, much like climbing a ladder. However, there are times when they encounter setbacks or forget to utilize these skills, feeling as though they've slid down a chute, almost starting anew.

Another game analogy I employ is "Candy Land." In this game, certain cards allow players to advance, symbolizing small victories and progress in a relationship. Conversely, the same cards can sometimes result in moving backward, mirroring the unpredictable nature of neurodiverse relationships. A particularly poignant comparison is getting stuck in Candy Land's "Molasses Swamp," where players wait for a specific card to free them. This scenario resonates with many neurodiverse couples who feel as though they're watching others advance effortlessly in their relationships while they remain stuck, hoping for that one breakthrough that will help them move forward.

These analogies encapsulate the challenges and complexities neurodiverse couples face as they work to redefine and understand what marital satisfaction means for each individual. Let's delve into what our research study with the 322 participants revealed about how they perceive and experience marital satisfaction in their own marriages.

Marital Satisfaction

This section focuses on the concept of marital satisfaction within neurodiverse marriages, emphasizing the differing perspectives of autistic/neurodivergent (AS/ND) and non-autistic/neurotypical (NA/NT) spouses. Many studies discussing marital satisfaction provide specific definitions or criteria to define the term 'marital satisfaction.' However, in our study, this wasn't necessary. We were more interested in exploring what marital satisfaction meant to our participants. As we delved deeper, it became evident that the AS/ND spouse's experience of satisfaction differed from that of the NA/NT spouse. The chart below shows which of the spouses tended to be the most satisfied overall. Our findings show that 68% of the AS/ND partners had a neutral or favorable view of their marriage. In comparison, only 35% of NA/NT spouses reported a neutral or favorable response to marital satisfaction.

Do we, the authors, believe that a satisfying and fulfilling neurodiverse marriage is possible? Absolutely.

Do we, the authors, believe that a satisfying and fulfilling neurodiverse marriage is possible? Absolutely. We also recognize that neurodiverse relationships are inherently complex and necessitate a lifetime of mutual teamwork and accommodation. To gain further insights, we conducted semi-structured interviews with 23 AS/ND partners from the larger sample, focusing on their perspectives and perceptions of marital satisfaction.

Marital Satisfaction: A Comparison of AS and NT Partners

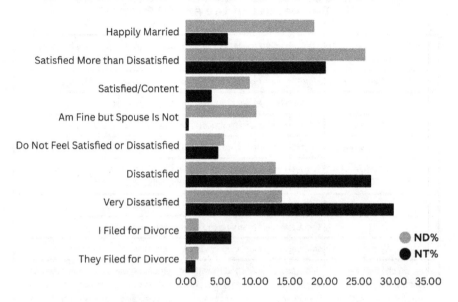

Satisfaction of Contentment Themes from the AS/ND Perspective

When there is not conflict
When we are doing a shared activity that I enjoy
When there are not demands or pressure on me
When my spouse appreciates me or recognizes that positives I contribute
Being respected/accepted as an individual and acceptance of my differences
Doing activities we both enjoy, having fun together
When we are acting as a team
When they encourage me to do new things and pursue passions and interests
When we were having sex or having sex more regularly or more physical touch (this was expressed from males primarily and only 1 female on the spectrum)

Themes of Dissatisfaction or Discontent from the Perspective of the AS/ND Partner*

Feeling the Autism/Asperger's is blamed for all our marital problems (noted primarily by those in a mixed-neurology relationship and 1 of the double-neurodivergent relationships)
Feeling criticized or that I am not enough or meeting needs or expectations
Not enough alone time to decompress or engage in my interests
Being told repetitively my spouse is not happy or healthy and I am the cause
Constant conflict/heightened emotions in the home environment
Lack of physical affection, touch or sex, which is lacking or nonexistent due to marital strain or sensory issues (this was noted by half of the men and only 1 woman)
Feeling my spouse wants me to be neuro-typical
My spouse regrets marrying me or threatens divorce
We are in an in-home separation or living in separate rooms, which I do not want
Having children with autism or special needs and the added demands/costs of their needs (note that participants did not regret having children or adopting children with needs, but not knowing about their own autism and needs and increased pressure on marriage and family with children with needs was the theme that arose)

*Themes derived from 23 AS/ND partners from the semistructured qualitative interviews

Most research on marital satisfaction predominantly reflects the perspective of the non-autistic/neurotypical (NA/NT) spouse. [2,3,4,5,6] Our study, however, focused on the ND/AS spouse's viewpoint. The top themes that indicated satisfaction revolved around: the absence of conflict; encouragement to pursue personal passions and interests; sharing interests with their spouse; receiving appreciation for accomplishments; and acceptance of their differences without undue pressure or expectations. Among the male participants and one AS female, increased sexual intimacy was also associated with higher marital satisfaction. Additionally, we explored the factors contributing to dissatisfaction or discontent. The most prominent issue was the attribution of all marital challenges to either the individual or their autism, particularly noted in mixed neurology marriages as opposed to double neurodivergent ones. Other general factors of discontent included: feeling criticized or blamed; lack of sufficient alone time; any form of conflict; and a perceived shortage or withdrawal of physical affection, especially for those who value physical touch. Additionally, there are nuanced aspects to consider, especially when discussing the intersection of faith, beliefs about physical intimacy, and the complexities these bring to neurodiverse Christian couples (NDCCs). These aspects will be elaborated on further in later discussions.

Advice from Adults on the Spectrum to NT Partners

Slow down, we have slower processing/Give us time to think and respond
Alter your expectations/Will not ever be NT/Please stop comparing our marriage to other NT-to-NT marriages/I can't give you a Hallmark or Disney move marriage
We love you, but we do not always know how to show it
We want to emotionally support you and connect, but we struggle with the *how*
When I am dysregulated, give me time to regulate
Communicate one topic or need at a time
When there is a need or concern, a gentle start up or softer approach
I need appreciation or affirmation when I have done something well/Only hearing my failings and mistakes is demoralizing, hurtful, discouraging, and depressing/Encourage my strengths and what I do bring to the marriage or family
Everything feels all or nothing or pass/fail that I am one mistake away from separation or divorce, and that affects my mental health
Just because you are NT does not mean I am by default incorrect or my perspective is wrong

To foster empathy and understanding in a neurodiverse marriage, it's essential to consider what the ND/AS spouse needs from their NA/NT partner. The primary request from ND/AS spouses is for their partners to *slow down* and allow them time to think and respond. My husband Dan and I encountered this challenge due to our differing processing and discussion speeds, and we've developed two effective strategies to manage it.

 ## Effective Personal Strategies for Navigating the Maze of Communication Differences and Differing Processing Speeds

In the past, I (Stephanie) would approach Dan with time-sensitive information, overwhelming him with details and immediately asking for his opinion. This approach made him feel bombarded and pressured to provide solutions or opinions instantly, which wasn't feasible. Our differing styles — my decisiveness and preference for quick planning versus Dan's inclination to ponder, research, and keep options open — often led to a deadlock. Dan would point out the difficulty in making decisions quickly, as new information might lead to better solutions. However, not every decision can wait for optimal conditions. Recognizing this, he asked for more time to contribute meaningfully to our discussions.

Before the era of texting, we used email as a communication tool, which suited Dan's learning style. He could process information and conduct his research without the immediate influence of my emotions. For non-urgent decisions, I would compile an email with research and thoughts, giving him the space to form his response. We would then set a time later in the week to discuss the matter and reach a decision. This approach reduced pressure on Dan, allowing him time to thoroughly consider the information and add valuable insights to our discussions. Our strategy has evolved but it continues to be a positive part of our communication process.

Another strategy we've adopted is to categorize our discussions. I'll give Dan a heads-up about the nature of the conversation I want to have. This pre-discussion coding is especially useful when differentiating between relational, logistical or financial matters. We've become proficient in handling logistics and finances, but for topics involving relationships and emotions, we've found a different approach to be effective.

For these more emotionally charged discussions, such as those on spiritual growth or relational issues, we start by writing in a shared notebook. I'll jot down my thoughts and questions, allowing Dan the time and space to process them. He can then reflect on what he wants to say or ask. This method of initiating conversation has led to more successful and productive live discussions, whether over a meal or during a walk.

There are typical polarities presented in many neurodiverse relationship books: in addressing these, I (Stephanie) have recognized that I cannot sacrifice my emotional and relational needs, nor can I expect Dan to process emotions at my pace. Similarly, Dan understands that he can't expect me to forgo my needs or handle all decisions and relational matters single-handedly. Building empathy and making accommodations for each other has been key to moving past the stuck points in our relationship.

One crucial lesson we've learned is to focus on one topic at a time. Although this can sometimes be frustrating for me, it's necessary for productive discussions. I often remind myself to let go of speed and instead choose to have a quality conversation with less conflict. Prioritizing quality and harmony over speed and efficiency has proven more beneficial. Overloading Dan with too much information at once led to reduced engagement from him. By finding the right balance in the speed and volume of information, we've successfully navigated our way out of many challenging phases in our relationship.

Growth Tip: Effective Coaching Strategy

Our research also revealed that a significant frustration often mentioned by the ND/AS spouse is the NA/NT's tendency to compare their relationship to idealized marriages portrayed in the media (i.e., Hallmark or Disney films), or to other neurotypical (NT) couples, or to an ideal "Christian utopian" marriage. These unrealistic comparisons are linked to another common issue: the difficulty to mutually and effectively express love. Here, even popular frameworks like those suggested in *The Five Love Languages*[7] can prove challenging in the context of neurodiverse relationships. The ND/AS spouse may feel confined to expressing love in their inherent love language and struggle to adopt a new one, leading to frustration when their efforts don't seem to resonate with their partner.

To address this, I often recommend the book *Love Needs*[8] to couples who have begun the work of healing from their crises and trauma. This book broadens the scope of love languages, presenting 30 needs identified through extensive professional counseling. The process begins with an assessment where each partner ranks their top 10 love needs. The back of the sheet provides space to list these top needs and to note two specific ways each need can be meaningfully met, tailoring the general concept to specific, personal preferences.

In practice, I advise couples not to tackle all 10 love needs at once, but to start with needs ranked 8-10 to build consistency and positive momentum. Gradually, they move to addressing needs ranked 5-7, then 3-4, and finally 1-2. This approach helps to mitigate potential clashes between differing neurotypes by starting with the 'easier' needs. However, in cases where the relationship has suffered from abuse or neglect, and one spouse has been predominantly accommodating the other, the imbalance must be identified, and the approach modified accordingly. In such situations, the couple first works on addressing the love needs of the more depleted spouse, fostering a sense of balance and reciprocity. This process aims to halt negative cycles and restore mutual trust and understanding, with the ultimate goal being a balanced and reciprocal partnership.

This book is intentionally titled *Uniquely Us* to address the common pitfall of comparing one's relationship to idealized standards. This title reflects the understanding that joy and satisfaction in a relationship are highly individual and, as mentioned above, may not resemble portrayals seen on TV or in other couples. This is especially true when considering messages from mainstream Christian marriage resources, which often set unrealistic goals and expectations that are particularly challenging for neurodiverse Christian couples (NDCCs). The addition of "gracefully" to the title underscores the ongoing need for grace and empathy in navigating the complexities of a neurodiverse marriage.

Our approach does not offer simple solutions or guarantees for a perfect outcome. Instead, we believe that through personal responsibility, a growth mindset, and the adoption of practical tools and strategies, couples can address their mistakes, reassess their marriage beliefs and theology, and work through trauma or abuse. These steps, though challenging, can lead to contentment, satisfaction, and even fulfillment in a neurodiverse marriage.

Another common challenge for AS/ND spouses is the frequent criticism or mis-interpretation of communication about relationship issues. As authors Stone and Heen highlight in their book *Thanks for the Feedback*,[9] it's crucial to learn to "difference spot" and "right spot." While not specifically about marriage or ND couples, this book is a resource we recommend to our clients, accompanied by a free self-study course available on our website. Learning to receive and balance feedback, combining appreciation with constructive coaching, is vital for breaking negative communication cycles. Many AS/ND spouses feel they are constantly being evaluated, with every mistake potentially leading to drastic consequences. However, this doesn't mean that addressing hurts, setting goals, and maintaining accountability should be avoided. Rather, it's about reframing how feedback is perceived and shared, a key skill for moving beyond the impasses in a relationship.

Finally, let's look at common comments made, specifically by a male AS/ND partner on what attracted them to their female NT/NA spouse.

- *She was kind, sweet, praised/encouraged me*
- *She saw potential or things in me I did not see*
- *She said she accepted me for who/how I was*
- *She is bright/intelligent/ could carry on heady or substantive conversations*
- *She was fun and liked some of the same things I liked (but with less intensity)*

When things changed, after the diagnosis and entering counseling the male AS/ND spouse said:

- *I thought she was kind/sweet but now nothing I do pleases her*
- *Why can't she say what she means? Why does she expect me to guess her thoughts? Why is my being direct/honest wrong?*
- *She says we "don't connect"/"have intimacy" I have no clue what she means by these words*
- *I thought she knew my quirks/eccentricities/nuances/differences and accepted them; now all she brings up is how I need to change and how terrible of a person I am*
- *She says, "Why can't you do this or that like so-and-so's spouse?"*
- *I feel nagged/bullied/criticized*
- *I wonder why I bother trying, nothing is right*

In the next chapter, we will look at marital satisfaction and dissatisfaction from the perspective of the NT/NA spouse. But for the NA/NT spouse, what is an action point or information that could be helpful to know in your marriage? And what does that mean when offering grace and empathy to your ND/AS spouse?

Outside of the Maze: Dan's Insights and Hindsight Learning

I (Dan) observe that the tension in the "Prodigal Son" Bible story is relieved when it's revealed that the father has been watching for the son, and he comes running to meet him. The NIV's[10] phrasing (in Luke 15:11-32) is that the father saw him from "a long way off." This is a picture of waiting in patient expectation. The son was welcomed home, regardless of his actions, words, and thoughts from earlier days. The father demonstrates this: "love never fails" – a picture before 1 Corinthians 13 was written. Such endurance and hope by the father are not easy to maintain. Some days – many days – we don't feel anything like it in our neurodiverse marriages: yesterday was too much, and today isn't looking any better.

What I know is when you recognize that someone is trying and they are beginning to do something different, it is rewarding. When Stephanie rephrases something to be clearer, or when she starts a conversation a week before she is ready to have it, I am rewarded by feeling seen and understood. I know she likes decisions and a decision made quickly. I am not like that. We have used the metaphor that I am a slow-cooker (crockpot) and she is an "Instant Pot" or microwave. Each of those appliances has a purpose, and something good in one isn't usually good in the other. So, when I see she has surrendered her preference and leaned into mine, that shows she wants me involved. She believes I have something to offer and that what I have is worth the cost of surrendering her preference. When I follow through on this, it shows that I am receptive to her. For instance, if she starts a conversation on a Monday with an agreement that we continue it on a Thursday, and I am ready and engaged when Thursday comes, she is 'rewarded' for preferring me in this way. If, however, I am not ready because I didn't do the research (or whatever was required) or I say I don't want to and I don't engage with her, I am showing her that I don't value her or what it took for her to approach me against her instincts. Likely, she won't do that again until I follow through and repair what I have broken. Establishing a pattern of follow-through will build trust and create a "benefit of the doubt" when you occasionally don't. And when you don't, it's important to apologize and repair the relationship, quickly.

We have learned (and still are learning) about our different skill sets and about which of us is better at a specific task.

We have learned (and still are learning) about our different skill sets and about which of us is better at a specific task. This is in everything: from cooking and cleaning to technology and finances, to navigating social situations, to what I wear when I go out in public. We lean on this understanding. It doesn't have to be via traditional husband and wife roles; it needs to work, first and foremost.

This next suggestion is for the couple that is already teaming well to work themselves out of the maze. (If this isn't where you are, then this suggestion may not be for you – yet.) What makes things work is the combination of solving the daily mini-mazes along with maintaining the "hopeful expectation" shown by the prodigal son's father. You are regularly in the expectation that this act of love (expressing things the way your spouse can best receive them) will yield a welcome ear. At the same time, one must fend off the temptation to become resentful like the older brother in the story. That mental conflict is real: perhaps you have felt unseen for so long and have not received a reception of joy or celebration; you don't want your spouse (the younger brother) to experience any grace.

How is your spouse reaching out to you in their approach? They may have started looking for the way out of the maze and might be asking you for an assist. As the receiving spouse, recognizing this and reciprocating both in appreciation and like behavior is how you move this forward. Think of it as a turn-based game, where it takes one step from each of you to complete the turn. What needs to happen next to get closer to the exit of this maze? It is all about context. What has happened in the last 30 seconds, 5 minutes, hour, and perhaps even yesterday? Is repair needed? What about the situation is like one you've experienced before? Conflicts usually have patterns; they are often not unique. You may have seen this before. What lessons from history can you draw? Conflict and curiosity are good teachers, if you allow them to be. How does your spouse's pattern work? What makes things turn out better? If you don't know, have you asked?

The call to action is for both partners to act with "hopeful expectation" while pushing back the temptation to be withholding or resentful. Then when it is your turn, complete the step by continuing down the road. Remember, the younger brother didn't turn and run when he saw his father approaching. He didn't hide. He knew that where he had been and what he had done – despite the shame – wasn't comparable to the goodness of living with his father. It is this hopeful attitude that finds a way out of every maze and keeps the relationship moving forward.

When I (Dan) see Stephanie reaching out and using an approach that works for me, it creates a desire in me to do good in return. To set realistic expectations, this wasn't something that happened quickly for us. It didn't 'happen' at all; it became a daily choice. This involved much trial and error, and it still does. Much of it wasn't predetermined nor preplanned; we didn't have a coach helping us to find these things. Even with the ideas of this chapter and book, a reliable strategy for exiting the maze is as much a matter of endurance as it is desire. What is also true is that when you recognize it working once, the taste for more success grows.

If what I have described isn't where you are, then it is time to decide what you want. If you are content in whatever state your relationship is in, then changing may not be something you want to do. If this is you, I would ask, how does this align with God's design for marriage? Are you *partnering* with each other to show glory to *Him*? If neither of you is thriving, I would suggest that it is being observed by others. God is not being glorified by your relationship. If one of you is pretending in public (church) to have marital satisfaction, then I would wonder if the pretender is doing what God would want or what their partner wants. If that is you, are you stuck in appearances or tradition? Is there a role you expect of yourself, or that you think others expect? Perhaps you have set an expectation that your *image* is important, and therefore, others need to pretend so it isn't tarnished.

Ask God to search your heart, and if you are courageous, ask your spouse.

The call is to be honest with where you are with God, yourself, and your relationships. Search yourself. Ask God to search your heart, and if you are courageous, ask your spouse. Be willing to accept the feedback that is given. Staying in denial doesn't help. Pushing someone away doesn't help, and certainly, ignoring the One that can reveal doesn't help.

What Stephanie and I hope for is healthy people producing growing relationships. That only happens when both parties are engaged and see their reality for what it is. They listen to each other. They give grace and receive grace. They are kind in word and deed. They are everything 1 Corinthians 13 says love is. They are patient with themselves and each other, and they endure. They know this life is not all there is, but they also know that the "abundant life" is available now. It can be experienced in the land of the living. Choose this day: abundance or desolation. And tomorrow you can choose again.

Personal Story: Intentionality is Key

*(Excerpts used with permission from **An Intentional Marriage:***
***Tools for a Stronger Relationship**, by Brian Hight).*

My marriage's Doomsday Clock was at **23:59:57** and I was asleep and unaware of my world. At **23:59:58** a sense of unease roused me, but I was unable to identify the cause. As the clock flicked to **23:59:59** I woke to the harsh reality that my marriage was about to collapse or explode. I didn't know what would happen, but I suddenly knew I was the problem, and if my marriage was going to survive, I had to change my attitude and my actions. **INTENTIONALITY:** An attitude of purposefulness, with a commitment to deliberate action. (Dictionary.com).

Our world is teeming with distractions and incessant demands on our time and attention. It is no surprise we slip into ruts and habits that keep us moving without thinking and responding without reasoning. We shield ourselves from the relentless barrage of information by relying on these familiar patterns and habitual responses, but in doing so, we risk becoming disconnected from the world around us and the people who share our lives.

It is all too easy to shut down and stop noticing, responding, and caring. Consequently, we can jeopardize our health and well-being. This can affect all areas of our lives, most significantly, our personal relationships. We end up living an unintentional life where events and people are taken for granted. I will share how unintentionality took a toll on my relationship with my wife and jeopardized my marriage. My mental wiring (Autism Spectrum Disorder, Level 1), my introverted personality, and my upbringing all contributed to the difficulties I experienced, but they were not the primary issues. The real problem was that I had stopped investing in my marriage. I was living an unintentional life. The journey towards intentionality requires commitment and focus, and as with all major endeavors, you will need tools and skills to help you reach your destination. This journey is not a one-time fix, but a lifelong commitment to seeking the best in yourself, your world, and especially in relationships. My journey towards intentionality commenced during a relationship crisis when I came face to face with the stark realization that I had ceased to engage with my wife on a deep and meaningful level. It became clear to me that I had gradually failed to prioritize her or our relationship. While I had been aware for years that our marriage was far from what I had envisioned, I felt utterly lost and unsure of any viable solution. I was unable and unwilling to see my own culpability for the demise of our relationship because I thought everything was my wife's fault. I was blind to my own harmful attitudes and actions. Unfortunately, it required a crisis before I was willing to confront and acknowledge my own attitudes and the damage they caused. The realization and acceptance came after a profound epiphany about my attitude.

There must be a commitment to the journey, otherwise the goal of an improved relationship cannot be achieved. Nothing of lasting value happens by chance or without effort. As I began to consistently live from my new mindset, my expectations for my marriage changed from expecting a future of mediocrity to flourishing in the renewed reality of a close and meaningful relationship.

My wife, who was a counselor, has often said that people habitually do things because there is a payoff from the action. It might be easier to ignore an issue than confront necessary changes, or there is less effort required to live with some pain than to practice new habits in the hope of a new outcome. Or simply because there is a measure of security in living with a known circumstance rather than risking change for an unknown result.

It is a certain fact that if nothing is done, nothing will be achieved. The issue that remains is whether the level of risk of the unknown is greater or less than the level of commitment to change.

Growth Tips to Navigating the Maze Gracefully

- As you continue to read, you will find there are often different levels of satisfaction for NDCCs. When you hear from your spouse that he or she is hurt, dissatisfied, or wanting out of the marriage, what do you do with this information? Are you curious to find out about these hurts or do you dismiss these hurts or needs with defensiveness or spouting your good intentions? How do you offer grace and become curious about your spouse?

- In order to find mutual satisfaction and build tools and skills to be better *equipped* as a couple, you may need the help of a neurodiverse trained coach or counselor. Becoming better equipped is stage 2 in neurodiverse couple work. While we (Dan and I) did not have a coach to guide us through this maze, my (Dr. Stephanie's) background in counseling and communication was helpful as we discovered our trial-and-error process. When a marriage is in crisis or a negative cycle, a guide is often necessary to help you get unstuck from this maze. Referral information for those trained under the International Association of NeuroDiverse Christian Marriage is found on the "Referrals" tab at *www.christianneurodiversemarriage.com*. Many of the contributing authors of this book are trained counselors or coaches. Find a guide (coach) that can meet your needs. Not only do you want a neurodiverse-trained coach, but you also want one that is a fit for *you*. Reading this book is not enough to get you unstuck from your maze, but it is a starting point.

- The strategies that we (Dan and Stephanie) mentioned work for us as well as other couples. Find your communication strategy that meets both your needs (for slowing the process *and* for getting a resolution to an issue). Remember: ignoring the problem or conflict does not make it go away. It will make it worse.

- Ask yourself: Am I committed to change? What does change look like? How do you know when you are ready to change? Barbara Grant's chapter (6) will help you examine your readiness to change and outline some strategies. If you are ready to be intentional and engaged in the work, it helps to make necessary changes in yourself before trying to change the marital dynamic.

$\mathscr{Chapter\ Three}$

Navigating the Maze of Expectations and Marital Satisfaction From the Perspective of the Neurotypical or Non-Autistic Spouse: A Tale of 2 Marriages

REV. DR. STEPHANIE C. HOLMES AND REV. DAN HOLMES, MS (A NEURODIVERSE CHRISTIAN COUPLE)

n the previous chapter, the table on marital satisfaction indicated the differences in marital satisfaction as reported by AS/ND and NA/NT spouses. Of the handful of couples who were both on the spectrum, there was only one couple where both spouses indicated they were satisfied in the marriage. We will further discuss the different nuances in the types of neurodiverse couples, but for this chapter, the focus is specifically on an NA/NT spouse married to someone on the autism spectrum. When the following blog was available on our website, many wives resonated with author Nicole Mar's (pseudonym) account of being an NA/NT wife:

I am the wife of a man with Asperger Syndrome (AS/ND) traits. About 15 years ago, I met him — the man of my dreams. It was during a hurricane, and I was standing at the front door of my apartment complex, a divorced, broke,

mother of one. I didn't have the money to escape the hurricane, like the other tenants in my complex. And I was too depressed to care enough to do anything about it. Yet, I was worried about the welfare of my child, so my child and I stood watching the hurricane loom closer and closer.

Suddenly in comes my knight in a baseball cap and Levi's jeans. He looked at me and complimented me for having moved my vehicle to a part of the parking lot where a tree couldn't fall on it. I was amazed by his casual tone and relieved not to be alone in the building. I think my toddler was relieved too. In her young effort to keep the conversation going, she blurted out, "Excuse me, sir. Why don't you have a mustache?"

He replied, "Excuse me, ma'am. Why are you so short?"

We all laughed. He told me he was stuck in the apartment because he'd gotten off work too late to be able to leave. Now the weatherman was saying to take cover, so he'd done what he could to prepare for the storm. We headed to our individual apartments. I glanced inside his place as he opened his door, only to be completely mortified by what he called doing "what he could." He had all his furniture up on box crates. His windows were all taped. He had batteries, candles, canned food, and cases of water in view.

I went into my apartment and prepared dinner over my gas stove since the power had already gone out and the food in my refrigerator would soon be no good. Feeling more and more dread, I decided I needed a way to continue the conversation with this neighbor because I'd done absolutely nothing to prepare for the storm. He was our only hope.

About an hour later, I took a deep breath and knocked on his door. "Hey, neighbor. So, what are you up to?" He replied, "Just sitting in my tub waiting out the storm."

I laughed again. What a relief to laugh. "Are you serious? Do you plan to sit in your tub the entire night?" "Yes, that's what the weatherman urged us to do for those who don't have a basement, but I have a transistor radio, and I think the storm is still a couple of hours out." "Oh, in that case, do you want to play a board game at my place?"

"Okay."

We played Scrabble by candlelight. It felt romantic, and I laughed throughout the game, winning with every play. To me, he felt safe, consistent, and easy to please. But I had recently gone through a divorce. I didn't want to get into another relationship. Somehow, I felt like he could be a friend. He wouldn't force a relationship on me.

Fast Forward eight years later. We each dated each other and then came back to the comfort of our friendship time after time. We decided to get married. I would describe marriage to a person with AS/ND traits as very high highs and dreadfully low lows. A roller coaster ride that goes on and on but evokes the same extreme reactions. Our marriage was at first exhausting, and then eventually just plain scary.

It's been several years since we got married, and with God's help and guidance, we figured out what was challenging with our marriage. We didn't know about Asperger Syndrome (ASD) all those years we spent getting to know each other. Plus, I was his "special interest," so the symptoms were pretty well hidden, and he was masking.

Marriage was like a light switch. Suddenly he seemed to go from a sweet, intelligent, and generous man who adored me to this asocial, moody, tightwad who could spend days away from me without a second thought. And for him, I went from a supportive, forgiving woman he adored to a nagging, bitter, weeping complainer.

We're making it work. Day by day. Okay, sometimes hour by hour. But we're still here. I want to share our journey and our story with you.

When I (Stephanie) have shared our story or taught workshops, I usually refer to my neurodiverse marriage in two ways: I quote Charles Dickens, from *A Tale of Two Cities:* "It was the best of times, it was the worst of times. It was a season of light, it was the season of darkness, it was the spring of hope, it was the winter of despair." I explain that mine is a "Tale of Two Marriages." My experience of marriage before Dan's diagnosis of autism was not going well, and Dan's experience was going well. For Dan, ignorance was bliss; but for me, what I did not know *did* hurt me, repeatedly. I may also refer to our marriage as our first marriage (NC: lived in North Carolina) and our second marriage (GA: lived in Georgia), yet we have never divorced. The differences in satisfaction for me are as different as living in two different states. Had I participated in the study 15 years ago, I would have checked the box of "very dissatisfied or very discontent," and Dan would have checked, "content or satisfied." Today, with knowledge of our neurodiversity and by doing intentional work to build a marriage we both thrive in, we would both check "happily married and satisfied." We will talk more about how we changed ourselves and our marriage in later chapters when we discuss neuroplasticity and intentionality.

The study that we conducted in 2023 had far more NA/NT wives as participants than other demographics. Let's look at the differences in marital satisfaction from the point of view of the NA/NT wife, who sees the marital challenge quite differently from her AS/ND spouse.

Answer Choices	Responses
Lack of connection or emotional intimacy	83.49% (273)
Communication on a daily basis is difficult/misunderstanding/lack of attunement	80.12% (262)
Conflict does not get resolved/conflict is avoided	75.54% (247)
My spouse/partner does not seem to understand my point of view/perspective	74.92% (245)
Sexual relationship	70.95% (232)
Emotional dysregulation of my spouse (formerly called melt-downs)	58.41% (191)
We do not have friends or as many friends with other couples that we both enjoy	57.19% (187)
Emotional shutdowns: my spouse will emotionally shut down and we will not speak for long periods of time	54.74% (179)
Lack of overall communication (lack of courtesy check-ins, updates on schedules, logistics)	54.45% (178)
We do not spend time together in shared activities (note: watching TV does not count as a shared activity) or experiences	52.91% (173)
My spouse/partner is not curious or does not appear interested in me	50.76% (166)

Question 26 asked this spouse "At what point did it seem things changed in your relationship?" (or as Nicole Mar put it, "the switch flipped"). The following chart indicates the answers received by the different NA/NT spouses:

Answer Choices	Responses
Other (please specify)	21.10%
After the wedding/honeymoon	19.27%
First year of marriage/living together	17.13%
After the first child was born	13.76%
I am not sure we were ever really connected or both satisfied in this relationship	9.79%
First month of marriage/living together	8.26%
After engagement	6.12%
When we had teenagers	2.75%
When the kids left home	1.83%

In the first category, "other" represented a compilation of answers, including: during the COVID shutdown; when he began working from home; during a financial crisis or changes in finances, a move, or a job transition; when a child/children were diagnosed with

ASD or ADHD; when we got custody of his (or my) kids; when a parent moved in with us; or during a health crisis (his or hers). The options of "other" as well as the others listed above all indicate a major change in life or transition. When we think of human development, it is common to refer to developmental milestones or life stages. Married life has developmental milestones and changes, and as many have observed, *change* is usually difficult for those with autism. Change, however, is a consistent part of life. Dr. Peter Vermeulen, in *Autism and the Predictive Brain, Absolute Thinking in a Relative World*[1] writes, "The theory that the prediction system of an autistic brain is different from that of the non-autistic brain is still very recent. In particular, we think autism is associated with an inability to flexibly adjust the degree of precision in a different context. Or to put it in slightly different terms: when making predictions about the world, when learning and updating its models of that world, and when dealing with sensory information that deviates from those models, the autistic brain seems as though it is affected by context-blindness" (pgs. 36-37). He explains that to the autistic brain, the world is filled with unpleasant surprises that were not predicted and appear random. Thus, life changes can create enormous stress for the autistic person, which often produces stress for the non-autistic spouse.

The AS/ND spouse may minimize or deny that there are problems to solve proactively, which then burdens the NA/NT spouse with stepping up to field the problems alone. Often the AS/ND spouse may be averse to asking for help or getting open about the stress that change has brought and may instead handle the stress by masking (acting as if all is well, especially to those outside the marriage) or spending more time alone or in special interests. This solitary way of handling stress becomes ineffective for the marriage, as it further burdens the NA/NT spouse, who is likely more relational and desires outside help and support. When this spouse begins to tell others there are problems in the marriage and with the AS/ND's behaviors, outsiders don't often see the truth of what is happening and may dismiss or question the NA/NT's complaints and cries for support. This experience of not being believed or taken seriously has been frequently reported by NA/NT spouses: it evolves over time and is hard to understand, especially by those it is happening to. In the world of neurodiverse relationships, it has come to be known by a somewhat controversial name: "The Cassandra Syndrome."

In Greek mythology, Cassandra was the daughter of King Priam of Troy. The capricious god, Apollo, fancied her and decided he must have her, and as a god, he was used to getting what he wanted. However, Cassandra did not fancy him the same way, and Apollo cursed her with the gift of prophecy (accurate prediction) with the twist that no matter how many times she accurately predicted events, she would never be believed. Cassandra lost her mind. See the connection?

An additional frustration for the NA/NT occurs when, during times of change, they tend to have better predictive abilities and fewer predictive errors than their AS/ND partner. However, no matter how they try to give advice or warnings to their spouse (i.e., "If we do not plan for A, then B will happen" or "This is how we could/should prepare for this situation"), the autistic spouse can be dismissive of their predictions. No matter how many times the NA/NT spouse is correct, the autistic spouse's tendency towards predictive failure causes them not to heed the warning. When preparations or evasive maneuvers don't happen and the change or disaster ensues, AS/ND spouses are often surprised and can even blame the NA/NT spouse for the outcome. In the interview portion of our research, I asked one autistic spouse, "How often would you gauge your wife is accurate in understanding social or family situations?" His answer was, "I would give her a high 80s or 90%." I followed up with, "How often when she suggests a plan or alternative course of action, do you heed the warning or change course?" He replied, "Rarely. I mean how does she know what will happen?" I then asked, "Don't the numbers you provided (at least 80% accuracy) indicate a change in course direction is likely warranted?" He said, "You would think so, but probably not. Each time is a new situation to me whether or not she was accurate before is not relevant."

Clinically, Cassandra Syndrome closely resembles *Complex-PTSD* (C-PTSD), which has finally been included in the *ICD-11* as a legitimate diagnosis.[2] *The ICD-11* description includes the following: "Complex PTSD is characterised by severe and persistent 1) problems in affect regulation; 2) beliefs about oneself as diminished, defeated or worthless, accompanied by feelings of shame, guilt or failure related to the traumatic event; and 3) difficulties in sustaining relationships and in feeling close to others. These symptoms cause significant impairment in personal, family, social, educational, occupational or other important areas of functioning."[2] Since adult autism is largely under-diagnosed, many neurodiverse couples are only now beginning to realize the connection between emerging symptoms of Complex-PTSD as an unfortunate result of the autism diagnosis being unknown for many years of the marriage. The NA/NT spouse is especially vulnerable to not having their lived experience believed by their AS/ND spouse or their adult children, family, friends, counselors or pastors.

While various blogs and podcasts have provided different definitions for the Cassandra Syndrome, this is a compilation of symptoms: negative self-image or loss of self-identity, anger and emotional dysregulation, various anxiety or trauma responses (OCD, panic), hypervigilance, flashbacks or triggers of trauma, physical illnesses, and weakened immune system. Of the 20 NA/NT women I interviewed in the second portion of our study, 18 had developed an autoimmune illness during the course of their marriage, stating their clinician had linked their illness to recurring stress. Several studies link ongoing and unrelenting stress to mental or physical illness,[3,4,5,6] and while autoimmune disease has genetic components, stress is recognized as the trigger for at least 50% of autoimmune disorders.[7] The 20 AS/ND men were asked if they had any autoimmune illnesses, and only 1 had an autoimmune condition. While some of the AS/ND partners expressed dissatisfaction or not having their sexual needs met, they did not report a stress-related illness or condition.

Several studies link ongoing and unrelenting stress to mental or physical illness.

In the interview portion of the study as well as the open-ended questions at the end of the survey, the second reason for "the switch flipping" seems to be masking or camouflaging. Dr. Tony Attwood and Dr. Michelle Garnett describe, "A person with autism can acquire successful social and interpersonal abilities by observing peers and people in general, analyzing and interpreting their social behavior, and then copying the observed social rules and convention, thus effectively camouflaging their social difficulties. The person creates a 'social mask'."[8] Masking was once considered to be prevalent only in autistic females, but research shows both males and females use masking or camouflaging.[9] Attwood and Garnett also stated that because masking or camouflaging autistic traits is prevalent, this can delay a proper diagnosis or identification, as the autistic individual will build compensatory behavioral strategies over their lifespan. But often, when "at home," neurodiverse people may dispense with these strategies. As I interviewed the NA/NT wives, a common refrain about such changes in their spouse were described as "a bait and switch," "Jekyll and Hyde" or "a flip" or a major "switch." The authors of this book do not contend that the autistic spouse willingly, knowingly, or maliciously deceived those they were dating or marrying, but for the majority of those in this study, the autism was not identified until after the marriage, when the individual was already over the age of 30 (and often older). Thus, not only was the NA/NT spouse unaware of the autism, but so was the autistic person. Only 5 of the 108 autistic individuals who took the survey were identified before the age of 19, and 10 more before the age of 30. For the NA/NT, the person they fell in love with (or as Nicole Mar called her "knight in shining armor') suddenly changed. What happened?

In addition to changes in masking behaviors, another theme that has emerged in research as well as in our study: that it is not uncommon for a girlfriend/fiancé/spouse to be the object of the autistic person's "special" or restricted interest. The *DSM-5*[10] defines a restricted interest as a "fixation" that is "abnormal in intensity and focus." Such interests can be in anything from topics, hobbies, collectibles and objects, and even people. The interest itself does not have to be odd or abnormal, it is the intensity of focus and amount of time pursuing the interest, planning for the pursuit, thinking or imagining details about the interest, and the energy spent in the interest that set it apart. These special interests can change over time. In interviews for *Autism Parent Magazine* and *Autism/ Asperger Digest*, Dr. Attwood said, "A special interest tends to have a 'use by date' of 3-5 years," though some can remain over the lifetime. In the study, many wives observed they thought they had been a "special interest" when the couple was dating. When I asked one AS/ND man to describe how he chose his wife or what attracted him to her, he said, "Easy. She paid attention to me and after asking several girls out online, she said yes, so she was the one!" In another interview, I asked the autistic husband what he thought marriage and partnership would look like, and he said, "Well, like dating but we live together. I would also have someone to come with me to watch me do my things or participate with me in my interests."

In another survey for an article I wrote for the American Association of Christian Counselors in 2016,[11] I asked NA/NT wives about their husbands: "While dating, what were the qualities you admired about them?" The responses compiled from 30 wives include:

- *His boyish charm/ nativity/ social immaturity/ awkwardness around me*
- *He was quiet/ shy/ aloof/ mysterious/ reserved/ stable/ honest*
- *He was interested in me/ Went out of his way to show me he liked me/ almost obsessed with me*
- *He wasn't like the other guys*
- *Intelligent/ smart/ kind of geeky in a cute way/ felt he would go far in his line of work*
- *Felt he would stable/ good provider/ good father because he got along with children*

The second question asked these wives why they were in counseling at this time. Answers included:

- *He is rude/ cold /aloof/ selfish/ He only cares about himself*
- *He is embarrassing often in social situations and does not seem to care*
- *I feel like [there's been] a bait and switch! The interest he once had in me while dating, is now shifted to other interests and he ignores me, like I was once a special interest and now I am not*
- *He is so smart but cannot seem to progress at work and never seems to understand what I am communicating. He is stuck in a rut at work or cannot keep a job*

- *He is not attached as a spouse or parent*
- *Those stupid obsessions/ interests/ hobbies he would rather spend money and time with those than me*
- *I don't feel like I can rely on him or respect him*
- *I feel alone/ isolated/ rejected/ de-valued/ unimportant to him*
- *Whenever I try to have a conversation, he gets combative/ he hammers me/ he shuts me out/ he says I am nagging/criticizing*

One of the first things I address in ND couple's coaching is that NA/NTs entered their marriage with expectations of an NT-NT marriage. When the wife hears about Asperger's/ autism, she may first feel elated that "this was not in her head" and that "I've tried everything and thought it was all me," but there now is a label or name for the behaviors. She will likely have to grieve the loss of the marriage she thought she was getting (NT-NT). I make it clear that our coaching goal is not to meet the expectations of an NT-NT marriage, since this is not what exists. The goal is to reexamine the expectations and optimize the marriage in light of their neurodiversity and to strive to reach a relationship in which both can feel marital satisfaction.

Though having expectations of an NT-NT marriage can lead to dissatisfaction for these couples, the survey accounted for this by asking participants what the challenges or issues they experienced being in a *neurodiverse* marriage. The following chart is a combination of the top reasons both spouses felt strife, tension, or dissatisfaction in the marriage. I have chosen the answers that were given by 50% or more of the participants.

In the next chapter, we will look at comparisons of those elements as reported from the AS/ND male, AS/ND female, NA/NT female, and NA/NT male perspectives. But I want to go back to the previous Chapter 2 to look at what the AS/ND spouses said brought marital contentment or satisfaction and compare that to what NA/NT spouses said. The AS/ND spouse listed the following: a lack of conflict; encouragement to pursue own interests and passions; doing their thing of interest with their spouse; appreciation of what they bring to the marriage; acceptance for their differences; and no pressure, asks or demands. The AS/ND males (and 1 female) were also named as having more sexual relations. Dissatisfaction was described as: feeling criticized or blamed; not having enough alone time; any form of conflict; and having their autism blamed for the marital challenges. In contrast, the NA/NT spouses were looking for: better emotional intimacy and connection; better and more frequent communication; more quality time doing shared interest activities; sharing the mental load and household chores; co-parenting and shared responsibility with the children; and having their AS/ND partner initiate time with them and the family as well as spending less time in a restrictive interest doing things alone. Both the male and female NA/NT in the study expressed that: they want their AS/ND to pursue them; be curious about them; seek to understand their perspective; and be open to negotiating and problem-solving collaboratively. More than simple male-to-female differences, there is a fundamental difference in what brings satisfaction and contentment – each partner's needs frequently are directly opposed.

Self-determination theory (SDT) posits that all individuals, despite their neurotype, desire or need competence, autonomy, and relatedness to foster volition, motivation, or engagement to achieve creativity, persistence, and enhanced performance.[12,13,14] Wehmeyer and fellow researchers[15] argued that throughout the centuries, a debate emerged between religious groups and leaders over the concepts of free will and determinism. The authors of this book believe in free will: God put the tree of the knowledge of good and evil in the Garden of Eden, and He gave Adam and Eve the freedom to choose obedience and not to eat of it. Religious groups still argue today concerning free will. The philosophical belief that events and human behaviors are determined, or a result of a specific preceding cause, dominated intellectual thought until the turn of the 20th century, with the emergence of the field of psychology.[13] In the 1930s, psychologists began to argue that humans, while mammals, are distinguished from other mammals because they have thoughts and free will that influence behaviors and outcomes, which challenged the theories of Freud and behavioral psychologists who believed primarily in determinism.[13,15] As research expanded and the fields of personality psychology and motivational psychology emerged, psychologists studied people's intrinsic motivation and individual personality to coin the phrase *self-determinism*.[13,15]

In the 1970s and 1980s, early research by Richard Ryan and Edward Deci[12] argued that people have an intrinsic need to be self-determining and to be able to master their challenges. The three key elements of SDT are autonomy, competency, and relatedness.[12] *Autonomy* is far more than agency or independence. In their work, Deci and Ryan defined autonomy as "being the perceived origin or source of one's own behavior." Other research linked autonomy to Abraham Maslow's concept of self-actualization, which includes self-esteem, self-respect, and positive feelings about one's self-driven need to meet one's potential.[16] Control is seen as the opposite of autonomy. The use of extrinsic rewards, punitive measures, imposed goals, or consequences for various behaviors would be viewed as *control* to someone seeking autonomy.[13,16]

This concept of *autonomy* is highly valued, especially by those on the autism spectrum. A new acronym was recently introduced in the study of autism, known as *PDA*; in the clinical field this refers to *pathological demand avoidance* (or *pervasive demand avoid-*

ance).[17] If you were to look up PDA on internet sites or blogs written by individuals using the hashtag *#actuallyautistic*, these would say PDA signifies a *pervasive demand for autonomy*. The PDA Society stated that while it is a human trait to avoid demands from time to time, they define demand avoidance as, "not being able to do certain things at certain times, either for yourself or others, and also refers to the things we do in order to avoid demands." Within Autism, the autistic person may not only avoid demands or situations that trigger anxiety or sensory overload, but avoid anything that disrupts routines, involves transition, involves something of no interest to them, or which they deem is pointless, or any request or suggestion that is perceived to as a demand.[17] PDA involves "an irrational quality to the avoidance" which can be a dramatic reaction to feeling controlled, even by "a tiny request."[17] The PDA Society of the UK[17] posts an extensive list of what someone on the spectrum may perceive as a demand:

1. Time: This can include asking for the time of someone or giving up time to do something else of less preference.

2. Plans: This can be the making of plans, which for some feels like being tied down and not allowed to pursue one's interests or better opportunities that may occur, but it may also be interrupting the person's carefully made plans.

3. Questions: This can include being expected to answer a direct question or being questioned about a choice.

4. Decision: This can include being asked to make a decision or stand by a decision once the person has changed their mind.

5. Uncertainty: Those on the spectrum have an intolerance of the unknown and uncertainties; therefore, there is a high need to know and feel agency and control of their schedule, environment, and day.

6. Praise: For some, praise can feel like a demand or expectation that the action will be carried out again or can be improved upon in some way. Praise can bring stress to some.

7. Transitions: The need to change from one activity to another, especially if it is from a preferred activity to a lesser preferred activity.

8. Expectations: These can be expectations that one places on oneself or expectations from others that may include following through or keeping your word about an action.

9. Sensory overload and sensory integration difficulties: These can arise within the person or from the environment, and with overload can come the sense of being overwhelmed and perceiving things as threats that may not be a threat to others.

10. Other people's energy and presence: Sometimes another person being in the same room or proximity who is not talking or placing a demand can be a perceived threat or demand because of the unknown or uncertainty that the person may or could ask for something or change the schedule.

11. Preferences: Wanting to do a preferred activity or special interest instead of tasks, work, household chores, etc.

To explore the dynamics of PDA and autonomy in neurodiverse marriage, let's consider a real-world example: I worked with a couple who struggled with the issue of *follow-through*. The wife felt burdened by carrying the mental load of household responsibilities (despite both partners working) and expressed frustration over her AS/ND husband's broken promises to help with chores. He would commit to tasks but then fail to execute them. In a coaching session, we devised a plan, allocating specific chores to each person, which were to be documented in a binder when they were done. The husband initially showed enthusiasm, choosing chores he felt inclined towards or even enjoyed. However, when it came time to perform these tasks, the binder, which was meant to be a tool for accountability, was perceived as imposing demands. He saw his wife's expectation for him to fulfill his commitments as controlling. Even though the husband had agreed to complete a home task, like "x", upon returning from work, instead he consistently prioritized his personal activities like online research. Although in sessions he acknowledged the need to better share responsibilities with his wife by limiting his "research for pleasure" to only 3 or 4 hours a day, being monitored to ensure he followed through felt to him like a demand, triggering emotional dysregulation. Such repeated failures to keep promises can erode trust in a marriage, and the AS/ND partner may appear increasingly unreliable. This inconsistency and lack of follow-through can lead to relationship strains and exhaustion for the NA/NT spouse, who is left uncertain about what to realistically expect and rely on.

A common manifestation of PDA is the perception by the AS/ND that their partner's suggestions, ideas, or alternative solutions are controlling and demanding. For example, if an NA/NT spouse proposes an idea about where to dine or how to arrange something, or offers any differing viewpoint, the autistic spouse might perceive these normal marital interactions (in which mutual influence is expected), as threats to their personal autonomy. Even simple comments can be misinterpreted by the AS/ND as attempts to control them or criticism.

A typical scenario in neurodiverse marriages involves the AS/ND spouse acknowledging their forgetfulness or executive function challenges and requesting text reminders from their partner. However, if reminded, they may refuse to act, asserting that the reminder itself is a form of control. This paradoxical response can be enormously frustrating for the NA/NT spouse. Contrasting autonomy with relatedness, Ryan and Deci noted the importance of combining autonomy with *competency*. They defined relatedness as not just social connection but as a communal sense of *belonging*.[12,13] This concept aligns with Maslow's hierarchy, where belonging is crucial for self-actualization.[16] They further explained that relatedness and social context imply a sense of teamwork, belonging, and support, rather than constant social interaction.

For the NA/NT spouse, seeking more connection and relatedness is about feeling part of a marital team. Their suggestions or queries are often attempts to foster attention and connectedness. In neurodiverse marriages, such NA/NT needs for greater relatedness can clash with those of the AS/ND partner, who may be driven by a strong desire for autonomy. In a later chapter, we will explore how joy, *hesed* (Hebrew for "commitment" or "attachment"), group identity, and the capacity for healthy connection are crucial for personal transformation and healthy relationships. These factors become even more significant when considering the additional challenges posed by traditional religious beliefs about male headship, wifely submission, and gender-defined marital roles; when those are imposed on neurodiverse couples it can further frustrate healthy needs and exacerbate a husband and wife's differences.

From the NA/NT spouse's perspective, their hope of having a life partner and teammate can get lost in confusion and hurt, due to their spouse's defensive reactions and accusations that they are critical or controlling. This ongoing relational disappointment and stress, if not addressed, can escalate to abuse and trauma, a topic we will delve into in an upcoming chapter.

This ongoing relational disappointment and stress, if not addressed, can escalate to abuse and trauma.

 ## Outside of the Maze: Dan's Perspective and Message of Prayer for the Worn and Weary NA/NT Wife

Many of the wives in our counseling and coaching practice are tired, hurt, worn out, perhaps numb, and near to being hopeless. They wonder if there is life in their relationship and if there can be life in them again. The dream they had on their marriage day is far from their reality, and while achieving that dream remains unlikely, there is still a question if anything can be salvaged. Living in a grey world that consists of existing instead of thriving (abundant life) isn't what they had in mind. With this in mind...

Genesis 1:1 says, "In the beginning, God made the heavens and the earth. Now the earth was formless and empty, darkness was over the face of the deep, and the Spirit of God hovered over the waters" (NIV). We'll follow the paradigm laid out in creation:

You are made. God created you uniquely and wonderfully (Psalm 139). He has a plan for you (Jeremiah 29:11). He has come to give you abundant life (John 10:10).

You may feel formless. Where do I fit now? Apart from the robotic actions of managing a household, what is my purpose?

You may feel empty. King James uses the word void. Void indicates there is nothing left. You are spent and nothing is returned. The law of sowing and reaping isn't working. You give and there isn't a 'pressed down shaken together and running over' (Luke 6:38) type of return. Life is draining life, and there isn't any life left.

Darkness is all you see. The hope, if there is any, is the size of a pinhole. Darkness is also on your countenance. You hide it when necessary. The loss of hope though, has drained the light from your eyes.All of that might describe where you are ... let's keep reading.

The Spirit of God is hovering over all. He sees the void. He knows there is darkness. Verse 2 comes immediately after, and changes things -- what was is no longer: "And God said, 'Let there be light', ..." (NIV). From here on, darkness is separated from light. What was once void, is teaming with life.

Due to copyright, we cannot quote the song lyrics, but I invite you to look up the lyrics or the actual song "Breath Miracle" by Red Rocks Worship, close your eyes, breathe, and reflect on these words. Make this a prayer and remembrance of the One who created you with a purpose.

Father, I ask that for those who read this and desire it for themselves. Furthermore, that You would be near them and draw them to yourself and that as 3 John 1:2 says they would "prosper even as their soul prospers". Amen

A relationship takes two. You prospering and thriving doesn't change your relationship (it can't hurt it), but it will certainly help you begin to thrive, not just exist, and cultivate life in those you care for, despite your circumstances.

Outside of the Maze: Dan's Hindsight Learning: A Message for the AS/ND Husband from *Embracing the Autism Spectrum: Finding Hope & Joy in the NeuroDiverse Family Journey*[18]

As I reflect back on the journey our family has taken, it's impossible not to acknowledge the moments I missed. I am Dan – the neurodiverse dad and husband. My role in our family dynamics wasn't absent, but it was passive. I would listen to the events, nod in agreement, and occasionally participate, but I realize now that my involvement lacked depth and presence.

From our girls' perspective, our weekends were filled with play and laughter. They had the essentials and more – a comfortable home, nourishing food, clothing, toys, and school. Dress-up and our playful game of "Freddie the Fish" became cherished memories. But what they couldn't see, and what I didn't communicate, was my advocacy for them. I left that responsibility to Stephanie. I didn't fully stand beside her in the challenges she faced while fighting for our daughters' well-being and future.

Regrettably, I didn't offer her the support she needed most during those times. The pressure and disappointment that grew in her heart were outcomes of my absence – not a physical absence, but an emotional one. I was there, yet strangely distant. I didn't realize the pain she carried underneath her outward frustrations. Each complaint or irritation was part of a larger theme that I failed to see, a theme that would eventually manifest in ways I never expected.

My silence, my passive approach, robbed her of a partner in navigating the storm. I lacked engagement not only with the practical challenges but, more importantly, with her. I failed to express curiosity about her feelings or experiences. I was oblivious to the depth of her struggles, and this lack of presence allowed negativity from the periphery to seep in unchecked.

When I say "silent," I don't mean just words. I mean a wholehearted engagement with her – a commitment to understand and cherish her. My generosity was one-dimensional, and my gestures of love were often limited to empty promises. While I didn't need or want much myself, I projected this onto her. This one-dimensional approach left her feeling unfulfilled, longing for a connection that extended beyond material gestures.

My lack of interest and curiosity further exacerbated the divide. While she was a person with many projects and tasks, I didn't make the effort to share those interests. I didn't communicate that she was cherished, that her presence in my life was a gift. I realize now that I should have fought for her attention, for moments of togetherness that communicated her intrinsic value to me. Finding creative outlets for these expressions of love could have alleviated some of the pressure. It wasn't about grand gestures, but consistent efforts to connect. Investing in each family member, and truly engaging with their worlds, is an invaluable endeavor. It might require effort and practice, but the rewards are immeasurable.

This level of engagement should be ongoing, not limited to challenging periods. Building joy and connection within the family should be a constant effort. It's not something that expires when children grow up, move away, or start families of their own. Even when distance separates us, the affirmation that we are interested in their lives remains vital.

The journey of life often disappoints, revealing that even in places where we expect righteousness, there can be wickedness. Yet, these trials are growth opportunities. They refine us, teaching us resilience in the face of adversity. Our burdens, whether light or heavy, connect us as humans, and as Christians, we are called to support one another through these trials.

Bearing our crosses is a difficult path, one that Christ himself walked. It's not meant to be easy, but through it, we find strength and transformation. In times of light, when our burdens seem manageable, we must also be prepared to share the load of others. Galatians 6:2 reminds us of this responsibility, urging us to bear each other's burdens. In some ways, I could do that for others before my wife and children. We also must bear each other's burdens as spouses. Generosity and charity should begin in your own home.

As I look back on my journey as a husband and father, I see where I fell short. I recognize the importance of active engagement, of communicating love and interest through actions and words. My hindsight reflection serves as a reminder to all parents and spouses – that our roles are not merely passive. We must actively invest in the lives of our loved ones, building connections that withstand the challenges of life. As a neurodiverse husband and/or father, who are you building community with? If you lack the skills to be the husband or father needed by your family, who do you admire or have as a role model to learn these skills from? When your wife gives you a bid for attention makes a suggestion or tells you of her pain do you listen, or do you dismiss her concerns? Do you give yourself a pass because of your neurodiversity or are you still angry or in denial about your neurodiversity and unwilling to make changes to be the man God called you to be in your marriage and home? Neurology is a reason that things are different or challenging in your marriage; it is not a valid reason to not strive to be the best husband and father you can be or continue to learn skills that build joy and attachment in your home.

Chapter Four
Navigating the Maze of Similarities and Differences Among Different Types of Neurodiverse Couples

BY REV. DR. STEPHANIE C. HOLMES

U p to this point in the book, the focus of neurodiversity in couples has been on the type of neurodiverse couple where the husband is AS/ND and the wife is not. This combination is the most common neurodiverse couple seen by the authors in their coaching practices, but AS/ND women are commonly missed and diagnosed later in life after several misdiagnoses. Dr. Natalie Engelbrecht,[1] a female clinician who is on the spectrum, wrote that historically autism was seen more as a male diagnosis,[2,3] and males were diagnosed at higher ratios than females, but she contends there is a diagnostic gender bias. In the recent past, the diagnostic ratio of men to women was 10:1, but the current quoted male-to-female ratio is estimated to be 4:1, and some estimate 3:1.[4] Current research has even suggested a shift to 3:4.[5]

Women on the Autism Spectrum
Dr. Engelbrecht highlights the male bias in autism diagnosis, attributing it to factors such as camouflaging, special interests, and prevailing autism stereotypes. Engel-

brecht[1] noted that clinicians often require a higher symptomatic burden for diagnosis in females compared to males. Women must exhibit greater distress or dysregulation to be diagnosed and are often diagnosed later in life. This delay is partly due to their ability to camouflage autistic traits, allowing them to manage well enough in life and careers. Additionally, the special or passionate interests of women on the spectrum are typically less eccentric and more socially acceptable, contributing to the diagnostic discrepancy.[6,7,8]

Bargiela[9] and colleagues reported that females on the spectrum face a higher risk of misdiagnosis or of remaining undiagnosed. This issue arises because symptom research and criteria have historically been based on male presentations of autism. One common misperception among clinicians is the belief that a woman is too social or socially motivated to be on the spectrum. However, recent research suggests that females on the spectrum may simply be more social, have greater social capacity, and maintain more friendships than their male counterparts.[10,11]

Dr. William Carroll,[12] in his dissertation on the autistic female phenotype, cites Duvekot,[13] Lehnhardt et al.,[14] and Whyte and Scerf[15] who suggest that autism manifests differently in females. These females may exert more effort to appear neurotypical or camouflage their symptoms. Carroll's 2020 research, drawing on Hull and colleagues,[16] proposes that the female autism phenotype includes unique challenges in social relationships, such as increased social conflict, interests that are less mechanical and more relational, and internalizing difficulties manifesting as anxiety, depression, and eating disorders. Additionally, these females may make appropriate eye contact and tend to use prepared social scripts.

Carroll's approach to studying the female autism phenotype was distinctive. Instead of interviewing parents about differences in presentations, he conducted interviews with adult non-autistic sisters of autistic females. These sisters often serve as close, non-primary caregivers. Carroll's research aligns with Hull's 2020 findings. Through in-depth interviews, he discovered themes reported by the non-autistic sisters: these included higher conflict with friends and siblings due to the black-and-white thinking of the autistic sister; co-occurring manifestations of anxiety, depression, and eating disorders; more relationally focused special interests; and a heightened motivation for social interaction.

Professor Tony Attwood and Dr. Michelle Garnett[17] stated that a common choice of partner for an autistic woman tends to be an autistic partner rather than a non-autistic partner. According to Crompton and fellow researchers,[18] two autistic individuals marrying allows for the individuals to be themselves without masking, which can positively impact mental health. Autistic-to-autistic communication is reported to be more comfortable and less anxiety-provoking, due to similarities in communication styles.[17,18] Strunz and fellow researchers[19] found higher marital satisfaction in neurodiverse couples where both partners were on the autism spectrum. Other benefits of both partners being on the spectrum may include shared interests, a shared need for solitude and time with separate interests, and less need for highly social events.[21]

However, there is another neurodiverse couple type that is comprised of an autistic woman and a NA/NT partner. Attwood and Garnette[17] said that the non-autistic husband who is married to an autistic female has likely fallen deeply in love with her and seeks to make her happy; he also provides social, emotional, and practical support. Their research indicated that a non-autistic partner who is friendly, outgoing, talented, and socially motivated can see the potential in their partner and accept the autistic traits, and they may be willing to accommodate preferences around social situations and sensory sensitivities. The autistic female is more likely to be satisfied in the relationship if she feels safe and supported, especially if her partner is tolerant and compassionate when she is agitated or dysregulated for various reasons. However, they report from their clinical experience (and research by Ying Yew and associates[20]) that both the autistic and non-autistic partners may also report low satisfaction with emotional communication, amount of leisure time together, and intimacy.

The autistic female is more likely to be satisfied in the relationship if she feels safe and supported, especially if her partner is tolerant and compassionate when she is agitated or dysregulated for various reasons.

While our survey on neurodiverse marriage received over 300 respondents, the overwhelming majority of respondents were non-autistic female partners (NA/NT). Fewer respondents (108) reported they were on the autism spectrum (AS/ND). Of those 108 autistic respondents, 21 were biologically female and the remaining 87 identified as biologically male. Only 7 responses were from neurotypical men married to a female autistic partner. From the survey, 20 couples were chosen for qualitative interviews to compare similarities and differences among types of neurodiverse couples.

Question 18 in the survey asked respondents to check as many boxes as they could that reflected the challenges and complexities they experienced in their neurodiverse relationship. The charts below reflect the themes that occurred in 50% or more of the respondents' answers:

Relationship Type: Male ND/AS and Female NT/NA

ND/AS Males Responses to Survey Question 18 to List Common Challenges in the Relationship*

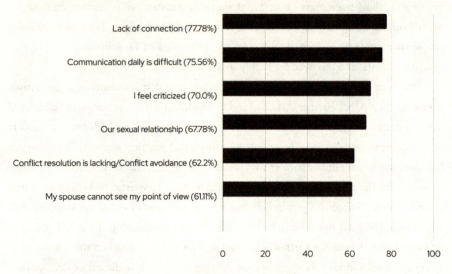

ND/AS Men n=87

* The chart reflects responses that were 50% or greater from the respondents.

Relationship Type: Male ND/AS and Female NT/NA

NT/NA Female Responses to Survey Question 18 to List Common Challenges in the Relationship*

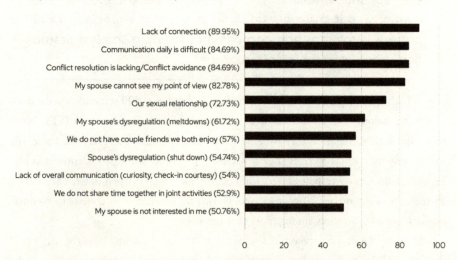

NT/NA women n=209

* The chart reflects responses that were 50% or greater from the respondents.

To compare satisfaction and dissatisfaction here, the NA/NT spouses have a greater number of issues that contribute to their dissatisfaction. For the AS/ND males after those listed on the chart, the next complaint for dissatisfaction is 48%, citing their spouses' emotional dysregulation and not having mutual couple friends. Then 40% stated there are no shared activities, followed by 37% who stated daily communication is difficult. No additional complaints from the AS/ND male perspective reached at least one-third of the responses. For the NA/NT women, at least 1/3 cited the following: they lack partnership in finances (one partner makes all the decisions), the state of finances, co-parenting, their time spent on their interests and passions, too much alone time, work-life balance is off, and my spouse's rigidity.

These charts share some themes that may be prioritized differently, but a few key differences between the AS/ND and NA/NT female responses are evident: the AS/ND female's list included *finances* and *co-parenting*. Overall, though, the NA/NT has more issues that lead to dissatisfaction. Question 19 asked respondents to choose their top 5 challenges. They were only allowed through the question's rule set to check 5 issues.

Relationship Type: Male Spouse Either NT/NA or ND/AS with Female ND/AS

ND/AS Female Responses to Question 18 to List Common Challenges in the Relationship*

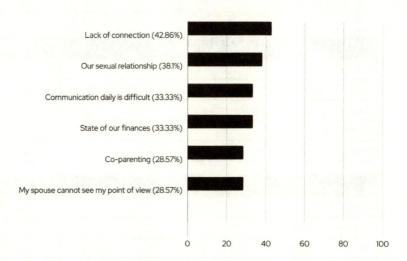

ND/AS Female n=21

* The chart reflects responses that were 25% or greater from the respondents.

Relationship Type: Male NT/NA Spouse with Female ND/AS

NT/NA Male Responses to Question 18 to List Common Challenges in the Relationship*

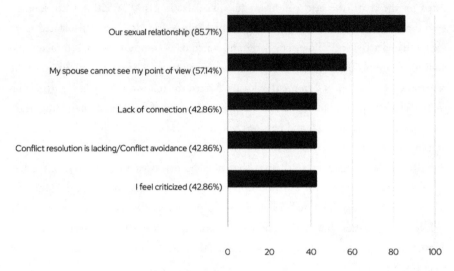

NT/NA Male Spouse n=7

* The chart reflects responses that were 25% or greater from the respondents.

Marriage Type: Female AS/ND to Either AS/ND Male or NT/NA Male

Responses to Question 19: List the Top 5 Challenges in your NeuroDiverse Marriage*

ND/AS Females (n=21)	Percent
Lack of connection	42.86%
Our sexual relationship	38.10%
Emotional dysregulation of spouse (shutdowns)	33.33%
Communication daily is difficult	33.33%
State of our finances	33.33%

NT/NA Males (n=7)**	Percent
Our sexual relationship	85.71%
My spouse does not see my perspective	57.14%
Emotional dysregulation of spouse (shutdowns)	42.86%
Lack of connection	42.86%
Conflict resolution is lacking/Conflict avoidance	42.86%

* The chart reflects responses that were 30% or greater from the respondents.
** Responses for NA/ND Males are not included.

Relationship Type: Male ND/AS and Female NT/NA

Responses to Question 19: List the Top 5 Challenges in your NeuroDiverse Marriage*

NT/NA Females (n=209)	Percent
Lack of connection	72.25%
Conflict resolution is lacking/Conflict avoidance	49.28%
Communication daily is difficult	42.11%
My spouse cannot see my point of view	36.36%
Our sexual relationship	30.62%

ND/AS Males (n=87)	Percent
Lack of connection	66.67%
Our sexual relationship	55.56%
Conflict resolution is lacking/Conflict avoidance	40.00%
I feel criticized	36.60%

* The chart reflects responses that were 30% or greater from the respondents.

Across questions 18 & 19 of our survey, the themes common to all neurotypes and genders were: lack of connection, sexual relationship, inability to have one's perspective seen (double empathy), and spouse's dysregulation. Interestingly, both the AS/ND and NA/NT males feel criticized by their wives, yet their sexual relationships were differently prioritized. All but the male NA/NT listed daily communication as difficult, and all but the female AS/ND-related lack of conflict resolution as a top five theme. The Female AS/ND was the only one to list the state of the finances as a top five theme.

Respondents to the broad survey were asked to indicate if they were open to doing a more in-depth interview, and if so, to leave emails to be contacted. I (Dr. Stephanie) was looking for couples who expressed being content or happy in their relationship, dissatisfied in their relationship, and very dissatisfied with their relationship. I was also looking for different types of neurodiverse couples. Originally three couples with AS/ND women and NA/NT men agreed to be interviewed, but one couple dropped out, with the wife stating she was becoming stressed about being interviewed. Three couples where both spouses were AS/ND (or double-neurodivergent) participated in the interview process. (There is another prevalent type of neurodiverse couple where one spouse is on the spectrum and the other with ADHD, though we were not able to identify such a couple for an additional interview.) The remaining seventeen couples consisted of AS/ND husbands with NA/NT wives.

Double-Neurodivergent Couples: AS/ND to AS/ND couples

The three double-neurodivergent couples I interviewed all had very different experiences. ND Couple 1 were both identified on the spectrum before puberty and knew about their autism going into their marriage. They were the youngest of the three couples interviewed. The husband was identified as what was previously Asperger's Syndrome and she was diagnosed autistic. She said under new criteria she would be considered Autism Level 2, and he would be Autism Level 1. Both spouses said they were content or satisfied with their marriage, yet some aspects could be better. Both had grown up in religious households but no longer believed in religion. The wife considered herself spiritual but not tied to a faith tradition. The wife shared that she never felt she belonged in church; she was not included, and traditional gender roles of marriage would not work for her and her husband. Both stated in their interviews that they had genetics testing done, and the likelihood of having children with profound issues was too high for them: "We do not have the bandwidth for children with needs." They decided not to have children. They lived independently from their parents but indicated they received a lot of parental support. When I asked about what contributed to feeling satisfied or happy in the marriage, each separately mentioned they enjoy each other's interest or hearing about the interest, even if it is not one they shared. The wife said, "We can geek out on each other's interests and give space for those interests." While she would like to have sex more frequently, she said that they connect in other ways that are meaningful to them," but which may not look like a connection to others. She also stated, "We don't have to mask or pretend with each other." The husband stated, "It seems like we need each other" and "we give each other mutual support."

I asked each what could be better, or where do you see the challenges of both being neurodivergent or on the autism spectrum. Both indicated their biggest challenge was their different sensory profiles, preference for sexual activity, and dysregulation. She said, "While I am happy in my marriage, our relationship is challenging, I'm not gonna lie." I told each spouse that research indicates there may be fewer challenges when both partners are on the spectrum and they each replied, "No, that is not true." While he said he can support her when she becomes dysregulated and help her regulate, from his perspective, she is unable to do the same for him. "If I try to vent or let off steam, she will get dysregulated. So, she gets me and supports me on other levels, but I don't have someone I can vent to or just dysregulate, because it will impact her." He said that he is okay being touched by her, but in general does not prefer touch and he does not like surprise touch. He needs to be notified before being touched. She indicated that she is very sensory-seeking and would like to have more sex, but he cannot handle frequent sexual activity. Overall, the couple is happy together, but they shared that both being on the spectrum caused more challenges, and their communication is a problem due to many misunderstandings.

ND Couple 2 was also asked if they thought both being on the spectrum helped or hurt their relationship or if they found it easier or more challenging. The wife said, "It is only easier in that we understand the experiential perspective, but I think it doubles the challenges." The husband said, "If someone said it would be easier, that would be incorrect." This couple married without knowing either was on the spectrum; they have children on the spectrum, and the husband was diagnosed about 2 years before the wife's identification. The husband is in the STEM field (science, technology, engineering, and math) and the wife is an autism specialist who worked in the field before her diagnosis. Both spouses identified as Christians.

As a Christian wife, she was looking for a husband to be a strong spiritual leader who would encourage the family to grow in their faith, but instead finds that "he takes no leadership initiative." They indicated that they share similar values and agree on the big things, but daily communication and daily living are challenging. Because she had trauma in her background, she was misdiagnosed, and her autism was missed. Her presentation is more rigid, with stronger executive function skills and anxiety. His autism presentation is with ADHD, and he lacks follow-through and struggles with executive function. She feels she cannot rely on him to follow through, but he feels like his way of doing things gets the job done and that she is too particular. They indicated their three biggest challenges were communication, different sensory profiles (which impact their sexual relationship), and parenting styles.

The husband said both their children are on the spectrum, and one is profoundly challenged; the husband feels criticized when he does not follow through with the various protocols or structures their more autistic child may need. He is very conflict-avoidant, and the wife wants to settle the conflict and talk it through. Having worked in the autism field, when her first child was diagnosed, she wanted proactive approaches and strategies that required structure and protocols. She said, "We need communication tools that work for couples like us," and "Traditional approaches have not been helpful." The wife has more self-awareness but also carries a heavier mental load daily. She indicated she has autoimmune disease and GI issues. She said she is longing for deeper and more communication from her spouse, and he indicated he is happy if they are in the same room doing something they enjoy and "we don't even need to talk." A book that they said helped them understand different communication styles and listen to feedback was *Thanks for the Feedback*, by Stone and Heen.[21] Their differing sensory profiles are a huge challenge. He is sensory seeking and would prefer more sexual activity, while she is more averse to touch and could "do without it." They stated they were in a very hard season right now with neither satisfied in the marriage. Each said, "It is our faith in God" or "belief about marriage" that was keeping them together.

ND Couple 3 was the oldest of the three couples. Both stated that maritally they were not satisfied, with one identifying as "very dissatisfied." The husband said, "I think both of us being ND makes it harder, especially when you get married not knowing it." The husband was working as a chaplain with adults who had severe developmental disabilities. When he was being trained in autism, he began to identify characteristics in himself, which led him to seek a diagnosis. He stated that as a child he was dyslexic and had several learning disabilities, but autism was never assessed. After he was identified on the spectrum, the wife began to research it and found the criteria not only resonated for her but also explained their parenting experience with their now adult children. Both had family-of-origin trauma. She stated she fits the criteria for the autistic female phenotype "to a T," and now she knows why she felt she didn't fit in most of the time. "The Church doesn't understand us [autistics]. We don't fit in at the local church. We lack community." Additional challenges to the marriage included bad marriage theology (that focused on traditional gender roles and wifely submission), and the husband's sex and porn addiction. She shared she has used alcohol to self-medicate, and that they both have binged screens and food to self-soothe. Both have extensive health issues. Due to theology that was taken very literally, the husband's leadership style was more like a dictator than that of a priest or servant-leader. He stated, "We never had a good course or appropriate teaching on men and women or roles in marriage. I sat under teaching that said the man is the head of the home which meant more like the lord or practically a dictator. This really hurt our marriage." He confessed that his methods of child discipline "probably emotionally scarred my kids." When they met with a pastor to confess past porn use and get advice to navigate their sex life, the pastor counseled them to watch R-rated movies with explicit sex scenes.

She stated that for her, their sex life was the most emotionally painful aspect of their marriage; they navigated the porn and sex addiction either alone or with poor advice from people who did not understand addiction or autism. She stated there is trauma between them in their sex life: She felt pressured to have "duty" and "obligation sex" due to his past belief of being entitled to sex whenever he wanted it. She said that this, plus her sensory issues, has led to her disinterest in sex. She said, "I don't know if it is my trauma or sensory issues, but maybe I am A-sexual, who knows, but things make more sense now." Another of her complaints was that his parenting style was too harsh, and she felt like a single parent. Each spouse has specific sensory needs and preferences but as far as sexual touch, he is more sensory seeking, and she is averse. When I told each spouse that research indicated that communication between autistic spouses is more effective, they both strongly disagreed. Each said it does not take much for a misunderstanding to turn into an escalation and then dysregulation. When asked what marriage work helped them as a neurodiverse couple, they each said being in groups or having some sort of community, and learning basic communication and conflict-resolution skills, such as those taught in the course, they took on *Emotionally Healthy Relationships*.[22] The couple indicated they have stayed together because of their faith and religious views.

A few themes emerged from our interviews with these three ND couples: Communication was not perceived as easier but more challenging; competing sensory profiles and sexual preferences were difficult to manage; and it was challenging when the other spouse would get dysregulated. The two couples that had children indicated parenting styles were a point of contention and conflict. All three ND couples agreed that they could validate the other's lived experience and make room for quirks, decompression and the need for various interests. The three women indicated they longed for better connection and deeper communication with their spouses on emotional matters. ND Couple 1 indicated their decision to let go of faith and religion helped their marriage, while Couples 2 and 3 indicated that, though dissatisfied with the state of their marriage, their faith was the reason they remained together during their hard seasons. These three couples do not seem to resonate with the research that indicates autistic-to-autistic couples are more satisfied and doing better in their relationship overall; however, the previous research did not address sensory profile issues or each spouse's tendency to dysregulate. It is interesting to note that in the AS/ND to NA/NT relationships, dysregulation was mentioned as a major issue, while sensory preferences were near the bottom of the list.

Sensory Profiles

In discussing sensory profiles in autism, it's important to note that clinicians often only look for profiles that are hypersensitive (aversive) or hyposensitive (seeking) to sensory stimuli. Sensory processing is a complex subject, which is extensively reviewed by Carrol Stock Kranowitz in her books *The Out of Sync Child*[23] and *The Out of Sync Child Grows Up*.[24] Brown and Dunn,[25] along with various occupational therapy blogs, explain that sensory profiles encompass more than the five basic senses. They include variables such as the vestibular system (sense of head movement in space), the proprioceptive system (sensations from muscles and joints, perception of pain), the exteroceptive system (pressure, heat, cold, and pain), and conscious or subconscious interoception (the perception of internal bodily sensations, including emotional intensity and regulation).

In the case studies mentioned earlier, one spouse typically had an aversive or avoidant sensory profile, while the other was sensory-seeking or touch-seeking. When making a diagnosis, clinicians need to delve deeper than simply inquiring if a client or patient has "sensory issues." For instance, the MIGDAS-2 autism assessment, which I utilize, asks about pain tolerance, history of injuries or broken bones, tolerance for pain during activities, and lack of medical attention due to not feeling or realizing the extent of an injury. It also explores clothing preferences, responses to visual stimuli, and detail or pattern recognition. Questions might also cover preferences for lighting, reactions to temperature changes, and how individuals adapt to sensory changes like getting in and out of a shower.

Sensory processing can present distinct preferences or covert, unacknowledged issues. This is particularly true for unconscious interoceptive processing issues, where an individual might be unaware of their internal body states or unable to feel or understand the intensity of their emotions. For example, an AS/ND spouse feeling overwhelmed by their partner's emotions indicates interoceptive processing challenges. Brown and Dunn[25] identify four main sensory profiles: low registration, sensation-seeking, sensory sensitivity (heightened awareness of stimuli), and sensation avoidance. They note that individuals can exhibit a combination of these profiles across different systems or body parts.

For a comprehensive sensory profile assessment, an occupational therapist with autism training is most qualified. There has been a debate over the current inclusion of sensory issues in the *DSM-5* diagnostic criteria for autism (as these were not included in the *DSM-IV* for what was previously known as Asperger's Syndrome[26]). Though the impact of sensory issues varies among AS/ND individuals, it is undeniably significant. Clinicians should be cautious when dismissing an autism profile or diagnosis too hastily if the sensory profile is not immediately clear or known.

NeuroDiverse Couple Type: Autistic Women with Non-Autistic Men

Two couples completed the in-depth, semi-structured interview where the wife was AS/ND and the husband was NA/NT. As with the other couples, each spouse was interviewed individually, the interview was recorded and transcribed, and key themes were sought from each couple. In Couple 1, the NA/NT spouse said he was drawn to the confidence, independence, IQ, beautiful eyes, and wonderful laugh of his AS/ND spouse. He said changes came to the relationship when the first child was born, and with each additional child, he felt more distant and disconnected from her. They sought counsel from pastors and counselors but felt that "they tried to put us in a mold of what *normal* should be." The husband said that *The Five Love Languages*,[27] a book often given to couples, was a good book, but it did not help them. Though it specified his love languages, he said "Her love language is not identified in that book.... her love language would be more defined by what I don't do or what she does not want me to do." He stated he also tried doing *The Love Dare* (introduced by the faith-based movie, *Fireproof*),[28] and this was not helpful either. He said the most helpful book was Rudy Simone's *22 Things a Woman with Asperger's Syndrome Wants her Partner to Know.*[29]

He explained his dissatisfaction was mainly, "I'm lonely, feel unappreciated and invisible. I feel like I am here to do chores and bring a paycheck." After he made that statement, he smiled a bit and said, "I feel like the 'woman' of the relationship, and well, my wife has told me that too." He said he desired connection and better communication, as he feels mostly criticized or lectured to. He stated his coach has taught him boundaries, and so arguing happens less, but "she does not want to own up to her mistakes or take responsibility for where things are in the relationship. When I make a mistake, she would cuss at me or call me names." He shared that her use of shame, blame, and verbal vitriol is common when she is dysregulated. While this was improving at the time of the interview, the words spoken still stung, and he does not think she fully understands the impact of her verbal teardowns when she speaks in anger.

The AS/ND wife said she was drawn to her husband because he was a nice guy, smart and funny, but "when we started having children he changed, he wanted more attention. He says I am overly critical and not attentive to him." In her adult life, she had multiple health issues and went to the Mayo Clinic. It was during this process that a provider suggested she may be on the spectrum. Her first response was shock and disbelief, but as she read the criteria, it made sense. She said that she has researched and learned about the spectrum, and she is learning to be more patient, watch her tone, and try and work through conflict. Learning boundaries was also helpful, but she said that they still needed to work on conflict resolution skills. I asked her, as a Christian, what pastors or Christian counselors counseled or said that was not helpful. She listed these: pray your way to mental health, diagnoses are just someone trying to get their way, roles for women are legalistic, and men getting to do what they want because the wife is the support role. I asked her about love languages, and she said her love language is not in the book. She stated, "My love languages are loyalty and follow through."

I asked what satisfaction looked like to her in marriage and she stated for each of them to become more Christ-like with mutual respect, kindness, and teamwork in the home. She said, "I don't want to use AS for my crutch, but it's hard for ND women to conform to what society/church thinks they should be doing. I respond differently than other women. I am different from other women. I don't feel the Christian community accepts ND women. I feel ostracized." She said another great resource would be books or resources for AS/ND parents, as her children are all NA/NT and it is harder for her to parent them at times.

In Couple 3, the NA/NT spouse said overall he is content and he hopes they continue to grow and work on their relationship. He was drawn to his wife's deep faith and confidence, in addition to his physical attraction to her. Their journey to her diagnosis began with a son who was struggling with mental health issues, addiction and some recurring concerning behaviors; they began to suspect autism could be a possibility. When asked about what it was like finding out about the son and wife's autism identification, he said, "Knowing about AS helped. It helps me be less offended. It helped me understand her more… [I'm] now looking for where I see effort, and understanding how difficult relationships are for her." At one point the couple worked in ministry; he realized within the first five years there were differences and significant struggles for her as a pastor's wife, and that the expectations a church puts on a pastor's wife are already stressful, but even more so for someone on the autism spectrum. As a pastor, he often did pastoral counseling and read many Christian marriage books. He said none of them really helped their marriage. He stated, "These books, which I read most of them, made me feel more alone and hopeless." He encouraged pastors to get training and be more aware of neurodiverse Christian couples because pastors are not trained about differences in marriage like neurodiversity. I asked what improvement in the relationship would look like, and he said, "If she pursued me or were more interested or curious in me… I sometimes feel like a task she needs to do." He also smiled at some point and said, "I feel like the woman in the relationship, I just want to be seen." I asked him to give advice for those NA/NT men married to a woman on the spectrum, and he said to first learn about the spectrum and added, "You can feel slighted and grow resentful as an NT. You will need to look for her strengths and give grace. Being the NT man will require compassion and empathy."

The AS/ND wife said she was drawn to his kindness, his social nature, personality, and faith. She described him as a great boyfriend. She said, "I love my husband and our life together that we have created and our life together in our faith." I asked her about her experience in church and as a pastor's wife. She said there were challenges for her with so many social things, women's ministry, small talk, and greetings that just did not come naturally – she had to push through each week, and it was exhausting and she would then just shut down. However, being a pastor's wife gave her a role to fill, and having a role was helpful at times, but she was often depleted after church. "I'm not a people pleaser, but felt it was my duty to push through." She has not felt free to share about her AS identification in the church world. Because her husband is very social and outgoing, she said "I lean into him on social occasions." She described their connection as time together in activity, time without conflict or big emotions, and when they are focused on their spiritual life or becoming more Christ-like. She prefers time alone with him to connect; he shared he would like to have more time with her and the family, at social gatherings or with couples, but this is difficult for her. She would like to be able to do that for him but feels she can only do so sparingly: it takes a lot of energy for her to socialize in groups – even when the group is family – due to the nature of hosting, cooking, and preparing before the gathering. Then there are the social aspects, followed by the cleanup, and as a whole, this all becomes overwhelming for her. For this couple, the AS/ND wife does not go into verbal fights or lectures if she gets dysregulated; she is more prone to shut down, be silent, and retreat. With the couple becoming empty nesters, she finds it easier to focus on their relationship with the children grown, but when issues with their AS/ND son arise, it is draining and exhausting. They are learning to connect through travel, intentional weekends, and as grandparents.

NT men expressed a desire to be seen and known.

Both NT men expressed a desire to be seen and known and that they felt like the "woman" of the relationship, seeking the more attentive pursuit of their spouse rather than a checklist. Both men's attraction narratives fit the description of an NA/NT to an AS/ND partner given by Attwood and Garnett.[17] Both women were diagnosed later in life, and neither felt able to be free about their neurodivergence in the church world; they both felt the need to push through or mask, which they described as exhausting. One woman has been prone to verbal dysregulation and the other internally shuts down when overloaded. Both women expressed that connection is easier when there is no conflict or emotional tension in discussions. Both men would like to see more communication and connection in their relationships.

While there are aspects among the different types of neurodiverse couples that are similar, there are different power dynamics that can occur based on gender roles and physical strength and size. The NA/NT men whom I and other contributing authors have worked with have expressed that if their AS/ND wife has verbally exploded (dysregulated), abusive things are said and things thrown. These may not cause fear of domestic violence but are still experienced as verbal or psychological abuse, especially when criticism turns into messages of shame, blame, and denigration. For women married to autistic men who outwardly and verbally explode or throw and break things, there is a greater likelihood of trauma: these women fear physical harm due to size differences and often are financially disempowered if the husband is in control of the money. Though it is less threatening when an AS/ND partner shuts down, their NA/NT spouse (man or woman) can experience feelings of emotional neglect and abandonment.

In discussing this chapter with contributing authors who coach ND couples, a pattern often seen is that if the AS/ND wife tends to be more cognitively rigid, they may see counseling as a way to fix their NA/NT spouse; they resist taking personal ownership for their dysregulation or for what they say and do when dysregulated. Instead, they claim that they are the ones being abused. For those married to an AS/ND wife who is not as rigid (and may be taking ownership of her diagnosis and striving to self-regulate and improve), the husband may still experience degrees of loneliness. A few men have stated their AS/ND Christian wives have a "special interest" in humanitarian causes or helping people, and that this interest – while a good thing – can cause a lack of moderation in time management; the wife's desire to help people in the community or church may come at the expense of the husband or family.

As I conclude this chapter, I want to share advice from my youngest daughter about relationships. Our book, *Embracing the Autism Spectrum*,[30] is written from our family's four-person perspective on what it's like being in a neurodiverse family system. Erica, our youngest, who is non-autistic but has ADHD, speaks about the pain of living on the other side of her autistic sister's constant criticism and tongue-lashings. She offers this advice for AS/ND people who have non-autistic siblings, but certainly this advice applies to marriage relationships as well:

> To the sibling [person] that is autistic, please understand that being on the spectrum explains your behaviors, but it doesn't necessarily excuse them. If you say something [or do something] hurtful, even if that's not your intention, please take responsibility for the hurt and seek forgiveness and reconciliation. If what you said or did causes a rupture to the relationship with your sibling, parents [or other relationships], take responsibility for the impact caused. I understand that some social contexts might not make sense at certain points, but we're doing our best to accommodate you and your sensory needs and feelings and would honestly appreciate the same consideration from you. Quite often for those on the spectrum, emotional unawareness may be considered a strength or shield. For those of us who are not autistic, we do not have that ability. While you are unaware of the hurt you are causing because of self-referencing [due to challenges with theory of

mind], the sibling [of the other person in the relationship] can perceive and feel all of these emotions around them at all times. It becomes a superpower to the non-autistic and a heavy burden [for the others]. We need time to process and overcome [unintentional or intentional] hurt that has been caused. If you cannot recognize the hurt you have caused, it is more difficult for the non-autistic person to believe you will not hurt them in that same way again [and thus erodes trust] (p. 239).

I close the chapter with this additional observation: my AS/ND daughter may have been more cognitively rigid and experienced high conflict in her past relationships (including with her sister), but she also has a desire to belong and have friendships, which made her vulnerable to being manipulated and abused by so-called friends and boyfriends. Autistic female adults who have written[31] and spoken[32-35] about the female autism phenotype express that women on the spectrum may be naïve and easily drawn into abusive relationships and not know how to get out of them. In our podcasts with Thomas Pryde[37,38] of the Psalm 82 Initiative[36] (which rescues and removes women from abusive marriages), he says that his ministry is seeing an increase in non-autistic women married to abusive and rigid autistic men; additionally, he finds that autistic women have been enduring abusive marriages to legalistic and controlling non-autistic Christian men, due to false religious beliefs about divorce and adultery being the only justification for it.[37,38]

This chapter only scratches the surface of what is known about autistic women and their relationships with an autistic or non-autistic spouse; certainly, more research is needed in this area to better understand the female phenotype of autism.

Chapter Five
Navigating the Maze of Neuroscience and Neuroplasticity From Enemy Mode to Joyful Foundation

BY REV. DR. STEPHANIE C. HOLMES & REV. DAN HOLMES, MS

I (Dr. Stephanie) struggled with how to introduce this chapter on neuroscience and neuroplasticity. Do I try to give a summary or a more comprehensive view of the different wiring or neurodiversity in the autistic brain? Do I try to explain various brain structures and the differences in neurotypical or neurodivergent brains? Would the reader care? How much does the reader want to know? My goal for the chapter is to briefly discuss some neurological differences, why they matter, and the *hope* that neuroplasticity brings to this discussion.

Let me start with an "aha" that came through an email exchange I had with neuro-theologian, Dr. Jim Wilder. What is a neurotheologian? It is someone who has studied the intersection of neuroscience and theology. Our (Dan & Stephanie's) introduction to Dr. Wilder was by our pastors and fellow author Barbara Grant, through his book and podcast called, *The Other Half of Church: Christian Community, Brain Science, and Overcoming Spiritual Stagnation.*[1] If you had a psychology class, you may have heard that the left side of the brain tends to be more logical and analytical, and the right side of the brain tends to be creative. Through this book, we learned so much more about the left and right brain. However, as I was reading more material by Wilder and his associates – who identify different parts of the brain as the *joy center* and the *relational circuits* – I had questions. In a personal email to Dr. Wilder on October 22, 2022, I asked a question about what he calls *Enemy Mode*:

> *I know your ministry focuses on restoring whole brain health and relational community, but as I am reading about the importance of the posterior cingulate cortex, the right cingulate cortex, and the right orbital prefrontal cortex concerning enemy mode, I wonder if someone has damaged or does not have a fully developed PCC or imbalance in the orbital amygdala circuit, would or could this person be stuck in enemy mode? I wonder about the implications of what to do if someone is stuck in enemy mode because of how the brain is wired.*

Dr. Jim graciously responded on October 29, 2022:

> *You are right that people with any kind of disturbance in the development of the posterior cingulate, amygdala, or PFC are going to be very easily dragged into enemy mode. The autism spectrum is at high risk of overloading the posterior cingulate with even "normal" intensity input. That is the key as you suspect.*

The autism spectrum is at high risk of overloading the posterior cingulate with even "normal" intensity input. That is the key as you suspect.

We had the opportunity to have Dr. Wilder as a guest on our podcast[2] and we asked him for a summary of the right versus left brain function. Dr. Wilder stated,

> *It really wasn't understood, even as late as 30 years ago in the 1990s, when Dr. Damasio went to try to test how the right hemisphere worked, he couldn't find any ways of testing it because no one could quite figure out what was going on, and it turns out that the right hemisphere runs faster than the left. It's a sort of identity control. One way to say it is whenever we wake up, we wake up knowing who we are. We don't have to stop and figure that out again. We think we simply just know it all the time. The brain is actually figuring that out about 6 times per second, saying this is who we are. Then,*

the left hemisphere runs slower, and it's very good at focusing in on details and runs at a conscious speed which is 5 times or cycles per second. If we want to get really focused; the left hemisphere is good for that. If we want to know who we are and how to act, the right hemisphere is primarily in charge of that sort of thing. And of course, the whole brain has both who we are running well, and we're focusing on the stuff we need to get done, and when you get those two things together, you have a pretty good day.

Dan asked Dr. Wilder why that was important. Dr. Wilder responded,

Well, it would be a real problem if we kept forgetting who we were, if we got so focused on a problem and we were, like, who am I again now? We'd have to refigure that, so what we call character or identity is this combined sense of who I am in the situation right now. What are my options? What are my values? The left-hand side of the brain is unable to see the whole picture at the same time. It's always focused on some detail. It's the thing that we'll miss seeing - the forest - because you're looking at a tree. It'll pick up a detail. It'll turn someone you care about into a problem to be solved instead of a person to be lived with. It will get you so focused on work that you forget your daughter's birthday. All those kinds of things. So, if it runs just by itself, we do get a lot of things done, but we also cause a lot of relationship damage. Sometimes, what you do to get things done, the end justifying the means, means that you end up violating your own values. We don't actually act in terms of what's important. On the left side is all our vocabulary and thinking and conscious thoughts, and that's where most people put their Christianity, so they can talk and think like Christians... but when something goes wrong and they have their fast reaction, they don't react inside at all like Christians, and then you end up having to constantly be monitoring and trying to control your own reactions, because Christianity is not in the fast track unless it goes out of an attachment, an actual connection to God and to others.

Let me (Dan) give a brief overview of the basics before we go further into Dr. Wilder's work. According to Dr. Wilder[2], the brain's two hemispheres, known as the left and right sides, have traditionally associated the left brain with logic and the right brain with creativity. Dr. Wilder's material presents a different perspective: it emphasizes that the right hemisphere is more relationally oriented, while the left is more process-driven. Furthermore, these hemispheres operate at distinct speeds, with the right-side processing relational aspects more rapidly than the left. This suggests that we understand and react to relational dynamics faster than our conscious thought processes can keep up. The left brain, being slightly slower, follows behind in this cognitive processing. Essentially, the right side of the brain is continuously searching for our place in the social world and informing the left brain for processing and action. When the relational aspect of your thinking is interrupted, the left side of the brain continues functioning, but it does so without the influence of your relationships, or whom and what you hold dear. And, if your brain is also in an alarm state, what you might be processing and reacting against is not perceived as relationally neutral – it is relationally harmful (enemy mode). How do we counter this? The "four soils" outlined by Dr. Wilder in *The Other Half of Church*,[1] are the keys to transformation. A brief overview follows.

The Four Soils: A Framework for Growth and Connection

1. *Joy* - "I'm Happy to Be with You!"

This first soil, Joy, is akin to the unconditional happiness seen in a dog's greeting. Yet, joy is different than a temporary state of happiness. It represents a fundamental human need: the joy of being *together*. This soil fosters relationships that are grounded in positive, enthusiastic engagement, where one's presence is a source of enjoyment for others. It's about creating an environment where mutual enjoyment and acceptance flourish. Yet, joy and happy are different.

Joy is different than a temporary state of happiness

---

2. *Hesed* - "Loyal Love"

Hesed, a Hebrew term often translated as 'loyal love', embodies the idea of unwavering commitment and presence. It reflects a divine attribute, illustrating a love that is steadfast regardless of circumstances. In relationships, this soil is about creating a sense of security and trust, ensuring that individuals feel supported and valued unconditionally, much like the Biblical narratives of God's unwavering presence.

3. *Group Identity* - "Who Are My People?"

This soil delves into the sense of belonging and identity within a group. It's about understanding and embracing the values, behaviors, and beliefs of one's community. In this context, individuals are encouraged to align with their group's positive attributes, reinforcing a sense of belonging and shared identity. This soil nurtures relationships by fostering a collective sense of purpose and belonging. Marriage is about defining "us" and "we," and how "we" as a married couple can do things in a way that reflects and honors Christ.

4. *Healthy Correction* - "Propelling Towards Betterment"

Unlike shame-based correction, which diminishes self-worth, healthy correction is constructive and encouraging. It's about guiding individuals towards their better selves (what the group/couple identity has defined as 'better'). Just as Amos used the plumb line as a standard against which the moral and spiritual alignment of Israel was measured (Amos 7:7-8, KJV), healthy correction in relationships serves as a moral guide, helping individuals to align their actions and attitudes with the values of the group. This form of correction, therefore, is not about toxic shame (identity crushing or character assassination), but about providing a clear, upright standard, akin to a plumb line, that guides us towards our better selves, which for Christians is growing in your Christlikeness. If someone is trying to give a healthy correction to hopefully produce Godly sorrow and repentance, the individual receiving the correction may perceive it in a toxic or negative way, due to their identity triggers,[3] therefore it is imperative to learn to be a good receiver of feedback in order to develop a growth mindset instead of a shame-based or fixed mindset.[3]

What do *joy* and *hesed* have to do with anything? Can you have joy and hesed in a neurodiverse Christian marriage? Yes – if you are intentional about it! Let's start with the joy center of the brain and why I (Dr. Stephanie) originally reached out to Dr. Wilder after reading his books. Where is this joy center? Is it different in neurotypical and autistic brains? Can the joy center be turned *on* or further developed? Yes! Dr. Wilder and others[4] stated that joy is the foundation of maturity and growth and that with a firm joy foundation, one can increase resiliency and manage stress. In *Daring Greatly*,[5] Dr. Brené Brown adds that joy is important to have in your armor to combat unhealthy or toxic shame. Under toxic or unhealthy shame, according to Brown, one will protect oneself, blame others, rationalize the behavior, and offer disingenuous apologies. Joy is powerful! Where have we heard that before? Nehemiah 8:10c (NIV) says, "For the joy of the Lord is your strength!"

Where is the joy center located? According to Wilder's study and additional research, in the right orbital prefrontal cortex (OFC). Are there any differences in the OFC for the autistic brain? Yes. Rowland[6] is becoming a controversial name in autism research for stating that autism is over-diagnosed and for focusing on autism as a disorder instead of a difference; however, his research discusses four parts of the autistic brain that are different concerning neurophysiology. First, the *cingulate gyrus* (CG) is the part of the brain that focuses attention; the CG can keep the autistic person trapped in the left frontal lobe of the brain. Second, the left frontal cortex in the autistic brain has dominant alpha frequencies (8-12 Hz) to beta (12.5-30 Hz), which Rowland says is the opposite of how the non-autistic brain functions. These higher alpha waves in the autistic left frontal cortex appear to overcompensate for the diminished ability to access intuition from the right side of the brain. Third, he notes there are underdeveloped neural networks in the right frontal cortex associated with social connectivity. The fourth area of difference is the amygdala, which plays a central role in the expression of emotions and how a person sizes up a threat or experiences fear. Together, he explains, the different functioning of the CG can suppress the feelings of emotions. Rowland states that the autistic person is incapable of feeling fear, and if a person can feel fear, they are probably not autistic. The authors of this book disagree with Rowland's assessments that autism is over diagnosed and that those on the spectrum cannot feel fear. However, his study of differently functioning brain structures correlates with other studies that also name these same structures as functioning differently, but his hypothesis and conclusions differ somewhat.

Harden et al.[7] studied the OFC in autistic and non-autistic brains using functional MRI. The researchers describe the OFC as heavily involved in multiple functions, including emotional and cognitive processing, and learning social behaviors. The findings concluded there were disturbances in the autistic brain's OFC, but not because the structure itself was abnormal. Girgis et al.[8] also studied the OFC of autistic brains and confirmed the importance of the OFC for social-emotional processing, and that the circuits which run from the OFC to the amygdala are core components in how emotions are processed. Girgis and fellow researchers wanted to study the then-recent hypothesis of Bachevalier and Loveland,[9] which suggested that abnormalities in the orbitofrontal-amygdala circuit may play a key role in emotional dysregulation and social-emotional processing in autism. O'Doherty et al.[10] and Völlm et al.[11] suggested the area to be studied more specifically in the OFC was its right lateral subdivision. Völlm et al.[11] also suggested that the medial prefrontal cortex as well as other structures influence the capacity for having theory of mind (ToM involves empathy, intuition, and inferring others' emotions). Girgis and researchers8 found implications that the left hemisphere of the autistic brain is dominant in knowledge-building, to the detriment of the right hemisphere. Further, the researchers suggest that if someone continues to choose isolated activities that build knowledge over relationships, this can further exacerbate the differences in the right to left hemispheres.

Does this sound familiar yet? While knowledge, new activities, and intense, passionate interests are important to the autistic brain and person, moderation is needed for relational circuits (RCs) to improve. The authors of this book advocate the need for passions and interests and alone time, but not to the detriment of relationships. There is a time and place for intense focus and individual time, as the brain needs both *joy* (high energy) and *shalom* (rest or quiet). There is a need for moderation and finding those rhythms within yourself and your relationships. This call for moderation can also be found in the writings of the Apostle Paul, specifically in Philippians 4:5 (KJV), "Let your moderation be known unto all man. The Lord is at hand;" and 1 Corinthians 10:23-24 (NKJV), "All things are lawful for me, but not all things are helpful; all things are lawful for me, but not all things edify. Let no one seek his own, but each one the other's well-being." Special interests, passions, and hobbies have their place in restoring peace or a resting state in the brain, but there must be vigilance that these do not replace relationship or relational joy-building, or there will be neurological and relational consequences.

Wilder reminds us that joy-building cannot be done alone in solitary activities. When I stated to Dr. Wilder on our podcast, "But those on the spectrum would say they may be happiest when they are alone in their interest," Dr. Wilder reminded me that joy is not equivalent to happiness. He said the person may find peace or rest in pursuing those activities alone, but it is not *joy*-building, as building the joy center in the brain cannot be done alone. Why? As Dr. Wilder states in Chapter 2 of *Joy Starts Here*,[4] joy simply means "someone is glad to be with me" (p. 7). Dr. Wilder continues about the importance of joy, explaining that joy enables us to grow strong, loving relationships; it is a high-energy state for the brain, and it is essential for healing and growing strong identities. The good news for those with underdeveloped joy centers (or OFCs), according to Dr. Wilder and other researchers, is that the orbital prefrontal cortex is a part of the brain that continues to learn and grow over one's lifetime – *neuroplasticity!*

Chris Coursey, one of the co-authors of *Joy Starts Here*,[4] and co-author of *Relational Skills in the Bible*[12] reminds us that while our brains have neuroplasticity, and that the OFC can change, you simply cannot *pray* joy into being:

> *It can be tempting to spiritualize some things that are not meant to be spiritualized, so an important distinction must be made between God's domain and our domain. Maturity and relational skills require effort and work on our part. Would you pray a vegetable garden into existence, or would you be like Adam and tend the garden? (p.9)*

Coursey reminds us we can pray for resources and opportunities and the right coach or mentor, but building joy and relational skills will require our work, effort, and practice. This is where the phrase "gracefully navigating the maze" in our title comes into play. For those with neurotypical brains, relational skills may come more easily, but the joy center can also be affected by trauma and lack of attachment from either our family of origin or the current relationship. Both spouses can build their joy centers. In *The 4 Habits of Joy-*

Filled People[13] and *Daring Greatly*,[5] the authors list appreciation and gratitude as ways to start building joy and erasing toxic shame.

The next soil, *hesed*, is about attachment. Are you *there* for me? Are you *for* me, and for *us*? It can be difficult to build joy with someone who treats you like an enemy, is adversarial, and does not appear in words or actions to be for you. Before we speak to 'enemy mode,' what is hesed or attachment about? We (Dan and Stephanie) had the opportunity to interview a clinician who specialized in attachment theory and attachment repair, Dr. Jesse Gill. On our podcast,[14] we asked Dr. Gill to give a layman's definition of attachment, and he replied, "Knowing you exist in someone's mind when you are not present." For a more in-depth discussion of attachment styles and how our family origin can impact our attachment style, tune into our podcast with Dr. Gill[14] or read his book, *Face to Face*.[15]

In our podcast discussion, we spoke about how it is important to know your attachment style and what you brought with you into the marriage, but you do not have to have the same attachment style with your spouse as you did with your family of origin. If you were insecure, you can learn to build secure bonds, or as Dr. Wilder and co-authors say in *Living from the Heart Jesus Gave You*,[16] move sus from *fear* bonds to *love* bonds. A male client on the spectrum once asked me, "Wait, if I'm on the spectrum and have lower emotional intelligence, doesn't she just have to give me grace and live with what I have to offer?" My reply was, "I have to believe that if you are a Christian and in a relationship with Jesus if you strive daily to be more like Him and develop the fruits of the Spirit, you will grow in emotional intelligence." Later that day, in my G-mail inbox, the book titled *Emotional Intelligence in Christ*[17] popped up, with an emotional quotient (EQ) assessment and tips to grow your EQ by patterning your life around the fruit of Spirit, anchoring yourself in self-control. I don't want to make it sound so easy, like "3 steps to a new you," but Dr. Gill shares this in his book:[15]

> *Modern research shows that God made our brains in wonderful and resilient ways. Our brains can recover from trauma, rebuild new brain tissue, and compensate for areas of damage and underdevelopment. We may also have new experiences that help us reprogram our brains and teach us healthier ways to connect. However, I think it is important to note that it is quite automatic for us to rely on strategies for attachment that we learned during the earliest years of experience (p. 29).*

Many come from families or backgrounds that perhaps used toxic or unhealthy shame, and this negatively impacted their attachment style. Some have had trauma in their neurodiverse marriages that have led to *low joy*, and *high conflict*. Wilder and his co-authors talk about *Trauma A* and *Trauma B*. In *Joy Starts Here*,[4] Trauma A is when there is the absence of good or necessary things like secure attachment. Wilder further explains that this type of trauma can look like neglect, rejection, abandonment, or withdrawal from a relationship. Trauma A will lead to low joy and can build insecure bonds as well as fear bonds in the home. Trauma B is about the bad things that happen to us, such as any type of abuse or events that exceed our ability to function or cope. Furthermore, Dr. Wilder says what is traumatic for one can be less so for another, and that trauma can distort our sense of identity because something in our experience has not yet finished processing. You will not be able to build love or fully secure bonds if there is either ongoing trauma in your marriage or unhealed trauma from your past. You will not feel *hesed* or secure attachment when there is trauma present, and this will lead to low-joy marriages and families.

Trauma A has been described in *Living from the Heart Jesus Gave You*,[16] as not experiencing certain demonstrations of love from a *parent*. I have listed these same items from the perspective of a marriage relationship, which include:

- Not being cherished by a spouse
- Not experiencing delight in your spouse's presence
- Not having a spouse who sees you or will hear your pain
- Not receiving large amounts of daily, non-sexual touch (hugs, embrace, touch)
- Not having time together for fun
- Not having access to resources
- Being made to feel dependent or that resources are scarce
- Not doing hard things together
- Not resolving conflict
- Not making plans together
- Not having the agency to use one's gifts, talents, skills or abilities to develop one's potential.

This list of Trauma A triggers describes the state of most neurodiverse Christian marriages when a couple enters marriage work. But the hope is, it does not need to stay this way!

A continued cycle of trauma can turn relational circuits (RCs) off and lead a couple into "enemy mode." As Dr. Wilder said, with the differences in the functioning of the autistic brain, it is quite easy for the AS/ND spouse to slip into "fight/flight" enemy mode with their spouse and those they love. When one is in enemy mode and not aware they are in it, they may also believe their spouse is in enemy mode, even if they are not. How do you know if you are in enemy mode? In the book *Escaping Enemy Mode*,[18] Wilder offers this definition: you see a person whom you usually *want* to be with as a threat, interruption, or problem to be solved. Dr. Gill stated that when we feel threatened or sense harm, we are each wired differently in our protective states for *fight* or *flight*. But enemy mode, according to Wilder, can be spotted, and we can learn to turn our relational circuits back on! When the RCs are off, enemy mode can occur with one or both parties; and when one spouse is in enemy mode, if the other is not mindful, they can end up in enemy mode with them. Joy, hesed, group identity, and healthy correction will not be received or built during enemy mode. In *Escaping Enemy Mode*,[18] it explains that when you see yourself through your "as if" or "self-perspective lens" (based on your aspirational self), instead of as your *real* self, you are more prone to go into enemy mode. How to reduce and minimize enemy mode? By increasing your mindfulness and self-awareness of the impact you are having,[3] learning to self-rescue (regulate or pre-regulate), learning to be intentional about turning on or keeping on your relational circuits, and accepting healthy correction (or a call back to your *best* self, rooted in your identity in Christ). Ray Woolridge, co-author of *Escaping Enemy Mode*[18] and a retired US Army Brigadier General, cautions that if you have military training, the "soldierization process" may also make you more prone to enemy mode. (We have a self-study or coaching course available if you are ready to take your next step out of enemy mode into relational mode.[28])

We hope that you, the couple, navigate change, growth, and transformation in yourself and your marriage by knowing about these differences in wiring and neuroplasticity. If you are a marriage helper, we hope to support you in knowing where you can help couples target growth, remove trauma and build relational skills, and help them set realistic goals while keeping neurological differences and challenges in mind. Lastly, we want both couples and helpers to become "horsemen spotters." These are criticism, contempt, defensiveness, and stonewalling (Dr. John and Julie Gottman named these in reference to the Four Horsemen of the Apocalypse[19]). Any marriage, neurotypical or neurodiverse, will be doomed if they habitually have even 1 of the 4 horsemen in their marriage. Gottman's research has shown these four horsemen will destroy your relationship if you allow them to run wild in it. These behaviors will lead you straight to enemy mode, so if any one of them consistently reoccurs, check your relational circuits and become intentional about getting out of enemy mode. If any program, counselor, or pastor promises to turn your neurodiverse marriage around in months, be skeptical. There is no fast track to reducing trauma, building joy, and hesed. Your long-term goal should be *mind and heart transformation*, not short-term behavior modifications. The definition of the transformation sequence, according to enlightenment thinking, shown in *The Other Half of Church* is: Transformation = truth + good choices + power.[1] However, Dr. Wilder points out a critical piece is missing in this formula – *love*. Without love that comes from hesed, there is little transformation. In *The Solution of Choice*[20], Dr. Wilder and Marcus Warner explain the importance and function of love in discipleship that leads to transformation. "When hesed replaces truth as the foundation of discipleship, the whole model self-corrects. Placing love at the core of the transformation process allows truth, choice, and power to play their proper roles and not bear a weight they were never intended to carry." They continue, "Developments in modern brain science have made it clear that any model of transformation and character change must be anchored in the development of a love bond with God and His people" (p. 68). Therefore, the transformation equation should look like this: Transformation = attachment (hesed) > truth > good choices > power.

You will need to ask the Holy Spirit to empower you to seek the truth, even if that means taking a look at what might be incorrect theology and doctrine, which you have may been taught over the years by respected spiritual leaders. Through knowing the truth, you can then apply it through new actions and better choices, but knowledge and truth are not enough for transformation. You can read Scripture, this book, and all of Wilder's materials, but if you stop there, you will only have read some books and acquired knowledge and built more pathways in your left brain. The real step of change comes in moving from *reading* the Word, to *doing* it. And that doing be motivated and driven by love (hesed) for one another. This is what we are exhorted to do in James 1:22 (NIV), "Do not merely listen to [or read] the word, and so deceive yourselves. Do what it says." We must let the motivation of the doing be hesed (love) that is rooted in a Christ-based identity: an attachment to our heavenly Father, and displayed to his people, especially our spouses. Ray Clendenen in a word study on hesed[21] explains, "when someone went beyond what is required or expected, showing a special kindness, love, mercy, etc. that is hesed. God wants more from us than our loyalty, He wants our devotion." He went on to explain that our spouses want more than loyalty or duty – they want affection, tenderness, and love above the call of duty or obligation: this is hesed. A reminder of love is given to us in 1 Corinthians 13, which is often called the "love chapter". Verse 3 says, "If I give all I possess to the poor and give over my body to hardship that I may boast, but do not have love, I gain nothing" (NIV). Verse 8, "Love never fails. But where there are prophecies, they will cease; where there are tongues, they will be stilled; where there is knowledge, it will pass away" (NIV) and the chapter ends with verse 13, "and now there remains faith, hope and love. But the greatest of these is love" (NIV). Without love (hesed) you cannot be transformed, and your marriage cannot be transformed.

We want to affirm that if you each do your work, remain intentional, remove trauma, and learn communication and relational skills, your neurodiverse Christian marriage can be joyful and fulfilling.

We (Stephanie and Dan) want to finish the chapter by sharing our personal journeys of how we learned to apply the above material. We want to affirm that if you each do your work, remain intentional, remove trauma, and learn communication and relational skills, your neurodiverse Christian marriage can be joyful and fulfilling. It is important to be clear that while we believe you can improve your relational and amygdala circuitry, and that this change will build relationships and interpersonal relational skills, we are in no way saying that someone would no longer be neurodivergent.

Outside of the Maze: Stephanie's Insights and Hindsight Learning

In a previous chapter, I (Stephanie) shared "the tale of two marriages." Several years ago, Dan and I had two very different experiences in our marriage: I felt completely miserable and trapped, while Dan felt fine and content. (To understand the entire narrative of our marriage and family system, I invite you to read our first book, *Embracing the Autism Spectrum: Finding Hope & Joy Navigating the Neurodiverse Family Journey.*[22]) I want to share how I began to apply joy-building to change my mindset, not in a prescriptive or condemning way, but to simply tell how I found my way out of the maze in which I (and my marriage) was trapped. When I look back before 2008, I would not have called it a maze, but a labyrinth with gauntlets and hurdles and giants opposing me. I felt like a prisoner, with no hope of seeing a different future for myself, my career, my daughters, my walk with the Lord, or my marriage. I was living the first part of Proverbs 13:12 (NIV) "Hope deferred makes the heart sick." I had goals and dreams and big ideas, but in my mind, I was stuck. I felt like I was put on "hold", that no one saw the real me, and no one wanted to know what I was going through. My identity was based on how I helped or served others because as a "helpmate" and Christian, that is what I believed I was supposed to do. As a child, I had been taught the lyrics to this old song:

J is for Jesus for He has first place,
O is for others you meet face to face;
Y is for you in whatever you do,
Put yourself third and spell JOY.[23]

Just last year when I began diving into his work, Dr. Wilder even commented, "If you learned JOY was Jesus, Others, and You, that is not JOY – that is something else entirely."[2] What became obvious in hindsight, was that my life had been without true joy, and nothing I did or accomplished was bringing joy.

The years 2001-2008 were challenging years for me on all fronts. I felt lost in my life, with a loss of self-worth and identity, confusion in my vision of who God was, and even anger at God. I was disconnecting from my faith community and carrying a lot of shame that I was not a "good enough" Christian wife and mom. From when my daughter Sydney was 3 until age 9 (through her diagnosis, pre-school, and elementary years), I was known by each of the seven North Carolina schools she attended as "Sydney's mom." This did not imply a warm welcome or a positive, "we're so glad to see you and be with you" from any of the schools' staff members. It was the opposite: not only were the schools not happy to see me, but our relationship became very adversarial when they would not implement her individual education plan (IEP). Their focus was on their opinion of my "bad parenting" instead of on the goals and outcomes we had jointly agreed on at the IEP meetings.

Being at church was also difficult for me during these years. There were also some strained relationships, and very few receptions of "I'm happy to see you" or "I see you and want to know you." I would sit in the sanctuary each Sunday morning and stare at the box with the red LED lights to see if number 27 would come up, signaling me to come get Sydney from the nursery or children's program. Her behaviors at church were not understood as autism. Instead, they reflected badly on me for not being a good parent or disciplinarian, able to raise a Godly child. I know this because of the number of books her Sunday school teachers gave me on parenting and discipline. I was also given advice (in small women's groups) that if I submitted enough, kept my husband sexually satisfied, stayed small, obeyed authority, and lived a perfect Godly life, my circumstances would improve. This added toxic shame and condemnation to my life. I had been a woman full of passion and goals, a spunky go-getter, but during these years I was a shell of myself, walking amidst broken dreams, loss, and grief. I felt very alone: unseen, unknown, unheard, and unwanted. I channeled what energy I had into my girls, getting the resources and therapies they needed for their developmental issues. My identity came to be about my advocacy for them, and my floundering counseling career about advocating for others. In subtle ways, I was told my needs did not matter, that the Christian life is all about sacrifice and death of self and that God only cared about "my holiness, not my happiness." In 2007 and 2008 I had several miscarriages, first of twins then, two additional miscarriages, which I faced alone. I felt like a failure as a woman because I couldn't produce a "quiver full of children." I was in a very dark place and began to wonder, "Why am I even here?" and worse, "Do I even want to be here any longer? What if I disappeared?" By 2008, it was becoming obvious I was without joy. So much so, that my dad, who tended to over-spiritualize things, decided he was giving us all spiritual names so that he "could speak something that was not yet into being." Ironically, what name did he give me? *Joy!* It was annoying and frustrating at the time. He would come up with any and every reason to contact me, just to say, "Hi, Joy" or "What is going on today, Joy." Joy, Joy, Joy – ad nauseum. I was beginning to hate the word *joy*, but I soon realized that joy and hope were missing in my life. There was nothing to look forward to, and no one I felt was truly happy to see me or knew the real me, especially not my husband. Who could I tell about all that was happening to me and what I was feeling? If I wanted to share about my marriage issues or my questions about God, there was no safe place in my spiritual network or family to have those discussions; my dread, misery, and fears compounded as an echo chamber inside my head. Though we knew about our daughters' neurodiversity, we would not begin to discover the neurodiversity in our own marriage until 2014 – 2015. I blamed the challenges in our marriage on the taxing circumstances and financial strain of providing numerous therapies for two special needs children and of getting to all their therapies and resources each week.

Fast forward: when I was finally at a breaking point, in anger and desperation I reached out to the new pastor at church who was an outsider (meaning he was the first pastor who had not known my history in the church because he had come from Oklahoma when our church was in transition). He invited me into a discussion of how I truly felt about myself, my life, and God, and he gently guided me to examine some of my thoughts and feelings. He invited me to look past my difficult circumstances which were skewing my vision of God, and I began to see who God really was, and that He was *for* me. It dawned on me that there is no exclusion clause in Jeremiah 29:11 (NIV); though the verse was written to God's people in exile, the words of Jeremiah spoke truth and hope to my heart,

> 'For I know the plans I have for you,' declares the Lord, 'plans to prosper you and not to harm you, plans to give you hope and a future. Then you will call on me and come and pray to me, and I will listen to you. You will seek me and find me and when you seek

me with all of your heart, I will be found by you,' declares the Lord, 'and I will bring you back from captivity'." (Jeremiah 29:11-14 NIV).

Right there, Scripture was telling me that my identity, my hope, and my future are in the Lord, not my marriage, family, or career.

Right there, Scripture was telling me that my identity, my hope, and my future are in the *Lord*, not my marriage, family, or career. *He* is happy to be with me and *He* is for me! Another verse that would be life-giving to me was in the story of Joseph. In Genesis 50:20 (NIV) Joseph notes that what was intended to *harm* him, "God intended...for *good*, to accomplish what is now being done, the saving of many lives." I still remember where I was standing in my North Carolina living room on the day when I declared that, no matter what happened in my marriage, family, or career, "I would be okay!" So began my journey towards a *joyful* life, of rooting my identity in Christ and my relationship with the Lord, first and foremost. I began to seek out and find relationships where I could speak my needs, be known, and have reciprocal healthy friendships and community. Instead of fighting Sydney's school system, we decided to move to Georgia to get the resources she needed. We wanted to find a school that was *for* her and us, that would come alongside us instead of opposing us. Dan made a career move and began to dream of what his career could become. At this point, there began to be some big changes in our marriage, and the "giants and gauntlets" were starting to be removed from the marital maze we were navigating. With some obstacles removed, I began to imagine a path forward.

When Sydney was in high school, we realized that Dan, too, was more than likely on the spectrum, and that we would need to approach our marriage differently. We began to shift away from "traditional" gender roles, and to look at our marriage and family through the eyes of our strengths and skill sets. We shifted our responsibilities and chores to share the load based on our capacities and neurotypes, not our gender roles. I have excellent executive function skills, so planning and details are in my lane, and let's face it, Dan is a better cook. (Admitting that used to bring me shame that I was not doing my job as a woman!) We shifted from Dan cooking only on weekends to Dan taking over the kitchen. He had been saying to me for years, "Just give me one thing. I can only do one thing at a time. One thing." We still collaborate and plan meals and our schedules together, but we have two very different skill sets that now complement each other. Once we leaned into complementing our *skill sets* (versus strict *complementarian* theology), we were on our way. At this point in our relationship, we better understood who each other was and who we were capable of becoming; we restructured our responsibilities and became curious about getting to know the other person. What I realized in studying Dr. Wilder's work, is that my order of the four soils starts with *hesed*, then *group identity, joy building* and *healthy correction*. I could not build joy with Dan until our marriage was free of "Trauma A" triggers. After I realized he was *for me* and *for us*, we began to build joy in our relationship. But it started with each of us doing our own work to find ourselves and our identity in the Lord, then removing the negatives and building on our strengths. We began calling each other higher to be our true selves in Christ and encouraged each other's gifts and neurotype.

While our marriage was growing and the fear bonds releasing, we still yearned for a stronger connection to each other. This final piece would be forged through a series of new trials. Fortunately, before these trials hit we had gained communication skills and an understanding of each other, so that when the trials came, we could face them together as a team. While the COVID lockdowns of 2020-2022 were difficult for many, a brief synopsis of our experience includes me finishing up a doctoral dissertation, injuring a shoulder and not being able to receive treatment for months, and a tree falling on our home, displacing us to a rental (also for months). Then, the week we were packing up from the rental to return home, a second tree fell on our house, damaging it and ripping out the main electrical wires. This was followed by our move to another rental, where, within the first few weeks, a third tree disaster occurred: a huge tree limb (the size of the tree) fell on both of our vehicles and the rental home, which forced us to move again! We were moving all around the metro area of Atlanta, without a car and facing a housing shortage. At the same time, my dad was diagnosed with stage 4 cancer, and Dan's dad was diagnosed with yet another cancer (both of our families were far off in North Carolina). Moreover, there was uncertainty in Dan's workplace, as the company he worked for relied on markets and gatherings, and COVID was disrupting many things. Amidst all those trials, stressful things were also happening in the lives of our teenage girls. Fortunately, Dan's dad would go into remission, but sadly, in 2023 my dad's cancer became his ride home to Jesus. If we had still been in fear bonds and trauma, I do not think we would have made it through those difficult years. What follows is not a prescription (or a promise), but rather, the steps we took to bridge connection and intimacy.

First, we took a course on how to lead marriage ministry together. The leaders asked the participants to take an inventory of their met and unmet needs, and to discuss these with their spouse. Dan brought up that in the past, we enjoyed recreational outdoor activities, and he said he would like us to do more of that on weekends (during the COVID lockdowns, it was best to do things outside). We eventually took up bike riding as an intentional activity together, with the goal of riding at least once a month.

Shortly after this course, we began reading the books *Emotionally Healthy Spirituality*[24] and *Emotionally Health Relationships*[25] by Peter Scazzero, and we made more life-altering shifts. We also began teaching group studies on these books in our couples coaching practice. While we had always kept Sundays set aside as a day for church gatherings, we realized we had both neglected to have a Sabbath and rest period each week. We needed, as Peter Scazzero said, "a rule (trellis) of life." We implemented the Sabbath slowly, starting with a few hours and working up to our target of taking a full day without paid work and chores. For us, Sabbath is not the elimination of physical labor, but rather, a rest from *toiling*. Based on travel schedules, we might do this Friday to Saturday, Saturday to Sunday, or if Monday is a holiday, Sunday to Monday. We saw that recreation was missing from our lives individually and as a couple, so we tried out new shared activities and began biking and hiking. Now, if there is decent weather, we try to get outside and do something together, even if it is enjoying our backyard. We decided to invest some money in our backyard so it could be a place of rest and respite (once we were back in our home). We each had our daily "quiet time" or "devotion time," but we wanted to connect with God more deeply and to share that as a couple. While both of us grew up in church and are avid readers regarding our own study time, we had not developed the habit of studying together. The *Day by Day*[24] devotionals by Scazzero is now one of my favorites to connect on, as well as *The Forty-Day Word Fast for Couples*[27] by Tim Cameron (about limiting toxic words that kill relationships). We have notebooks for the various devotions we are doing together, and when we are studying a book or workbook, we each start by writing. We then deepen what we're learning by discussing it over a walk or dinner.

Next, we realized (and still must work on this) that our schedules were out of control, and that sometimes we were too tired to enjoy our Sabbath together. We needed a touchpoint during the week, which became "at-home date night." Each semester, we look at our work calendars and choose a day to focus on "us," so we can experience joy-building or shalom together. In Wilder's work, *The Other Half of Church*,[1] he explains that while our brains crave and run on the fuel of joy, quieting/shalom and grace are important as well. Our at-home date night is restful, quiet and joy-building because we are together and doing a low-energy activity. One of our favorite things to do now is watch our "joy channel." We have curated photos of joyful, peaceful moments in our marriage and family, and Dan displays them on the television; we watch random moments of our life pop up and reflect, in gratitude and appreciation, about what brought us joy in that moment. Dr. Wilder said in several of his works that gratitude and appreciation are the first steps to building joy; the research of Brené Brown[5] concurs. With work travel, this at-home date is not possible every week, but we prioritize this intentional time together without working, choring, or checking emails. It is a focused time to stay connected in the moment with each other. As we watched our joy channel, we realized we hadn't had many new adventures and travels together, due to the COVID lockdowns. So now, traveling together and joy-building on vacation (while completing my 50-state quest) has become a priority. (At the time this book is being written, only 3 states remain!) We have even learned to travel together for work in a more positive way, making sure to have a date night each evening when the workday is done.

While I'm not going to discuss our physical intimacy in detail, I can say that we now have the best physical and sexual connection we have ever had in our marriage. When I moved out of the mindset (and bad theology) that sex was for *him* and was my *duty* as a good Christian wife, our intimate life changed. (In her 2021 book *The Great Sex Rescue,*[28] Sheila Gregoire argues against false teachings, such as a Christian wife's "duty" to have sex at least three times each week, so as to keep her husband pure and from cheating.) How did our sex life improve? It stopped being about the *physical* act of sex and fear bonds, and instead, celebrated the *relational intimacy* and *connection* we had built on all levels. For us, this led to more frequent sexual connections, curiosity, and pleasuring each other.

Our journey out of the "maze" – which went from realigning our roles, to wanting better connection, to enjoying at-home date nights – has been a three-year process that began during the hardest trials of our lives. Finding your way out of the maze is not easy to do. Life and schedules and weddings and more trials (and trees) can happen! For us, when we both began making joy, hesed and our identities in Christ a priority, we found a way to share the load of building connection and intimacy. In doing so, we have entered into a healthier emotional, spiritual, and sexual marriage that is satisfying and fulfilling for us both.

I can tell you without hesitation that, given where Dan and I now are in our neurodiverse Christian marriage, I would not trade our marriage for any that I know of, including for an NT-to-NT marriage. I could have never seen this coming or imagined us to be where we are, but God empowered us to commit to joy, hesed, group identity, and to offer each other healthy correction (or feedback) from a growth mindset, without shame and condemnation. Marriage work, as you saw in this narrative, first begins with each individual doing their own work to become emotionally and spiritually healthy! Two healthier individuals can decide to form a healthier and more reciprocal relationship. Where does alone time come in? We factor that in as well. We each have interests and passions, and we give one another space to pursue those. The difference now is that we *talk* about it. We ask each other if there is something the other needs or wants to do (like Dan pursuing the study of Hebrew or Biblical geography or a particular book, and my knowing he wants time to do that, or time to be alone outside and decompress). With such communication, I can plan things to do that help *me* decompress, and we are both getting our needs met. Communication and intentional planning provide the alone and couple time we need to rest, travel together, or simply "be" together. Do we have it perfect? No. But we have learned through Wilder's work that when we have a disagreement or get into enemy mode (one or both parties), we can turn our relational circuits back on and "re-friend" as soon as possible to minimize relationship damage.

Many of the neurodiverse relationships we work with fail to learn how to *repair*. Many couples come to coaching with decades of damage and trauma, and we do not weigh in on whether a couple should stay in their marriage or separate. However, Brené Brown[5] discusses "a particular sort of betrayal more insidious and equally corrosive to trust" (p.51). Not caring enough to resolve conflict, and not being willing to devote time, energy, and effort to the relationship is a type of betrayal that scars and does collateral damage. Brown[5] talks about toxic or unhealthy shame as the enemy of relationships because shame is intensely painful when we "experience or believe we are flawed and unworthy of love and belonging" (p. 67). She compares guilt to shame, wherein guilt is admitting you *did* something wrong or hurtful, and shame is believing *you* are bad or flawed. Working on your toxic shame is an individual journey, but couples can give each other correction or feedback in a way that produces healthy remorse and repentance (a call back to your true identity). However, no one can make you feel a certain way. If someone corrects the way you are building a fence or driving a car, they cannot make you feel like an idiot. If they call you an idiot that is one thing; if the person says, "Hey you are driving a bit fast or following too close and I don't feel safe," that feedback is about driving, with an observable fix, and not a character assignation. If you see that as control, criticism or contempt, that shame-based narrative and internalization is *your* work to undo. Brené Brown[5] said, "When you do something or say something that hurts some-one or act in a way you do not want to, confession releases shame. Empathy and under-standing toward others will bring you out of your shame hole." She continued that when you apologize or confess, you are making an admission of fault but do not have to absorb *shame*. If you are stuck in shame about the label of "neurodiversity" or if you receive any suggestion or feedback (even if done nicely) as criticism or contempt, you have work to do. Healing from toxic shame and rebuilding your core identity as grounded in Christ is possible, due to the *grace* Christ gives us! James 5:16a (ESV) says, "Therefore, confess your sins [wrongdoings, faults] to one another and pray for one another, that you may be *healed*."

Outside of the Maze: Dan's Insights and Hindsight Learning

We each reached our better individual selves in two very different ways. Stephanie mentioned she was in a bad state of mind in every aspect of life. That wasn't my experience. I didn't have desperation driving me to something different. As I have hinted in prior chapters, I could summarize my journey as "Taste and See." The Lord asks us to do that about him (Psalm 34:8, NIV). Applying that idea to life (beyond my spiritual relationship with God) means experiencing something different and recognizing that 'different' is better than what had been known previously.

I enjoy learning. I will read almost anything and be curious about how things work. I enjoy moments when knowledge from one domain applies to a different one. When I married Stephanie, she became one more domain or interest to pursue – to be interested in for *my* sake. I have also been described as curious. And for many years I thought I was successfully applying that curiosity to other people, especially Stephanie. What became evident is that I was curious about facts, data points, and other things in her world that interested *me*. What I missed was that I wasn't curious about her, for *her* sake. In all my wondering and questions, I missed being interested in *her*: her nature, character, dreams, disappointments, joys, and woes. I collected information (I still do); I did not show genuine, altruistic interest in *her*. Any interest I showed was typically self-serving.

It is also true that I wanted (and still want) to be with her. This wasn't a situation I was ambivalent about. I cared about her, our girls, and our relationship. What was simultaneously true is that I wasn't good at showing it. When presented with an opportunity to 'grow' together, I was rarely excited, but I was willing.

So, what does that have to do with "Taste and See"? As we started 'growing together' I noticed a richer, more abundant relationship. Each venture into a richer relationship beckoned me to explore further. Every step together healed, in a small part, the wounds from days gone by. Over the years, those small steps healed what I once thought would never heal and motivated me to continue the efforts.

As she mentioned, trees falling on the house, our rental and our cars happened during this time. Over many years I have seen that stress is something that overwhelms her quickly. The house situation was stressful, even traumatic for her, but it wasn't as much for me. It was simply what was happening. "Burden-sharing" while we lived in North Carolina wasn't something I did well. It is one of my shortcomings that created a great rift between us. When the trees began falling, I decided I was going to share the burden. No more pontificating about how this situation will one day be better or that this pain will cause us to be more resilient or that we should be content in our circumstances. That might be true, but it wasn't useful to say to Stephanie. It was dismissive. I hadn't *seen* her before, and I was determined to see her this time. I didn't get it right every time, but when I did, I noticed who we became was better than who we were. That was the "Taste and See." I changed my behavior: I turned toward her and *saw her*. Dr. Gottman refers to this as "responding to bids of affection or attention."[19] We have a choice to turn toward and lean into those bids or turn away and disconnect. I chose to lean in and pay attention to the bids. I *saw* her without trying to dig for more information and facts. I was learning to be curious about the right things. I was learning to put her first and validate her needs, even if they were needs that I did not have or understand. I was learning that the absence of information and my need to analyze the situation (and reserve judgment until there was sufficient evidence) wasn't as important as *believing* her. I was learning that the need for precision in details wasn't as high as I thought it was. I was learning to trust her instinct, especially when it wasn't *logical* to form that conclusion. In essence, I was learning that collecting information and analyzing it to form judgments were *preferences*, and they were my preferences. I had been valuing my preferences higher than I was valuing my wife and children. This wasn't a revelation that happened all at once: it was a gradual one, and it turns out those preferences didn't define me and were obstacles to us. I didn't quit being me. I am still eccentric. I have a very dry sense of humor. I can see patterns, but I still forget almost everything. I still can't recognize faces. I still have a particular fork in our drawer that I like more than the others and insist on using. More importantly, I learned that these types of things define my nature: they are who I am – my personality. But notice the difference: the first set of things are what I do and prefer. The second set is part of me. Those won't change.

As a general rule, I am content with how I work and who I am, and I am able to let go of things that don't impact my core. Doing so has honed those spots that were under-developed and has made me a stronger person overall. Each of my character qualities can be sharpened. That is what happened. When I lowered the value of my preferences and deferred to hers, I became sharper. There was a new found humility and openness. I am still not quick to share my inner thoughts. I am much more likely to do so than I ever was before – but only with her. It must be called out. I need to be invited. I am reluctant, but eventually willing to share verbally. For me, this is simpler in written form.

The various devotionals I was reading were, for the first time, usable. I had read devotionals before, and they were dry and boring. I lasted a couple of days at the most. This time, there was real value: I could recognize myself in the words. I could find ways to be different and grow better. What also began happening was that we started leading groups. We used various materials and combined these with the devotionals we were sharing. Now I not only had a book to read, but a group to read it with. We were creating a group identity that required group participation, and for me that meant spending time daily alone with God. That individual work created a desire to continue. My feelings of "I want to want to" became "I want to" – I *wanted* to spend time with God, and I *wanted* to grow our relationship. Those two things operated very well together.

I *wanted* to spend time with God, and I *wanted* to grow our relationship. Those two things operated very well together.

I'll refer to more of Dr. Wilder's material: In *Rare Leadership*,[29] he provides four habits of effective leaders. Let's first review how Wilder defines a leader. In this case, let's use the word 'initiator' as a synonym. This is the first person that takes the first action. Perhaps that action is internal, or it could be external. It could be calming yourself down or starting a conversation. We'll keep the definition within this simple form. We don't need the other traditional aspects of leadership for what we will talk about. Wilder and Warne uses the acronym RARE[29] to describe those four habits:

- *Remain Relational:* Keep relationships bigger than problems.
- *Act Like Yourself:* Does your current behavior align with your group identity?
- *Return to Joy:* Be your own referee – stop play when problems become bigger than relationships; refocus on what's important, then continue.
- *Endure Hardship Well:* Continue to grow your emotional and relational maturity during challenging moments.

Each of those thoughts is expanded upon in his book, and I encourage everyone to read it. I believe the one-liners are sufficient for what we need here. I will touch on each one but will spend more time on the last.

When Stephanie and I used to converse, I had a 'fix it' mindset: if she would only follow the steps I have laid out.

When Stephanie and I used to converse, I had a 'fix it' mindset: if she would only follow the steps I have laid out, this wouldn't be an issue anymore. That's the opposite of

"Remain Relational." In doing that, I focused on how she could solve the problem instead of on her. Perhaps she didn't want my help. She might have only wanted to talk, and this was a bid to *see* her.

I am an even-tempered person. Rarely have I exploded on anyone. It has happened though. I did not "Act like Myself" during those times. Sometimes it was aimed at inanimate objects; the lawnmower was the trigger for many of those moments. There was a time when I yelled at everyone. That is known as "The day daddy got the germ bug." And most embarrassing is the time I got extremely angry at our dog and almost strangled her. She ate my tent and camping equipment. In none of those situations, if you had been driving by or watching the replay, would you have thought this guy is modeling Christ-like behavior. I wasn't. This leads us to the next habit, "Return to Joy."

In those moments, what I should have done was watch myself (like being my own Jiminy Cricket) and call for a stop in the action. Next, ask myself, "Is what I am doing right now an expression of my best self?" When the answer is no, ask, "What do I require to deescalate my emotions and return to the situation with relationships at the forefront?" Sometimes it was right in front of me. The faces of the family showed that they were horrified by what I was doing. During the germ bug incident, everyone was crying and ran to their rooms. In the case of the dog, I did catch myself. My brain recognized what was going on and what would happen if I continued. It wasn't the possible loss of the dog that stopped me. It was the narrative that "daddy killed my dog" (and the dog's face) that turned the tide. Learning to be your own referee isn't easy, but there are usually external cues to help you, if you choose to see them. Now, I am much better and am more apt to quit a behavior when it is only a temptation. That doesn't always happen. I still have moments of weakness – driving in Atlanta for instance.

For my temperament, the change I have noticed the most is the last one, "Endure Hardship Well." You might think if you are even-tempered and rarely explosive, how can that be? What is true is that I didn't handle the challenges in a healthy way. I stuffed my emotions or ignored them. It worked until it didn't. From the outside, things looked like I navigated well. What I didn't recognize was I was storing my stress for another day. I didn't talk to Stephanie about it. I didn't talk to myself about it. I didn't gossip, curse or talk badly. It was the 'right' thing to do. I was, I thought, being very Jesus-y. Something happened I didn't like, and I moved on. It was that simple. That was my pattern. You could make a strong argument that I wasn't even relational with myself. I didn't (and still don't) have good self-awareness, especially when it comes to emotions and how others perceive me. In scripture, Jesus doesn't hide from his emotions. He gets angry, sad, frustrated, and happy. In all of those cases, he lives in the moment. He has feelings and expresses his emotions while ensuring the emotion doesn't *have him*. It is that part of endurance I had to learn. I am still not that good at it. It is still hard to talk about how I feel. Emotions still don't feel like they're important to me, nor of interest to anyone else. What I have learned is that Stephanie *is* interested in how I feel and always has been. For many years I kept my feelings from her; when I finally shared, it grew the connection between us.

The *Rare Leadership*[27] book is relatively new to us; we've only had it for two years, so what I've expressed in these terms is new vocabulary for me. I was able to do some things before I read the book. What is true after reading it, is I have a new vocabulary for doing new things. I have a new way to think about these things, and that framework makes it significantly easier to maintain growth.

It is important to remember that you only grow if you want to. Growth isn't something that happens to you. It is like the gym. You only get stronger if you use the equipment regularly. Driving by doesn't help, nor does having a membership and never going. You have to put in the time and effort. You only do that if you believe there is value. Growth is *valuable*. You might not know it yet, but that is the draw of "Taste and See" – once you experience what *can* be, you will likely want to continue.

The steps you take out of your "maze" will undoubtedly be different from ours. What is common are the milestones and strategies. The starting point(s) can be the same. The 'try something' and reflect can be the same. Being honest with yourself can be the same. When it comes to the details, you can work those out with each other. So, what can you start doing that will create a deeper desire to be with God? What are some preferences that you can let go of? And who can you start 'seeing' and being there for *them*?

 *Section 2*

What Can We Expect to Change?

Introduction

Change vs. Accommodations, Modifications & Strategies: Creating Realistic Expectations

BY REV DR. STEPHANIE C. HOLMES

A s we enter this next section, we want to provide strategies and insights for what can change in your neurodiverse marriage. Neurology is neurology, one's overall wiring is not expected to change, but we learned in the last chapter the joy center (OFC) can grow and each spouse can grow to be more relational and build relationship skills. Certified Autism Specialist, Barbara Grant will introduce stages of change and navigate first if both spouses are ready to bring about change from pre-contemplation to action steps. She will share how each individual is responsible for their own growth and when boundaries need to be put in place if there are recurring inappropriate or harmful behaviors. Motivation must come from within to bring transformation and true change. Part of what you can change is your expectations and comparisons to other NT-to-NT couples, repair any wounds and trauma, and heal from your past pain. Understanding and accepting who you are as a couple with realistic expectations is a great place to start this journey of relational change.

Communication challenges are one of the most cited issues in all types of neuro-diverse couples from daily planning to conflict resolution. Has it ever felt like you were speaking two different languages and that the simplest communication transactions can go awry? Neurodivergent and neurotypical people do use words and language differently, and often nuances and contexts are missed between a couple causing the double empathy problem. Former speech-language pathologist, Carol Reller will share from her professional background as well as tips and strategies she has found helpful in her own neuro-diverse marriage.

Have you wondered, does my spouse love me? If I was important to my spouse, he or she would remember our conversations and follow through on commitments. I know we had this conversation and made an agreement, and he or she says we never had that conversation, is he or she gaslighting me? Why can he or she remember so much about work or their special interest but cannot remember what I told him or her yesterday? What do all of these issues have in common? -Executive Function (EF). Challenges in EF are common with ASD and ADHD. Executive Function (EF) is the term commonly used to describe processes of the brain that we each need to use to accomplish each and every task that we wish to do every day. The more tasks we attempt to accomplish at one time, the harder this is, the more steps within each task the more stressed our neural processes become and the harder it becomes for us to access them to achieve our goals. This is a very practical and simplistic answer to a very complex question that neuroscientists and researchers are digging deep into to bring us to a better understanding regularly. Neurodivergent and certified autism specialist and life coach. Robin Tate will further explain EF and give tips and strategies to improve EF. Robin shares EF strategies from professionals and her ADHD lived experience.

Autistic author and life coach, Jeremy Rochford shares personal and professional insight on the importance of the acceptance of one's neurodiversity to move from shame to seeing the diagnosis as the ultimate life cheat code. Jeremy shares how curiosity about himself, his diagnosis and his wife had led to a happy and fulfilling neurodiverse marriage challenging the reader the type of neurodiverse marriage you have is up to you, better than imagined or worse than expected. If regulation is a challenge for you, Jeremy gives tips and strategies on pre-regulation and proactive tips for remaining regulated or noticing when you are becoming dysregulated sooner to minimize relational damage.

Jeremy and Charity (Team Rochford) talk about parenting neurodivergent children as a neurodiverse couple with different parenting styles and developing a strengths-based team approach rooted in the fruits of the Spirit. Many neurodiverse couples struggle with parenting due to communication and differing views about religion or scripture about parenting and the gender roles of parents.

Finally, Dr. Mary Jones discusses the additional stigma and bias that people of color face in getting proper diagnosis and support. Clinicians need to understand the bias they may bring to assessment when assessing autism in people of color.

Chapter Six

Navigating the Mazes of Change & Growth in Neurodiverse Marriages: Motivation, Boundaries, Acceptance & Healing

BY BARBARA GRANT, MMFT, CAS, NCC

What will this chapter help the reader do?

- Understand the considerations and steps needed to change, grow and heal.
- Learn practical "how to" strategies for growth.
- Embrace boundaries and identify obstacles that may be in the way.
- Recognize the connection between change and *repentance*.
- Align expectations with their present realities, while keeping hope in sight.
- Develop greater resilience and compassion for oneself and one's spouse.
- Embrace the power Christ gives us to mature.

Background

Neurodiversity has been a part of my family life since birth: I believe my mother's father and brother were autistic (very high functioning), and that there was a genetic and "cultural" influence of autism in my family growing up (also known as the *broad autism phenotype,* or *BAP*[1]). I believe this influence is what probably made my first husband (who was neurodiverse) seem so "familiar" to me (familiar, like *family,* comes from the Latin, *familia*). Neither I, my husband, nor our church counselors or therapists understood how neurodiversity presents or how it can impact self-image, thinking, behaviors and relationships.

My first husband and I (and his new wife) are now all best friends and monthly prayer partners, but after our 20-year marriage, we separated and then divorced. Sadly, we never had a clue what drove our conflicts, confusion and chaos. I eventually remarried another Christian man and 13 years later, I realized he was also neurodiverse. (He, too, seemed "familiar"!) I was already remarried when I finally had my 18-year-old assessed for autism (back then it was still called *Asperger's Syndrome).* They confirmed the autism, but unfortunately, they did not evaluate for ADHD (which now seems odd, since tests show that 40-80% of autistic people also have ADHD). The kid went another decade before a physician finally prescribed regular ADHD meds, which have proved enormously helpful.

After learning about neurodiversity and experiencing the personal and relational challenges it presents, I was led to become a trained biblical counselor. I then got several certifications for neurodiverse and trauma-informed coaching, and I even completed a master's in Marriage and Family Therapy. I've been coaching for several years now, and I share this background so that readers may know that neurodiversity is something I have lived with, lost with, and *learned* with! It seems the Lord had been equipping me for years to become a Christian neurodiverse couples coach, and it is now my joy to help others learn about and thrive in their unique neuro-profiles. Every day I witness people who are courageously growing as individuals, spouses and as parents - getting healthier in how they understand themselves and relate to others. This blesses *all* their relationships, including the one they have with God.

How Does Growth & Change Happen?

Neurodiverse couples are often in a state of *complex trauma*[2] by the time they finally discover their neurodiversity. The neurodiverse spouse may struggle with recurring *autistic burnout*[3], and the neurotypical spouse likely suffers from some level of relational and emotional neglect. Over time, their lack of knowledge and strategies causes them both to feel frustrated, estranged, and hopeless, even though neither ever intended to do the other harm. It is often one partner's level of distress (mostly the neurotypical spouse) which leads them to suspect or discover neurodiversity and to seek more effective help.

Change and growth happen in stages, over time. The *Stages of Change Model* was developed in the late 1970s[4] as a method of assessing an addict's motivation to change their habits. It remains a helpful framework to identify how ready someone is to change their patterns of behavior. The method suggests there are five stages of change:

1. Precontemplation
2. Contemplation
3. Preparation
4. Action
5. Maintenance

Precontemplation is when someone has no awareness that they could - or may need to – change, and *contemplation* is when they are aware but are weighing options and counting the costs of changing. They enter the *preparation* stage when they are beginning to get themselves and their resources ready to engage. *Action* happens when someone commits to change – their actions, thinking, expectations and behaviors begin to be noticeably different. Once satisfactory change has been achieved, *maintenance* becomes the focus, so that backsliding is kept to a minimum.

Though this model looks good on paper, in actuality it is not a linear process; people can bounce back and forth in these stages due to life challenges and distractions. But as Christians, we believe that we can "in all things grow up into him who is the Head, that is, Christ" (Ephesians 4:15b), and that "he who began a good work in [us] will carry it on to completion until the day of Christ Jesus" (Philippians 1:6b). Change and growth are *God's* plan for us, so if we lean into God, we are not alone in our journey of discovery and maturation!

Identifying What Needs to Change

When neurodiversity is suspected or discovered in a marriage, many things are called into question: Is this normal? Do other couples have this problem? Is someone to blame? Did God make a mistake? Did I marry the wrong person? What does this mean for our relationship, our kids, and our future? How do we fix or deal with this? What can I do and where can I get help?

A diagnosis or discovery of neurodiversity often brings a period of shock, grief, or maybe denial for one or both partners. (A diagnosis is not necessary, unless there are benefits to having one, such as accommodations that a workplace or school must legally offer because of the American with Disabilities Act). Letting go of past expectations and lamenting what is "lost" must happen as part of the acceptance and adjustment process. Curiosity is helpful: *what* exactly is neurodiversity, and how it is presenting in the marriage and family? Ignorance needs to be educated and support enlisted from informed, capable helpers. This may mean going outside of the church (or Christian) culture for help. While there are some Christian counselors trained in neurodiversity, the number is still relatively few. The secular book I most often recommend to learn about autism is *The Complete Guide to Asperger's Syndrome*[5], by Dr. Tony Attwood. His chapter on Long Term Relationships can shed much light on the dynamics in a neurodiverse marriage for both couples and counselors.

In the end, each spouse can only change themselves. This is perhaps the first paradigm shift to make: while we want to motivate, change or fix our partners, we can't. Christ instructed us to each "first take the plank out of your own eye, and then you will see clearly to remove the speck from your brother's/sister's eye" (Matthew 7:5b NIV). Putting pressure on a spouse to attend therapy/coaching, couples support groups, or read educational materials will usually backfire.

Making a Personal Decision to Grow

The word autism comes from the Greek work autos, which means "self." Autism is a self-referencing condition, and even highly functional autistic people can struggle with a limited theory of mind[5] (this is the ability to see a situation from another's point of view and a perspective that is maybe different, but equally valid to one's own.) A mistake many neurotypical spouses make (myself included) is to try and convince their neurodiverse spouse that they *are* neurodiverse. Each person must find their own curiosity and courage to explore their possibilities. Only when a partner willingly enters the *contemplation* stage do they begin to focus on their own opportunities for growth. As spouses progress to the *preparation* and *action* stages, it becomes most helpful if they can "stay in their lane." Bluntly, this means to mind their own business and learn the difference between what they can – and *cannot* be – responsible for.

 ## Growth Tips for Change:

- Assess how you are handling the knowledge that you (or your spouse) are neurodiverse.
- Evaluate what *Stage of Change* you think you are in (be honest).
- Consider what stage your spouse may be in (again, be honest).
- Get wise counsel and prayer support from safe, trustworthy and, ideally, qualified people.
- Learn about how neurodiversity can present, and what challenges it brings to relationships.

- With these insights in mind, revise your expectations for what change might mean in *your* life and your spouse's.
- Write out your *personal* growth goals and submit these to the Lord in prayer.
- Build a support team and get into *action*!

The What and Why of Boundaries

Identifying what *you* need and taking responsibility for identifying what you need will require defining your *boundaries*: ask yourself, "What do I need to be healthy? What can I actually control, and what must I let go of?" Boundaries have to do with your identity (who am I and who I am not or who I want to be). This is no easy process, as many Christian couples have built a large part of their personal identity on being "one flesh" in marriage (Genesis 2:24). But "one flesh" does not mean *one person*; if we are Christ followers, we are given a primary identity of being "children of God" (1 John 3:1) and called to put *God first* in our lives (Matthew 22:37). Are we able to trust God to help us and provide for our needs, whether our spouse does or not? Are we living for an audience of "one" (God)? Shifting our weight from self-reliance or co-dependence to God-dependence is another helpful milestone to aim for. Part of defining boundaries is taking ownership that one is responsible for their own safety and are not responsible for the way others perceive me or how they talk to me, but when someone does something that causes me harm or speaks to me in a way that is harsh or abusive, one can be responsible for their boundaries and communicating their boundaries in a healthy, clear way to another. Boundaries are about me and what I will and will not tolerate; they are not about making someone do what I want them to do because people have their own will and choices to make.

Identifying what *you* need and taking responsibility for identifying what you need will require defining your *boundaries*.

Most couples exhibit some degree of enmeshed or co-dependent thinking and behaviors. These are often unconscious, as they are learned in our families of origin. I've not yet had a client come into coaching with a well-defined sense of healthy boundaries. Few Bible studies and sermons seem to address this, and many Christian teachings over the centuries have actually generated guilt around having healthy individual boundaries ("don't be so *selfish!*"). Thankfully, there are now some excellent Bible-based resources that address this very topic: one I often recommend is *Boundaries: When to Say Yes, How to Say No to Take Control of Your Life*, by Henry Cloud and John Townsend[6].

A primary suggestion I give to all couples who begin coaching is to offer each other *grace and space*. By this, I mean that any habits of fighting, criticizing or controlling should cease and both spouses should shift their attention away from what they dislike in the other to working on themselves: what are *they* doing that contributes to the tension, confusion or dysfunction? What do *they* need to learn about their neuro-profile and how it differs from their spouse's? Couples very often report that giving grace and space has an immediate and positive impact on the tone and stress levels in the home. This, of course, is also of great value to any children. Declaring a "cease-fire" allows each partner to channel energy, focus and expectations towards their own opportunities to heal and grow.

Change in neurodiverse relationships takes a lot of energy. It's not a sprint, but definitely a marathon! Learning to develop habits of healthy self-care during this passage of healing is very important. Identifying and respecting each other's needs and limits (healthy boundaries) is both a way of loving and letting go of previous attempts at criticism and control. Needs are different than desires; needs are the basic requirements for physical, emotional, mental and spiritual health and safety. Desires are what we *want*. While having regular, edifying sex within marriage is desirable, it is not a *need* as been previously taught by many Christian books. Sometimes if there has been emotional damage, sex can be burdensome and even traumatizing. If a partner's healthy *needs* are not able to be met within the marriage, the partner should be free to explore meeting these needs through other relationships or resources (staying within the boundaries of Covenant marriage and using wisdom, of course!) Getting wise counsel and remaining transparent and accountable to one another is important in rebuilding trust.

Often, one or both partners in the marriage have not learned how to clearly communicate their desires or needs. Telling each other what one needs for health and safety may simply be a matter of *asking* (note: sometimes it's more effective to ask in *writing*.) If you're not sure you've clearly asked for one of your needs to be met, here is a script I have taught many clients to use, which helps them communicate their need in love. By using it, you are giving your partner the benefit of the doubt that they want to meet your need. I call this script a triple-decker "Love Sandwich." Here are the steps:

1. Affirm the other and the relationship.
2. Explain your need (the "Citation") *without blaming or shaming*.
3. Offer another affirmation of love.
4. Suggest what the change might look like (the "Invitation").
5. Close by again affirming something hopeful and positive about the other or the marriage.

When used, a Love Sandwich "need" message might go something like this:

1. (AFFIRMATION): I love you, and I know you love me.
2. (BOUNDARY): Therefore, when I share an idea or feeling, I need it to be respected and validated, instead of dismissed with anger or criticism. That kind of negative response makes me feel put down and discounted.
3. (AFFIRMATION): I know we both want our relationship to improve, so…
4. (INVITATION): If what I share tempts you to get angry or to criticize, please ask for a time out to process your feelings instead of saying something that might hurt me.
5. (AFFIRMATION): I have faith that you can accept this and join me in improving our relationship.

Unfortunately, simply stating your need may not be sufficient to get your partner's attention. While not intended, sometimes one or both partners have patterns of behavior that are deeply ingrained. These can have a hurtful and even unsafe impact; any kind of hurtful behavior (verbal, emotional, spiritual, physical, sexual or financial) is unhealthy and ungodly, and if it's ongoing, it may even be abusive. If there is ongoing abuse, then actual boundaries – with consequences – may need to be shared to protect the grace and space each spouse needs. Boundaries should first apply to oneself: if we can't control our behaviors, how can we expect our partner to make the same effort? Knowing our boundaries – or limits – is our personal responsibility. Boundaries are meant to be protective, not *punitive*. Example: by itself, a speed-limit sign on the freeway (a stated boundary) may do little to motivate speeding drivers to slow down; it's the risk of a *speeding ticket and fine* (the consequence) that may motivate drivers to control their behavior! However, some drivers may not be concerned about the consequences and speed anyway. The speed limit nor the consequence can enforce or control the behavior of one's driving. Even with the stated boundary (speed limit) and stated consequence (fine), one may still make the choice to speed because of their own will or choice or discount the consequence because they choose to do what they want to do- speed.

Deciding on appropriate consequences can be tricky. Think of a consequence as something that can escalate if the boundary keeps being ignored. Example: the initial consequence of a speeding violation is a ticket and fine. But most states allow drivers to attend traffic school to keep the infraction off their record and insurance. However, if someone is caught speeding again within a specified time period, they have to pay another fine, but they can't take traffic school again, so "points" are counted against their record, and their auto insurance goes up. If they speed again, their license could get suspended, and if they keep it up and fail to appear in court, their fines could skyrocket, they could lose their license for several years, and jail time may be in order. Escalating consequences, all for the same violation of speeding.

When implementing a boundary with consequences, you can use the Love Sandwich concept and add a consequence as a warning. An example might go something like:

1. (AFFIRMATION): I love you, and I know you love me.
2. (CITATION / BOUNDARY): I told you before that when I share an idea or feeling, I need it to be respected and validated, instead of dismissed with anger or criticism.
3. (AFFIRMATION): I trust you are trying to help our relationship improve...
4. (WARNING / CONSEQUENCE): So, if you get angry or criticize me when I share, I'm going to protect myself by leaving the conversation.
5. (AFFIRMATION): I have faith that you can accept this and join me in making our relationship safe and encouraging.

Separation (and divorce) are ultimate boundaries and consequences that unfortunately sometimes need to be applied. Separation can sometimes have the effect of motivating the other spouse to finally get into the *action* stage of change. However, those options should be very far downstream in the change process and should only be considered if there is ongoing abuse or other such behavior that threatens a spouse's health or safety. Decision support for separation ideally would come from a circle of wise and godly advisors who understand neurodiversity, as well as good legal and financial counselors. The return from separation should *only* happen once the spouse who has been asked to separate has taken responsibility for changing their own unhealthy or abusive patterns of behavior.

 ## Growth Tips for Boundaries:

- Spend some time listing out your true needs vs. your desires.
- Stop complaining and expecting your spouse to change; stay in *your* lane!
- Think about how your family of origin did (or didn't) have healthy boundaries.
- Identify unhealthy boundary habits that *you* can change.
- Use the Love Sandwich template to write out your needs and boundary messages.

- Consider sharing a boundary and consequence in *writing* instead of verbally: this helps make sure you share it in *love* and gives your spouse grace and space to understand and respond to it.
- Cultivate curiosity and humility when presented with your spouse's needs and boundaries.
- Prayerfully evaluate how you may unintentionally be enabling or even abusing your partner; get input from wise and informed advisors.

What's Behind Resistance to Boundaries and Change?

Developing a secure identity in Christ is essential when setting, communicating, and upholding boundaries. It's the strength and grace we have in Christ that gives us the dignity, courage and power to change. The apostle Paul wrote, "I can do all this through him who gives me strength" (Philippians 4:13 NIV). So, what trips us up?

People-pleasing is the number one reason most clients say they don't set boundaries: they are afraid of confronting and hurting someone's feelings and of being rejected. Conversely, when we do set boundaries and it provokes angry resistance or conflict in the person we have confronted, we often feel guilty and wrong for causing a conflict. ("Don't be so *selfish!*") We retreat in confusion and frustration and become enablers; we may even distance ourselves emotionally, stuffing our feelings until we become overly critical or controlling, overly anxious, or experience weight gain and/or physical illnesses (or a combination of these). It's almost like we're taking on the negative consequences for the other person's unhealthy behaviors! None of these responses are godly or promote resolution and reconciliation. They keep us – and our loved one - stuck in unhealthy patterns of insecurity and unresolved discord. In fact, it's unloving to *not* set boundaries ("love always *protects*"- 1 Corinthians 13:7a).

Neuroscience research is shedding light on how God designed the brain to function: this scientific work is producing neurological data about how we develop a sense of our identity starting at birth through young-adulthood, and how different parts of our brain function to help us survive and grow in wisdom. To some extent, the brain can evolve and mature throughout our lifetimes, especially when we are free to make mistakes and learn from them in a safe, loving relationship. Our brain's ability to evolve is called *neuroplasticity*[7].

Here's a very simplified explanation of neurodevelopment: We now know that if a baby is (or is not) lovingly cared for, it can directly impact their sense of security. They can feel accepted and safe or rejected and under threat of abandonment. This impacts how well they will come to trust and relate to others (also known as *attachment theory*[8]). If a child is traumatized by ongoing insecurity and fear of rejection (inflicted by parents, siblings or school bullies), they often grow to act out of their *limbic system* (their "survival" brain that responds to danger with unsettled emotions and behaviors like *fight, flight, freeze* or *fawn*). If a child is more secure, they will eventually learn to think out of their pre-frontal cortex (the rational brain) and find ways to self-regulate instead of reacting in anxiety, fear, and shame. Balanced brain development can support a person's sense of dignity, courage, curiosity and emotional resilience when faced with trials and threats. An often-overlooked aspect of childhood insecurity and trauma is that it can predispose us to humiliation (*shame*) instead of humility (*repentance*)[9]. Neuroscience also reveals that the workings of a neurodiverse brain can be similar to one that has been influenced by trauma: both ASD and ADHD brains can function in ways that may result in hypersensitivity towards rejection and shame (known as *rejection sensitivity dysphoria*[10,11]).

How does insecurity and shame interfere with boundaries and change? As children, these negatively influence our habits of thinking and behavior which impact our emerging sense of *identity:* we unconsciously behave as fearful, insecure beings. This is the opposite of God's invitation that we become "more than conquerors through him who loved us" (Romans 8:37)? How can we tell if we're insecure? Become observant: If we make mistakes and are challenged, do we readily accept and admit our shortcomings, and humbly change? (Again, God wants us to learn to do this, since Romans 8:1 says "there is now *no condemnation* for those who are in Christ Jesus"!) Or do we react in shame, covering ourselves with fig leaves and shifting blame like Adam and Eve (Genesis 3:7-13)? I confess that I have spent the greater portion of my life in fear, denial, shame and blame-shifting. It was only when I encountered and *accepted* the security and grace of Jesus Christ that I was able to renounce my shame-based identity and begin to live in freedom to learn and grow.

It is sad that, over the centuries, much of the church's teaching has unintentionally trained us to act like powerless enablers, and to then suppress our resentment instead of speaking the truth in love (setting boundaries). We are primarily afraid of rejection and abandonment. We become people-pleasers, or worse, self-reliant and insensitive to the needs of others. Neurodiverse and neurotypical alike, we cannot live in grace unless we admit that we need it.

Acknowledging and changing our habits of behavior is not an easy task – as Stephen Covey (the author of *The 7 Habits of Highly Effective People*) said, "You can't talk yourself out of a problem that you behaved yourself into."[12] When we commit to *action,* we being to learn bit by bit, uncovering habits and unearthing the wrong-thinking that motivated them. Then we have to rethink our motive and behave in a new way, repeating the new behavior until it becomes our new habit. Then we can tackle another habit and reform that. These are ways the apostle Paul described the process, "We demolish arguments and every pretension that sets itself up against the knowledge of God, and we take captive every thought to make it obedient to Christ" (2 Corinthians 10:5 NIV). And "do not conform to the pattern of this world, but be transformed by the renewing of your mind" (Romans 12:2a NIV). It's faith-building to know that *cognitive behavioral therapy* is nothing new – the Bible prescribed this thousands of years ago!

Everyone can learn and grow, if the obstacles of insecurity, fear and shame are identified and removed. Past trauma or neurodiversity is never an excuse for sinful, unloving behavior – God gives the Holy Spirit to counsel and guide us, and even though we will continue to make mistakes (and sin) for as long as we live in this fallen world, we are not under shame or condemnation. In 2 Corinthians 7:9b-11, Paul talks about the difference between the remorse a healthy conscience produces (*Godly sorrow*) and the blame-shifting, self-pity and "death" that comes from unhealthy shame (*worldly sorrow*). We see illustrations of these responses in how, when challenged by the prophet Nathan, King David humbly took responsibility for his sinful murder of Bathsheba's husband (*Godly sorrow*), compared to how King Saul dealt with his ongoing sin of jealousy towards David (*worldly sorrow*). Both Peter and Judas Iscariot betrayed Christ: Peter anguished about his sin and repented (*Godly sorrow*), while Judas tried to return the silver coins and chose to end his life (*worldly sorrow*).

In many ways, change and growth are all a part of ongoing repentance and sanctification, which are life-giving and relationship-protecting. We can't make anyone else repent and change; we can only choose to do so ourselves. But by choosing this path, we act as courageous examples to those we love, offering ourselves compassion when we fail and enjoying the grace and encouragement of Christ as we grow. This process humbles us and allows us to be more patient and compassionate with our loved ones as they wrestle with their own obstacles to change. If even one spouse chooses the path of growth, in time it may inspire the other spouse to do the same.

In many ways, change and growth are all a part of ongoing repentance and sanctification, which are life-giving and relationship-protecting.

Growth Tips for Overcoming Resistance:

- Prayerfully evaluate what ways you may be stuck in behaviors motivated by insecurity, fear and/or shame.
- Think about your family growing up; assess if you learned healthy boundaries and conflict resolution or if you learned how to people-please, hide, stuff your feelings and even blame-shift.
- If you discover that shame has motivated you, practice reforming your sense of identity in the grace of Christ. An excellent resource for this is *Victory Over the Darkness,* by Neil Anderson[14].
- Reset your goals to improving *yourself* (in Christ), and the marriage will most likely improve, too! If it doesn't, you will have developed the character strength and support you'll need to make wise decisions about moving forward.

Final Thoughts

While neurodiverse marriages present unique challenges, I've come to believe that once a couple understands and accepts their neurological differences, adjusts their expectations and learns new strategies for communication and conflict resolution, many of their remaining relational "problems" are not all that different from those of other couples. In both cases, healing starts with each individual and their commitment to learning and growing. Christ's teachings about grace, forgiveness and how to grow are essential, but they must be *applied,* not just admired. I've seen so many neurodiverse marriages become incubators of healing, growth and change, with blessings for everyone involved. In closing, I want to offer you hope that growth is possible for you and your relationship, too. As it says in Romans 5:2b-5 (NIV):

> ...*we boast in the hope of the glory of God. Not only so, but we also glory in our sufferings, because we know that suffering produces perseverance; perseverance, character; and character, hope. And hope does not put us to shame, because God's love has been poured out into our hearts through the Holy Spirit, who has been given to us.*

Chapter Seven
Navigating the Maze of Communication: Social Language Pragmatics

BY CAROL RELLER, MS, SLP

Communication. Seems like a simple word. You talk. I talk. We don't think about it a lot. Until something goes wrong. The message was misunderstood. A response was unexpected, or no response came at all. You begin to wonder what went wrong. You observe body language to try and to glean a meaning for what's happening. You question, but what you receive, again, is unexpected. You feel confused. Invalidated. Misunderstood. What is going on? What just happened???

Those were my questions for years.

Background

I am a neurotypical (non-autistic) person, and I began working in 1988, teaching in a special day class for communicatively handicapped 1st -3rd graders. I taught for the next 11 years. After that I served as an itinerant speech and language pathologist, and for 21 years I worked with preschool through high school-aged children. This was before any colleges offered training about *Asperger's Syndrome*, later called *Autism Level 1*. I am now retired.

In 1990 I married Greg; he is a brilliant man and has a kind heart. I fell in love with his intelligence, the way he used words so uniquely, and with his quiet nature. We had dates that weren't like any others I'd had. We went hunting for edible mushrooms in the hills, and we took a ferry to San Francisco to search for earthquake damage on the buildings after the 1989 earthquake. We shared interests such as hiking, camping and just being outdoors. Rocks were his special interest which led to his career choice of geology, and over time, I realized that he could tell me about each rock he owned, where it was from and when he got it. And he had *a lot* of rocks. After marrying, we began a family right away. Over the course of 8 years, we had three children. Communication seemed difficult about six months into the marriage, and I assumed this was probably because we hadn't lived together until then. But that's another story.

I first heard the term *Asperger's* in 1994. I didn't know a thing about it. I worked with younger kids in a classroom who were identified as severely handicapped, so I didn't come across it much. But later, when I changed jobs and began working with kids up through 8th grade, I noticed that kids who were identified as on the *autism spectrum* often acted in similar ways to Greg. They would tell jokes that didn't always fit the situation or were the type of jokes much younger kids would tell. The students were specific with their words, they focused on specific topics of interest, and they didn't understand other people. I worked on pragmatics (social language) with them and our goals focused around perspective taking, being able to think of two different reasons why a single situation could happen, flexible thinking, expected vs. unexpected responses to others, and gradients of emotions and idioms. Typically, the students with Asperger's passed most of my basic language tests with flying colors. They just weren't able to generalize to real life situations. I told Greg one night at dinner after a particularly strange interaction with him, "You act just like my kids at school." But I didn't yet make the complete connection that he might have Asperger's. We had been blaming all his behaviors on the fact that he was raised with an alcoholic father. He was so smart; I couldn't see past it. Once day in counseling I mentioned I should use my therapy materials with my husband. My counselor agreed that might be a good idea, but never suggested he was on the autism spectrum. I thought she was joking. Anyway, back to our marriage.

We live on five acres in the country. This means there are always projects to do. Big projects. Changing fence lines, re-building fences when the horse breaks through, laying out sprinkler systems, and finishing the top floor of our barn. You get the idea. Well, I love to work with my hands and be outdoors. Greg also loves this. He knows how to do lots of things because he reads *everything*. I, being a very curious person, like to learn by asking questions. Being shown how to do something works better for me than reading about it. I was raised this way by my dad and it worked well, however, it did not work well at all for me and Greg. He needs to focus on a task, and he can focus to the exclusion of everything else. He does not like to be interrupted because he processes his thoughts silently, in his head. And if things don't work as expected, he can have a very short fuse. I, on the other hand, process verbally. I wanted to learn, so I typically asked questions while he was in the middle of something so he could explain it to me. How did this work for us? It didn't. I would ask a question, and he would try to stop and answer, or he would ignore me - and all the while, his window of regulation got narrower and narrower. I couldn't understand why he was snapping at me. I would call these our $80 issues because that is how much a counseling appointment costs at the time, and it would take a session to discuss it.

After 25 years of marriage, we were still doing projects this way. It's not that we hadn't tried different things to help us. We had done years of counseling; we went through every marriage/communication class at church, and we had always tried talking things through. But we still didn't know what we were dealing with. Anyway, we began yet another large project: putting up a 400-foot fence that required an 8-inch-wide concrete strip under it. We had to sink poles into the concrete strips, so we mixed our own concrete and worked one wheelbarrow at a time. This took a few months. We had gotten to the point where we only had to say a few words to each other to get the job done. He would bring over concrete and I would say, "Start. Slow. Stop. Finished." Our 22-year-old son was home during a time when we had to figure out how to put the concrete around a tree. I was asking Greg questions, and he was trying to explain but was getting frustrated with me. I was growing more and more upset. Years of this had taken its toll on both of us. He went into the house frustrated. My stomach ached and my heart was racing. Then my son came up and explained what Greg had been trying to tell me. I felt amazingly calm. The way he spoke was soothing to me. They basically explained the same thing but with different words and a different tone. I felt compassion from my son. I told him how well he explained it and that he would be a great boss someday. But I couldn't stop thinking about how different I had felt when each of them had spoken. It was only a few days later (during another ridiculous misunderstanding) that I finally figured out Greg was on the autism spectrum.

Language

Permit me to "geek out" and give a bit of technical background to help us. There are many ways to communicate. The purpose of communication is to give someone else information or to connect. The information could be how you feel, what you are thinking, your opinion, what you need at the grocery store and so on. Someone needs to be the recipient and understand you for true communication to take place. Spoken language is only one part of communication. A psychology professor by the name of Albert Mehrabian from the University of California, Los Angeles, laid out this concept in his book *Silent Messages*[1]: his research suggested that 7% of meaning is communicated through spoken word, 38% through tone of voice, and 55% through body language (non-verbal behavior). This study focused on the communication of feelings and attitudes and not all communication in general. But it still says a lot about how important body language and tone of voice are to convey meaning.

Language is both the words we use and how we use them; speech is the sound of spoken language, such as articulation, fluency and voice.

Language is both the words we use and how we use them; speech is the sound of spoken language, such as articulation, fluency and voice. Language has five areas: *phonology, morphology, syntax, semantics* and *pragmatics*. The two main areas impacted by autism are *semantics* and *pragmatics: semantics* is the meaning of the words both on the surface and the underlying meanings. This includes labels, definitions, associations, how items relate to each other such as comparing and contrasting as well as multiple meanings of words, antonyms, synonyms, making inferences, and literal vs. implied meaning. *Pragmatics* is the use of language. It is often also called social communication. It includes the intended meaning of what was said. It deals with topic maintenance, turn-taking, social norms, perspective-taking, flexibility with language, gradients of emotions, and humor. It also includes non-verbal communication such as reading body language, reading a situation and facial expressions.

Language is also divided into *receptive language* (what we take in and understand), *expressive language* (what comes out as we speak; our expression), and *inner language* (all the things roaming around in our head and the conversations we have with ourselves that are not spoken).

Pragmatics and Autism

There are various ways diagnosticians assess people for autism spectrum disorder (ASD), which include different tests, interviews, reviewing childhood behavioral history (if the person is now an adult), and clinical observation. Diagnosticians also reference the *Diagnostic and Statistical Manual of Mental Disorders*[2] (*DSM-5*), which is a compilation of diagnostic criteria for various mental health disorders created by the American

Psychiatric Association. Some of the hallmark characteristics of autism that involve *pragmatic* language include the following (note: in my examples, I will be using "NA/NT" for the non-autistic/neurotypical person and "AS/ND" for the autism spectrum/neurodiverse person):

1. Difficulties in social and emotional reciprocity, including trouble with social approach, back-and-forth conversation, sharing interests with others, and expressing/understanding emotions.

    - NA/NT sits down with AS/ND and starts a conversation, and AS/ND responds in one-word sentences and continues looking at their phone.
    - NA/NT begins to share something personal and gets emotional, and AS/ND just looks blank or starts talking about something else.
    - AS/ND engages in fact-dumping, instead of taking turns and listening in a conversation with another.

2. Difficulties in nonverbal communication used for social interaction, including abnormal eye contact and body language, and difficulty with understanding the use of nonverbal communication like facial expressions or gestures for communication.

    - AS/ND doesn't know to move over when someone tries to share the same sink.
    - When socializing with others, NA/NT tries to subtly signal the AS/ND with facial expressions to stop talking, and the AS/ND loudly says, "What are you looking at me that way for?"
    - AS/ND doesn't realize that, when talking to someone who keeps looking around or looking at their watch, the person may want to end the conversation but is trying not to be rude.

3. Deficits in developing and maintaining relationships with other people (other than with close family members), including lack of interest in others, difficulties responding to different social contexts, and difficulties in *sharing* imaginative play.

    - AS/ND doesn't maintain friendships or doesn't have many friends.
    - AS/ND has difficulty approaching others and engaging in meaningful conversation.

4. Stereotyped speech, repetitive motor movements, echolalia (repeating words or phrases, sometimes from movies or television shows or from other people), and repetitive use of objects or abnormal phrases.

- AS/ND has a fascination with words and may repeat phrases from TV shows seen in the past as ways to facilitate conversation.
- Pedantic speech (explained later)

As you can see, social communication deficits are a large part of the diagnosis, which in turn has a large impact on relationships. Semantics and pragmatics are where the most language difficulties in a neurodiverse relationship land, and the two tend to overlap. Also, it is rarely the language difficulties in isolation: other things play a part, such as memory, executive function, compassion, feeling judged or criticized etc. For now, let's focus on the part language plays within social interactions.

Frequency, Intensity and Duration

Often when an NA/NT who is in a relationship with an AS/ND tries to discuss their issues with someone who *is not* in a neurodiverse relationship, they might describe the types of struggles they have in communication. After they give some examples, the person listening might say "Oh, my husband/wife does that too" and will then relate a story of their own. These listeners might disbelieve the ASD diagnosis, or they might be trying to relate to the speaker. What is important to understand is that while many of the traits of autism are seen at various times in neurotypical people, it is the *frequency* (how often it happens), the *intensity* (how strong of a reaction it is or how forceful the words) and the *duration* (how long the reaction goes on, if there is a meltdown, or if the person won't let go an issue or get resolved) that sets the neurodiverse relationship apart from what happens in a neurotypical relationship.

In Bill Nason's book *The Autism Discussion Page on the Core Challenges of Autism*[3], he talks about the difficulties behind communication and how NA/NTs and AS/NDs relate on two different planes: *literal* vs. *perspective*. As many others say, it's like they are speaking two different languages. Here is what Nason[3] says (pp. 263-264):

> *NT people speak with multiple meanings, and intentions, often with hidden meaning. Rarely is our communication literal to the word. Also, NT people usually assume that the same process occurs for people on the spectrum. So, they often infer certain perspectives and intentions on the person with autism that are not there. For example, the person with autism is often blunt and literal, saying it as it is! This often strikes NT people as rude and disrespectful, even though there is no intent on the part of the person with ASD (autism spectrum disorder) to be rude and disrespectful.*

In turn, people on the spectrum speak very literally, often meaning exactly what their words are saying. Consequently, they often read the language of others very literally, missing the hidden meaning between the words (perspective and intention of others).

Here are some examples:

Example 1:

Carol: (NA/NT): "Gosh it's hot in here. We really should open up the house."

Greg: (AS/ND): (Does nothing even though he is sitting right next to the door.)

Carol: (Opens up the house while walking around him and asks), "Why didn't you help me open up the house?"

Greg: "I didn't know you wanted me to do it now."

Growth Tip:

This was an implied request that Greg didn't infer, and I realized it happened quite a lot. It will help with understanding if the NA/NT calls the AS/ND's name out first to gain attention, and then states directly what she/he wants, i.e., "Greg, would you please open the slider now, since it's hot in here?" Sometimes he will say back, "Now?" and I have to make sure I am not snarky (since I already said 'now') and just answer "Yes, please. Now." He is probably just confirming, and not delaying.

Example 2:

Carol: (Referring to some fence repair work) "Today I was thinking we could move the gate over and just pound all those boards off."

Greg: "I like to *pry* them off, then you don't split them."

Carol: "You're taking me literally. I'm just talking about taking the boards down."

Example 3:

Carol: (Walks into bedroom where Greg is sitting in a chair) "What's up?"

Greg: "I don't know what you mean by that."

Example 4:

Carol: (Backing the car out of a tight spot, while Greg is out of the car, waiting and directing. Carol has a hard time telling if she's clear so she gives herself extra room. This particular spot takes lots of forward and back movement to get clear. Before she has finished, Greg gets into the car. She is surprised and when she finished backing up, she says) "I didn't expect you to dive in the car when I wasn't finished."

Greg: "I didn't dive."

Carol: (Realizing AS/NDs can get hung up on the semantics of a word or its meaning, and knowing many on the spectrum like language to be precise, e.g., Greg knew he didn't "dive") "I didn't mean 'dive' literally, but that you got into the car quickly when I wasn't finished moving the car."

These are examples of the confusion that happens with neurodiverse couples when one is prone to the use and understanding of literal language and one uses a combination of nuances, metaphors, hyperbole and various forms of figurative language while speaking.

Growth Tip:

Realizing this difference in language can help in understanding each other. Clarifying what was said or what you think you heard can be beneficial

Because of my husband's large vocabulary, occasionally we would play a game at the dinner table. I would open up the dictionary and turn to a random word on a page and ask Greg for the definition. We called it "Stump Daddy." He could always give the definition. I teased I was going to start calling him Webster (after the person who wrote the dictionary). Later I found out he actually started reading the dictionary at age 9, and continued to be fascinated by it, reading parts of it over the years.

Many AS/ND individuals have a high-level of vocabulary. They are also literal and want to be completely accurate with their words. However, their failure to "read" the audience they are speaking to often results in the use of a higher level of vocabulary than the situation or the audience requires. This is called *pedantic speech,* which is considered to have too much attention to detail, is overly formal for a conversational or casual setting (little use of slang), and often sounds a bit odd to others.

Examples:

- After a discussion about how my husband (AS/ND) was speaking harshly to me (NA/NT), I asked if he understood. He said, "I get it. The gravity and intensity for the conversation was not merited." What I was expecting was something like, "I'm sorry, I didn't mean to sound harsh." He wasn't wrong in what he said, it was just unexpected for the situation.

- I (NA/NT) looked at a children's book with my one-year-old granddaughter and there was a picture of a bee by a honeycomb. I said "Bee!" My husband (AS/ND) looked at the same book with her, and he said, "This is a hexagon. It's the most efficient way to fill up space!"
- "Look, the impudence of the bird!" (Greg's AS/ND response to there being bird poop on the window.)
- "You are beautiful no matter what you encase yourself in." (Greg giving me a compliment about my outfit.)

There are times when I love hearing him talk like this, and I understand what he is saying. Other times I ask why he said it that way, and we end up having issues about word meaning (semantics). Greg (AS/ND) mentioned that he spends a lot of time listening to what I say and then trying to think of a word in his vocabulary that matches it in meaning that makes sense to him, so he is basically trying to translate in his head what I'm saying into his vernacular. This is actually progress, because for years he would simply say his word out loud and correct me…. All. The. Time! That didn't go over well. I felt as though he thought I was stupid. So, he would say a word he thought would better fit the situation, then we would both have to explain and I would say, "That is exactly what I said," but he felt he said it better. Then the circle of explanations began and we started going round and round. We were essentially saying the same thing, but to each of us the meaning was slightly different.

 ## Growth Tips:

- If the listener (AS/ND or NA/NT) isn't sure what the word means, ask for clarification.
- If the speaker (AS/ND or NA/NT) is asked for clarification, give a meaning or a different word, realizing that not everyone has the same vocabulary.
- Both parties can come to accept that the other person may use different words for the same situation and that asking for clarification is not being critical – it is to create mutual understanding.
- Both parties should realize that they process differently. AS/NDs should consider that they are saying the word a different way to clarify and process, rather than to just correct the other person. NA/NTs should realize it is so the AS/ND can process and clarify and not necessarily to correct you.

No communication

I have read about a particular tool/strategy used by the military: when they are fighting an enemy, the strategy is to disrupt/scramble/knock out the communication of the adversary. This impacts their own efforts to communicate. The result is that no one knows what is going to happen and no strategies can be put into place. This can directly relate to the neurodiverse relationship. If there is no communication, that is, no one is talking, or one of you isn't talking, no one knows what the other person is thinking. Assumptions start occurring. This leaves you to try and guess or read body language. We know that reading body language in the neurodiverse relationship is not very effective for either party. Combine that with a neurodiverse brain that tends to have a negative spin and that might assume the worst, and things can go downhill quickly.

Often the AS/ND person doesn't know what to say or how to respond due to processing issues. Other times, the conversation stays in their head, as in *inner communication*.

Often the AS/ND person doesn't know what to say or how to respond due to processing issues. Other times, the conversation stays in their head, as in *inner communication*. Here is an example of when my husband and I discussed our niece, who was in competitive soccer in California. Greg had an *inner* conversation with himself, and then tried to converse with me without giving me the information he had been thinking about:

> **Greg:** "Well how old is she?"
> **Carol:** "She's 8."
> **Greg:** "Well she's not going to be catching any caribou up there."
> **Carol:** "What? What are you talking about?"
> **Greg:** "The caribou. She won't catch any."
> **Carol:** "Who? What are you talking about?"
> **Greg:** "The show we watched the other day. About the girl that went to college (in Alaska.)"
> **Carol:** "Please tell me how this relates to our niece or how you think I would know what you are talking about."
> **Greg:** "Well you watched the show with me. I can't explain it any more than I already have."

Growth Tip:

My AS/ND husband has said that for years he felt that everybody had the same access to all the information he did, so he figured a lot of his thoughts had occurred to everyone else, too. This is why he either doesn't say anything or he talks as if everyone has all his prior knowledge. If you are an AS/ND and you don't know what to say, sometimes it's OK to say just that: "I really don't know what to say;" "My mind is blank right now;" "Could we start again slowly;" or "I need a 10-minute break." All these are better than pure silence. I know it can be hard to even remember these things in the moment. It does take practice. If you are having a discussion in your head, and you try to start one up with another person, know that they don't know the *inner conversation* you have been having with yourself. The NA/NT can help by realizing that when this situation occurs, they can prompt some of these responses if the AS/NT is willing to have you do this. But don't prompt too many at one time.

Minimal communication

Sometimes there is communication, just very little. My husband feels the less words he has to use to get a point across, the better (unless he is talking about his special interest of geology and rocks). Sometimes I need more information to understand what he is talking about.

Here is an example – we were processing two baskets full of tomatoes to boil down and make into sauce:

> **Carol**: "Which pot do you think we should use? How about this one?" (I pull out a large pot.)
> **Greg**: "Sure, use that one."
> (We continue to process tomatoes, and the pot is almost full with only one basket completed.)
> **Carol**: "Oh my gosh we have a lot. I guess we should switch to our biggest pot."
> **Greg**: "That's what I was thinking in the beginning."
> **Carol**: "But you didn't say that to me."
> **Greg**: "I was thinking this one would be fine."
> **Carol**: "But you said you thought the biggest pot would be good, now you are saying you thought this one would work."
> **Greg**: "Because I did."
> (This lack of communication shares the same dynamic as the fence project example given earlier in the chapter: we had not fully discussed the chore we were working on ahead of time which led to confusion.)

Growth Tips (for projects):

- Before starting a project, sit down to discuss the project.
- Draw a picture so you know each of you have the same vision.
- Write out what each of you are responsible for.
- Set up break times to assess how it's going.
- If one has a question in the middle, ask if it's a good time to talk.
- Set up code words if necessary. (For our project we ended up using single words as he poured the concrete such as 'start,' 'slow,' 'stop,' and 'finished.' These were simple and we were able to communicate quickly.)
- Realize one or both people involved may need a break from overstimulation. Usually, it's the AS/ND person. Planning for breaks in general instead of plowing ahead is a good idea.
- Our mantra became "Relationship before task."

Body Language

When babies are born, and for the first year, they haven't developed spoken language, but they communicate. NA/NTs learn to understand their different types of cries and coos and to read their body language. They begin to understand when babies are hungry or tired, and they also read the situation: Is it nap time? Have you been on errands with them for a few hours? Many factors are taken into consideration. The same type of thing applies in communication with a person of any age. Body language is a significant way to communicate, and as we saw with the study by Mehrabian[1], when dealing with emotions/feelings and attitudes, it can often override words. I taught my students first to read the room/location/situation for data: How many people are there? Are you two alone? Are you at a party with many others? Are you hiking? Next, read the body language of the other person: Are their arms crossed and are they looking down as if they are upset? Are they holding a drink or chatting and seeming very calm? Listen to their tone of voice: Is it loud and harsh? Is it quiet? Is it escalating? Now here is the most challenging part: this step-by-step observation process can take time (years) to learn, but with intentional practice, it can offer much improvement in how well one person reads another.

Typically, the AS/ND individuals read body language and tone differently than NA/NTs. NA/NTs can learn to read each other pretty well, and if they aren't sure, they ask questions to confirm such as, "You look sad, are you sad about something?" AS/NDs also read each other fairly well, but in combination, the NA/NT and AS/ND (i.e., a neurodiverse couple) don't naturally read each other well. Body language is difficult for the person on the spectrum to understand; in turn they also don't use *typical* body language. Therefore, the NA/NT, who is more adept at reading body language, actually misreads the body language of the autistic person.

Example: For years as my husband and I walked together along the street or in parking lots, we would literally run into each other. He would switch to a different side of me at seemingly random times, and when I would head somewhere thinking he would head in the same direction, he would continue on his path, so I would run into him. It was incredibly frustrating. Why can't we even walk together? It wasn't until years later when he explained he was always wanting to protect me, and so to do this, he was making sure I was always on the inside of the sidewalk away from the street. He didn't explain this to me, however, and to get to his "outside" position he would go in front of me at each crossing to make sure he was on the outside. He also liked to walk down the middle of the row of cars so he could see both sides if someone backed out and I tended to stay out of the middle. I observed when I walked with friends, and when I tried to gently steer them in a direction I may want to go, there was never a problem. Once I found out what he was doing and he told me his rules, I was able to switch seamlessly at each intersection. It is kind of like a dance we have. We can now even continue to *talk* while doing it! This example shows both that we didn't read each other's body language and that there was no communication about what rules we were following.

 ## Growth Tips:

- It's always good to clarify your interpretation of body language. Be able to give your interpretation and accept it when the other person wants to clarify.
- If there is confusion, often one person may have an unspoken rule. If you have such a rule, understand that everyone does not automatically know what it

Social norms

Different situations require different communication. The way one speaks in a job interview is different than when speaking with friends. While playing sports, a different manner is used than with your spouse on a date. Social norms are the expectations of a certain type of language within a certain setting. For example, some conversations or discussions should be done in private instead of in front of others. Because those on the spectrum don't always read situations well, they may just use one type of language/word choice for all situations.

Humor

Looking online you can find websites that mention anywhere from nine to twenty different types of humor. A few types are:

- Witty or dry humor
- Self-deprecating
- Slapstick
- Word plays or puns
- Juvenile
- Observational humor

Because the AS/ND brain tends toward being literal, sometimes those on the spectrum don't understand humor, because humor often involves references to past events or movies and plays on words. There are many implied situations and subtle nuances. I have told my husband many times that if you try to make a joke that references phrases or a situation that would commonly happen, it may not be understood as a joke. If the person receiving the joke thinks it is funny, that doesn't mean that repeating the joke over and over makes it funnier. For example, my husband made a joke about my needing a lot of hair products for my curly hair. Initially, I found it funny. Since I laughed, he tried a few more about my hair and all the things I needed to do to it. After a while, it just sounded like cut downs, and it began to have the opposite impact than what he intended. Word plays and puns are big around our household. But Greg can take it to the extreme. Instead of the word 'avocado' he would substitute the word 'Avogadro' which is the name of an Italian scientist who worked with molecules. This wasn't just a one-time thing. It went on for years. I wondered if my children would ever learn the proper name of an avocado. Another substitution was 'fambily' for family. It wasn't a joke after the first few times. Actually, it wasn't funny to me at all, but he thought it was. Here is an example of Greg's attempt at humor:

> (I stand up in the back at church during worship every week.)
> **Greg:** (After the church service) "Where were you?"
> **Carol**: "I was in the back like I always am."
> **Greg:** "I know – that was my attempt at humor."

The next two examples are jokes that play on his 'Aspie' (AS/ND) nature. They are now common place in our house and put a little levity into our lives.

Example:
1. **Carol**: "I put up a filter for the spam on my email account and I haven't gotten any more spam, so my filter worked!"
    Greg: "I wish my filter worked better!"
2. **Greg:** (After making annoying noises) "I better stop before I annoy you.... See how smart and sensitive I am to those around me? I have *theory of mind*. See, I made an Aspie joke!"

Conversations

Having a conversation could be considered the peak of the language experience, as it can include just about any part of language and often at unexpected times. While you often start with a topic, the topic can change, but ideally, there should be a lead-in for the change, or a pause. Others can interject during the conversation, but it has to be at the right time or it appears to be an interruption. Jokes/plays on words can occur based on prior knowledge of a situation, so the listener must be able to recall that situation and understand the joke or word play without a lead-in. To turn-take in a conversation, questions are often asked. This requires recall of past events or fairly quick responses to not sound awkward. The speaker may start down an emotional path with the conversation, which requires empathy and understanding on the part of the listener. There are many moving parts, and the person with the neurodiverse brain often has trouble thinking quickly when an unexpected question is asked or an unexpected answer is received. Social norms are also somewhat confusing for an AS/ND person, so when to approach someone if they are already engaged in a conversation, or how to insert their topic to get it started can be difficult. Often those on the spectrum do something called scripting. I'll give some examples of my husband's experience with conversations and scripting.

Example 1: Since he was young, when he wanted to talk to someone, he would think about what he wanted to say and then would try to predict the response to that question. He would have an expected answer for that question and predict the next comment from the individual.... Therefore, he had a complete script for what would take place in the conversation. If the person didn't answer as he expected (they were off his script), his brain would lock up. He wouldn't know what to say and an awkwardness would occur. Sometimes he or the other party would say something that would get the conversation going again and sometimes he shut down.

Example 2: My husband and I went for a hike. We hadn't been to the location before. We walked in silence for a while. Usually when my husband talks at length it's about weather, rocks, the ground etc. As we walked, he began telling me about the rocks we saw. He was curious and went off trail to look at a few things. He explained to me what was there before the trail. He talked about the concrete culvert left behind and what the purpose was. He continued to share, and I found it fascinating. I told him I felt like I was on a site walk with him at work. Then I thought of an interesting question. "How is it that you can 'read' the ground, analyze what is going on without having seen it before, relate and generalize to other times you have seen these things, and yet it is so difficult for you to analyze and read people?" He stopped talking. We finally got past that I used the word "you" (which he feels puts blame and leaves him feeling criticized), and I explained I was just trying to start a conversation, which then made him feel like he had done something wrong since he couldn't continue it. After some silence, he said something interesting. He said that for years rocks and geology have been his special interest. He understands them. He also has time to research questions about rocks and process the information; however, for years, people have been a source of pain and confusion and he can't consistently make sense of how to read them. He stated, "People require real-time processing and I take longer to process complicated interpersonal interactions." He has improved in this over time, however not without intentionality and practice.

Listening

The opposite of speaking is listening. They both are necessary for a conversation to take place.

Example: I took a walk with my husband in the almond orchard that is next door to us. As we went through the rows of trees we were chatting. I was talking about the show *The Chosen* and the *Chosen-Con* conference that took place recently in Texas. I felt Greg's presence was slightly distanced. There was a tractor across the field in the distance, but we were nowhere near it. I continued to talk as we rounded a corner and there was dust from the tractor wafting in the air ahead of us. I felt Greg was not listening to me at all. Finally, I said, "I don't feel you are listening to me and your body language tells me you are not listening to me." He said he was trying to stay out of the dust. I said, "But I didn't feel like you were listening before we saw the dust." He had not asked me any questions, or given any 'uh-huhs' or anything to indicate he was listening, and he seemed distracted. I began getting a bit upset and raised my voice in frustration. This meant I was dysregulated. We ended up just not talking at that point. When we got back to the house, I looked up *active listening*. As I read all the things associated with active listening, I was reminded how important it is to have empathy and maintain focus, all the while thinking of how to respond. I tried to share what I had found out, and I apologized because I realized that many things in active listening are difficult for someone on the spectrum. At that point he couldn't hear my apology because he had also become dysregulated. His body language (crossed arms, crossed legs, glare on his face) told me he was mad. He continued to be dysregulated and told me strongly why he was mad at me. Finally, he shared that when the dust came, in his mind he was wondering if there were chemicals in the dust, if it was going to get on us, and would we breathe it, but that wasn't communicated to me. So, the whole miscommunication started with me feeling like I wasn't being heard, and then got more off-track with Greg not communicating his concern about chemicals. I didn't maintain composure, but got frustrated and dysregulated, which then led to him becoming dysregulated. Greg told me he was baffled by the whole conversation.

This could have been avoided in several ways. When I first felt like I wasn't being heard, I could have asked if he was distracted and if it was a good time to talk. When he saw the dust, he could have told me his concerns about chemicals. While I don't share that same concern, he is the geologist and has more knowledge in that area, so I could have validated his concern. We also could have just turned and walked the other way, but instead I became dysregulated. Often, if one person is dysregulated, the other one becomes dysregulated (co-regulation). It can also work the other way. If I had stayed regulated, he probably would have too. I then tried to talk the situation through too early when we returned home, because our dysregulation was still too fresh.

Considerations for Conversations:

- Is this a topic of special interest?
- Has this subject come up before?
- Does a decision have to be made?
- Is there blame involved?
- Is this feedback?
- How long will this conversation last?
- Is the person in the middle of another task and needs to be interrupted?

Growth Tips:

- There are many considerations and there is no one-size-fits-all solution to having a good conversation.
- If you find you have had a good conversation, talk with your spouse about what was good about it. Give helpful feedback about what you appreciated about the conversation.
- Recognize that when an AS/ND person is speaking, he/she is often translating in his head. This can cause the processing to be slower.
- To practice a conversation, set up a time (like at dinner time or after) and beforehand, each person can find a topic to talk about, think of a few interesting things to say about their topic, and formulate three questions to ask the other that are not yes/no questions. Practicing conversations helps to understand how they work.
- Practice active listening. Find a time when there are minimal distractions and start with a short conversation. Remember that practice will initially seem clinical (that is, it might be stilted/uncomfortable/choppy at first before it eventually becomes more organic and fluid.)

Example: Here is an example of when a conversation went well:

Greg: (Looking at his iPad) "Hey, want to watch this video with me?"

Carol: "What is it?"

Greg: "It's a fireside talk."

Carol: "What's that?"

Greg: "A guy sits by a fire and talks about stuff."

Carol: "I still don't know the content."

Greg: "Oh it's about kids in college."

Carol: "How long is it?"

Greg: "I don't know how to tell…. Oh, 45 seconds."

Carol: "Oh, 45 seconds? It's hard to believe it's only that long, but okay."

(Greg turns it toward me to let me watch, then starts packing up something and crinkling paper and bags.)

Carol: "I can't hear it now, and you aren't watching it, and it's 27 minutes long. Do you see what's happening here honey?" (I think this is an Aspie moment on multiple levels.)

Greg: "I'M MULTI-*ASPING*!"

(We both laugh.)

Carol: "I really want to watch this with you, but let's find a time we can do it, like at lunchtime."

Greg: "Okay."

There are many areas where this conversation could have gone wrong. I had to ask a few questions that could have put him off. I had to correct how long it was because the time difference was significant. I could have said I wasn't interested. But we used strategies we had learned, and we came to a solution without anger. He accepted my questions as being curious, and not that he had done something wrong. I showed my interest by asking to watch it at a later time, and he accepted that.

Final thoughts

Spoken language, active listening, body language, and pragmatic language are all subject to the difficulties neurodiverse marriages have with communication. But there is hope. With knowledge of your strengths and difficulties, and a desire to practice and learn, your communication and relationship can improve. My husband now realizes that social language is difficult for him, while for me it is a strength, so he now comes to me for help with texts and messages or even before he places a phone call. I am more than willing to help. I rely on my husband to remember directions, places we have gone, scripture interpretation, and a myriad of things his amazing brain can do that mine can't. Communication in a neurodiverse relationship will always have glitches, but if you learn from these and are willing to receive feedback while approaching each other with love, you just might enjoy the conversations that take place.

 ## Navigating the Communication Maze: Connection Challenge, Greg's Experience

This reflection is to share my experience putting something out there to connect with my wife as a task instead of really attempting a meaningful interaction. My plan was to share something with my wife thus establishing a relational connection (check that box), and then get back to my routine. But sharing something with another (and much more communicative) person (my wife Carol) is most likely to result in her wanting to provide a response. This back-and-forth is called communication AND is key to forming and sustaining the emotional connections necessary to build joy in our relationship. However, my plan which I must follow is to share (make the connection- did that) and then resume my routine (reading the news).

The share:

"Hey Honey, here is a funny headline: 'Goats can perceive human emotions based on the sound of our voice'!" I knew Carol would be interested because she is a communication specialist AND we have goats. This would connect with her in multiple ways could this go wrong? Read on and see.

My wife then asked a question in response to my share. Because I had not read the article and did not want to (I was just trying to share something observed during my routine and achieve a 'connection'), I then had to interrupt my routine and read through the article (what I thought she wanted based on her asking a question that could only be answered by reading the article). As I read excerpts from the article out loud to her, Carol focused on a new term that applied to speech and the interaction threatened to move even farther away from my plan/routine. Then Carol asked me to stop reading. So, I stopped reading the article and returned to perusing the news (resumed my routine), while she started discussing the new term.

I then noticed that Carol was dissatisfied and withdrawn. In the past, this is where I used to just shut down and bide my time until we needed to interact again. No repair, no additional thinking about it. Just relief that I was able to finish my routine and Carol and I could 'talk' again.

I had done it! I had shared to foster a connection and communicated with Carol...... but Carol was left frustrated because I did not hear her part of the conversation or participate with her in a back-and-forth exchange. I had just checked a box (on my own internal list) and being satisfied with having achieved this, tried to go on with my morning.

What actually happened was that I had 'shared' to complete the task of connection without actually communicating and connecting. After noticing the effects on Carol I began to think about what had happened:

- I shared something from my routine-I intended my share to foster connection with Carol
- Carol listened and started asking questions-the beginning of a conversation where we could really connect (if I would participate).
- I attempted to read the article to (at) Carol to answer her questions.
- As soon as an offramp was provided ('you can stop reading the article'). I disengaged and went back to my routine leaving Carol without a partner to her conversation. Carol calls this being gone-as in 'I can see that you are gone from our interaction now'

But was I really engaging with Carol or was I just trying to check a box? As I reflected on this event, I realized that if I truly want to connect with my wife in a meaningful way then I need to be able to flex a little after I put something out there. I can't interact and expect it to progress solely on my terms-it is not all about me, but about our relationship. I took a good first step with my share, but because my focus remained on getting back to my routine, I left Carol dissatisfied. This was not about the goats or the use of a speech term, it was about our relationship and building joy. I blew it this time. Next time maybe I can be more intentional about building a connection and less concerned about my routine. Then I could interact with Carol where she is coming from even though it takes me out of my routine. And after the connection is made via a genuine back and forth communication in which I remain fully engaged, I can return to my routine, and Carol can continue with hers. And both of us can be content with a connection made and a completed joy-building conversation. Also, I repaired by letting her know that I had this insight and this helped us to restore our relationship that morning.

Chapter Eight
Navigating the Maze of Executive Function Differences & Challenges: ASD, ADHD, AuDHD

BY ROBIN TATE, MA, MS, BCC, CAS

The Impact of Executive Function on Neurodiverse Marriages

This chapter delves into the complex topic of Executive Function (EF) and its influence on neurodivergent individuals and neurodiverse (ND) couples (when one or both are autistic). This subject is too vast to discuss entirely in one chapter. Dr. Holmes and I were aware of this challenge from the start. This chapter aims to provide a basic understanding of EF, its varied manifestations in autistic and ADHD individuals, and its impact on marital relationships. I'll also share practical strategies for couples and individuals to adapt to their unique cognitive strengths and differences.

In my coaching and education practice, I approach clients with genuine compassion, curiosity, and self-awareness, seeing them as individuals beyond any labels or diagnoses. My toolbox, enriched by extensive experience and continuous learning, includes a deep understanding of neurodiversity, marriage, people, and the impact of neurodiversity as displayed within adult couple relationships. These tools are vital for helping couples develop effective EF strategies aligned with their personal and joint goals. As we begin, it is important to note that EF skills tend to be a "means to an end." They present as a strength or challenge in meeting desired goals, rather than the ultimate objective of our work together.[1,2]

When addressing EF in ND marriages, where one or both partners are Autistic, it is important to also acknowledge each person's unique strengths and challenges. This chapter focuses specifically on EF and will overlook multiple other known elements that each person brings as an impact on their relationship. This is most evident as we look at case studies where only EF strategies are discussed to highlight this commonly overlooked neurological aspect and its impact. In relationships all of the strengths and challenges each person has exist as a dynamic and display as such within the context of life and marriage. It is important to note EF is not my only lens in working with a couple, and the following is scratching the surface to highlight the impact of EF challenges on the marital relationship.

What is EF?

Executive function (EF) is the term commonly used to describe the processes in the brain that we use to achieve every task we wish to complete. The more tasks we attempt to accomplish at one time, the harder this is; the more steps within each task, the more stressed our neural processes become and the harder it becomes for us to access them to achieve our goals. This is a practical and simplistic answer to a very complex question that neuroscientists and researchers are working on to bring us to a better understanding. EF has been proven to be a greater determiner of life skills and success than intelligence.[3]

EF challenges do not represent a stand-alone medical or psychological disorder or diagnosis. Rather, EF differences present as characteristics of multiple neurological, psychological, neuropsychological, and medical diagnoses.[4] EF challenges are common in people who identify as neurodivergent. These neurological challenges can range from struggles with simple tasks like remembering to eat to complex activities like managing a career, love relationships, and family life. It's valuable to recognize that EF is a fundamental part of every person's neural process, and vital for planning, prioritizing, initiating, problem-solving, and achieving goals. EF effectiveness can vary in all people, due to factors like stress, hormones, health, cognitive load, and aging.[2,3,5]

EF encompasses abilities related to self-regulation (SR), intelligence, and creativity, as shown in neuroimaging research. These studies reveal overlaps in brain areas controlling each of these processes, leading to distinctions between 'cold EF' (mechanical skills) and 'hot EF' (emotional regulation).[6] EF has also been proposed to be the same as SR, with dysfunctions that align with the deficits of ADHD.[7] In my experience, not considering both SR and EF risks unintentional harm and potentially leaves an invisible obstacle. Unacknowledged SR can paralyze individuals and couples in thinking about creating change rather than taking necessary action to reach a goal.

This mistake often leads to further confusion and hopelessness. Overlooking SR while having the expectation of EF skill development risks at least one person becoming consumed with shame and giving up. Developing strategies for EF necessitates more than accommodating tasks and time; it requires tangibly addressing the emotional regulation that is crucial for life and couples' relationships.[3,8,9]

The prefrontal cortex (PFC) in the front of the brain is known as the primary location of EF. It is interconnected with various other brain regions via neural networks. Damage to any of the brain regions, white matter, or neural networks can lead to EF Deficit Disorder (EFDD).[6,7] EF challenges are also associated with low dopamine levels, a neurotransmitter known for regulating pleasure and reward. Dopamine levels have been proven to be inherited; this neurotransmitter plays a role in addiction as well as other mental health challenges that people who display EF challenges are susceptible to.[3]

EF development peaks around 25 years of age, with limited growth in EF skills thereafter. Adults can still develop more efficient neural impulses while practicing EF skills, though it requires more dedication and repetition. This realistic understanding is essential when developing strategies with individuals and couples; it requires consistent effort to bring about each desired reliable EF skill change in adults. When delving into EF in ND marriage, it is helpful to remember that each person in a couple's relationship likely has both EF strengths and challenges.[2]

The Relationship of ADHD, Autism, and EF.

In defining EF, I have referred to both autism (ASD) and attention deficit hyperactive disorder (ADHD). Research shows that 50-70% of Autistic people also meet the criteria for ADHD, and these people have come to refer to themselves as AuDHD.[2,4,10] This high co-occurrence implies that the strengths and challenges that commonly exist for either an autistic person or ADHD person have the potential to present in either neurotype. Perhaps the percentage of people who have an overlap of EF strengths and challenges is greater than 50-70%, as research tends to account only for those who meet the diagnostic criteria for both ASD and ADHD. People can display EF strengths as well as challenges, which may limit them from receiving a diagnosis of ASD or ADHD, yet still present as a challenge in daily living.[2]

A 2016 research review[11] which compared EF in ASD, ADHD, and ASD + ADHD (AuDHD) populations revealed specific challenges in each group as well as consistent shared EF challenges across all groups. The ASD group had more significant challenges with flexibility and planning. The ADHD group had more significant challenges with response inhibition. The AuDHD group displayed the primary challenges of both the ASD (flexibility and planning) and the ADHD (response inhibition) groups. The other EF challenges that were studied included attention deficit, working memory, preparatory processes, fluency, and concept formation. These presented as challenges for each of the three groups in the same way. A more recent review[12] compared ASD and ADHD children and adolescents and found no difference in EF display between ASD and ADHD groups.

Although not accounted for in the *Diagnostic Statistical Manual* Fifth Edition (*DSM-5*),[13] it is common knowledge in the neurodivergent (autistic and ADHD) and research communities that symptomatically, women and men present differently.[14] While EF has not been proven to present significantly different in ASD and ADHD females vs. males, one study[15] noted a few individual processes may have gender differences: men may show a higher level of impulsive action along with a reduced reaction time, and females may be more avoidant of frequent punishment and have greater working memory. However, overall, measured differences were not enough to conclude gender bias concerning EF.

Research does show that EF is influenced by environmental variables like stress, socioeconomics, health, parenting, and age.[2] These findings reinforce that EF strengths and challenges can be different for all people, not just those who are neurodivergent. By identifying a person's strengths and challenges, each individual can begin from their current level of EF competence and work towards their desired growth goal. In my work, I am guided by a humanistic Rogerian approach,[16] utilizing concepts such as the "Zone of Proximal Development"[17] and "The Stages of Change"[18] to help each individual (or couple) develop EF strategies to achieve whatever goals are right for them.

In working with ND couples, I find it common that in an attempt to seek marital help, one partner (typically the wife, who usually identifies as NT/NA) suspects their spouse (typically the husband) is autistic and might have ADHD as well. Though not yet backed by research, my colleagues and I have observed a trend where one partner, often male, identifies as autistic at some point, and the other, typically female, later identifies that she has ADHD. This realization often emerges when exploring neurodivergent strengths and challenges and evaluating EF processes, so that the needs of each partner can be considered. Only then can a couple form authentic and mutual agreements. It is unknown if the ADHD in the partner who initially identified as neurotypical meets a true developmental ADHD rooted in childhood; ADHD characteristics may be the result of environmental stressors including the impact of an unidentified neurodiverse marriage and possible failed attempts at seeking outside help.[9, 18] Regardless of neurotype, my coaching and educational approach meets each person and couple where they are and helps them identify their unique neurological strengths and challenges. This process creates safety and identifies common goals and shared responsibilities which lead to the larger goal that they "become one" (Genesis 2:24 ESV) in their ND Christian marriages.

12 Commonly Identified EF Processes

As a frame of reference, I will list and define 12 commonly discussed EF processes.[2,20] With each process, I will provide you with a brief definition of the EF process as well as an example of a related strength or challenge. I will also give a brief description of the potential impact of the specific EF within the relationship of a couple. As you read you may find that you have some EFs that are strengths while others display as challenges: This may be fixed, or it may be determined by the context.

1. Response Inhibition: Another word for this is self-control.[2]

Example: When you decide to stick with a healthy protein diet that limits sugar, and the next day you find yourself at a birthday party with response inhibition; as a strength, you first weigh the possible reward or consequence, and likely opt not to eat the cake; as a challenge you may eat the cake without thinking.

Couple Challenges: A lack of self-control can look impulsive. This can lead to dopamine-seeking behavior, and unfortunately, addiction of many kinds. Dr. Jim Wilder calls such pseudo-seeking-joy things B.E.E.P.S (Behaviors, Events, Experiences, People, or Substances); examples are pornography, food, alcohol, sugar, exercise, gaming, gambling, etc. Addictions of any kind, in either partner, impact the marriage as a challenge. One partner may regularly worry about the unpredictability of their partner's decisions and ability to be safe or keep agreements. Addictions are different from special interests; passionate or restricted interests can provide a safe place for autistic people to relax.[8]

2. Working Memory: The ability to hold information in your short-term mind and manipulate it to use it.[2] Dr. Barkley talks about two kinds of working memory: *verbal* is using your mind's voice to talk to and remind yourself (this form of working memory is more challenging for autistic people); and *non-verbal*, which is yourself in role-play or imagination (used more frequently as a strength by autistic people). Using non-verbal visual working memory as a strength can result in a struggle to explain out loud how you solved a problem, even though you can visualize and move to the result.[7,8]

Example: When you need to run to the store for 3-5 items and do not have a written list, as a working memory strength (verbal or non-verbal) you may run in and come out with each of the items that you intended to buy including the correct size and brand; as a challenge, you may arrive at the store and leave with only one or two of the items on the list, which may or may not be the correct size or brand.

Couple Challenges: Incomplete projects; not showing up at a known event; chronically losing items like phones, glasses, and keys; upset and shocked over the credit card bill, even when both partners were aware of the purchases; agreeing then forgetting to keep them; an imbalance in relational roles. An individual strength in visual non-verbal working memory may help with tasks that require math. In a couple's relationship, the same strength can lead to unilateral decision-making. In ND marriages, typically one person is expecting and in need of mutually made decisions. Unilateral decisions tend to be experienced by the other partner as "controlling" and "excluding." If a couple is unaware of this tendency, it can also lead to one partner asking, "How did you do that?" and being confused by a reaction of "I don't know," or walking away upset and not knowing how to describe how something was completed.

3. Self-Regulation (SR) or Emotional Regulation: This can also be referred to as self-restraint or inhibition.[22] It is the ability to manage your emotions in a way that matches the situation and allows you to be productive.[2]

Example: You cannot remember the password to your bank account on a Sunday (bank closed) and you need to get into the account immediately. With SR as a strength, you stay calm and realize that you can call the 24-hour banking line to get the same information; as a challenge, you may become very frustrated, send angry emails, cry or yell about how stupid the bank is, and that it's crazy to have all of these passwords.

Couple Challenges: Unexpected shut down or explosion over the idea of facing conflict or the slightest suggestion of perceived criticism; disappointing your partner by not doing the planned activities or tasks that were agreed upon that day; intense lockdown arguments about who is right, only to realize many days later that it was a difference of perspective; yelling or sarcasm when your partner does something different than you expected; passive aggressive and aggressive retaliations, lying, addiction, blaming, name-calling, a lack of flexibility, negativity and shutdown are all signs of a challenge with emotional dysregulation; verbal, emotional, psychological and spiritual abuse, and/or a sense of fear and helplessness in each partner.

Example: As an obstacle, some people may struggle with alexithymia (a struggle to identify feelings in themselves and others).[23] In unexpected sensory situations, the autistic person may become dysregulated and need to move through the meltdown without punishment, to get to safety.[20] Multiple displays of SR are unique to neurodivergent people and important to understand, yet there are too many to define within this chapter. Their impact in ND marriage makes them worth listing in case you wish to explore them further; Reactive Sensitivity Disorder (RSD), Pathological Demand Avoidance (PDA), inertia, task paralysis, cognitive overload, melt-down, tantrums, and sensory overload. Also contributing to SR are commonly overlapping mental health challenges, such as PTSD, anxiety, and depression, as well as a deep sense of shame rooted in a lifetime of being bullied and excluded.[8,9,23,24]

4. Task Initiation: The ability to start a desired task when you want to start and/or when it's expected that you will begin.[2]

Example: You have a nice lawn and want it mowed weekly. With task initiation as a strength, you may mow the lawn every week at the same time, to assure that it is done consistently. You do not avoid beginning when it is time – you simply start. As a challenge, you may know you need to mow the lawn yet decide to clean the kitchen instead, delaying the lawn task. Even though you do *want* to mow the lawn, you cannot begin.

Couple Challenges: Tasks often have deadlines and there is usually one partner who keeps track of what is needed to be completed for the home, family, and couple. This person tends to see the need for a task to be initiated by a certain time to be completed by what they see as the deadline. This person is also aware of the consequences and rewards of initiating the task by a certain time. When each partner isn't aware of *task initiation* as a brain challenge, it can lead one or both partners to think that the person struggling with initiation is "lazy," "lying", "apathetic", and even displaying "passive-aggressive anger." To the partner attempting to manage the shared responsibilities, it can be translated to mean the EF-challenged partner "doesn't care about our family, what I care about, or me." Some of the experiences of SR that are unique to ND people may also contribute to an inability to initiate many kinds of tasks.

5. Sustained Attention: The ability to keep your focus on a task until it is complete and also cleaned up.

Example: You have decided with your partner to build a back patio in time for your daughter's birthday in a month. As a strength you can start and stay with the project, having it all cleaned up in time to prepare for the party; as a challenge you may find you are taking many breaks, seeking sugary snacks, or distracted by offers to go "hang-out" with friends. The project isn't completed on time, so you clean it up the best you can and promise to finish it after the party.

Couple Challenges: A home filled with half-started projects that "we are going to finish someday." For one partner, the reality that they do not have time right now but will get back to it when they can seem to be satisfactory. He or she may not be bothered or notice any "mess." For the other partner, this can be frustrating. Without awareness of EF, they may view their partner as lazy and embarrassing, they may express frustration in being limited in having guests or being denied the reward of the project completed. When their partner completes a task and leaves the clean-up unfinished, they are left to feel helpless and forced to clean-up, even if they are somewhat thankful that at least the task is complete.

6. Planning/Prioritization: The ability to lay out all of the what, when, where, why, and how of a task, as well as the ability to order tasks by importance (as dictated by intensity of need, deadline and sequence.) When understanding prioritization, it is helpful to consider *Central Coherence Theory*.[26] The brain of the majority of thinkers sees the "big picture" of a situation and then breaks it into parts in order of importance. Neurodivergent thinkers see the parts and then construct the "big picture" from the "bottom-up."[6]

Example: You have decided to build a garden: when planning and prioritization are a strength you assess the situation and see the first step is the need for a drain. You can organize the materials for the drain as well as order the materials for the garden. You begin with building the drain first. As a challenge, you may see the need to build a drain and the garden, choose to build the garden first, and then realize that you should have built a drain under the garden before completing it.

Couple Challenges: Without awareness, one partner may trigger frustration in the other at what they consider a simple question, i.e., "When will we do the taxes?" Shutdown or impulsive words can be said in reply, and the partner who is simply asking to know the "plan" to complete a task can quickly feel like the "enemy" for seemingly no reason. If one partner has expressed that a project has a high need or value and the other doesn't agree with this, it can lead to a sense of not being heard or valued. Commonly, one spouse may be working off of one plan while the other is working off of their own or no plan at all. This creates a sense of chaos and can lead to partners essentially living separate lives. Additionally, there can be anxiety from not knowing what the other partner is doing or when they will be available to them. They may be concerned that their partner will not carry out their responsibilities or agreements.

7. Organization: The ability to create and manage systems to keep track of your things (concrete or electronic), your responsibilities and your ideas.

Example: This can often be evaluated by looking at the inside of a person's phone or computer: Organization as a strength displays as organized folders by topic, only one or two tabs open at a time, important links are bookmarked and deleted when their need is complete, voice mail and emails are relatively up to date. As a challenge, you may notice that once you put a thing or idea away you forget it exists (object permanence).[27] Your laptop has all tabs that you deem important open, your files may all be on your desktop and may not be in folders. Email and voice mail tend to be overflowing and managed on an "as needed" basis.

Couple Challenges: Not having people over because one or both partners are embarrassed; one person setting up and maintaining all organization and at some point, becoming tired and frustrated with their partner who doesn't initiate or maintain organization; not being able to truly clean because there is too much "stuff" lying around. Not locating things anyone needs because there is no true system. When a system is established and agreed upon, it may quickly fall apart in the reality of a busy life. The partner who is struggling to keep up with the organization can experience a lot of shame at attempting but failing. The organized partner may express frustration and disappointment as well.

8. Time Management: The ability to manage time in the present and the future. The ability to predict how long a task will take and to operate within time restrictions. It also recognizes when time is important and can keep track of time.[2]

Example: You work at an office with an expected start and end time. When time management is a strength, you may have a morning and afternoon routine, you may manage your tasks at work to end at the desired time and reliably return home within a consistent time frame, except for one-offs. As a challenge, you say you will leave home and work at a specific time and often leave later than planned. Commonly, your partner calls or texts asking you to come home. When you make agreements to leave at a specific time and arrive home within a time frame, you may sustain this for a few days and then fall back into the same pattern of being late.

Couple Challenges: One person tends to take over managing time for everyone and becomes frustrated when they constantly need to ask their partner to take responsibility for managing their own time. This is a setup for the relationship to become more like a parent-child dynamic. One partner will tend to express frustration that their spouse is not reliable and that they don't leave for or arrive home from work on time. No matter what time they are given to leave for an event, their partner will not be ready. A sense of isolation can set in for the partner who is working hard to manage everyone's time. Friends and family make hurtful jokes about giving an arrival time that is earlier than the actual start time, acknowledging negatively that they notice the couple's pattern of arriving late.

9. Flexibility: Flexibility is both cognitive and behavioral. It is the ability to "shift" or change plans when something unexpected happens, or if someone introduces a different perspective or has a new plan.[2]

Example: You and your partner are talking about a vacation this year. You may immediately assume you will go to Disney World, as you have for the last ten years. Your partner excitedly introduces the idea of going someplace new. As a strength, you stay regulated and listen to your partner's ideas, and evaluate them as a possibility. As a challenge, you immediately respond "no", perhaps in a harsh tone. Your partner may become upset and attempt to talk about this. You may also be upset that they would even propose this change. Sometime later you may realize that you have gone to the same place for many years and that your partner is right: a new place may be nice.

Couple Challenges: Couples report that they cannot go to new restaurants together. They can't try new experiences or go to new locations together or with others. Some partners have stated that they are not "allowed" to move furniture or invite new people over. Only one person may initiate sexual intimacy successfully. Hidden unspoken obstacles get in the way of changing plans. Frustration and isolation quickly set in for one or both partners, as either or both may be afraid of their partner's reaction to the unexpected or novel.

10. Metacognition/Self-Awareness (Self-Directed Attention): The ability to think about what we think, know, and do about an idea or situation. It includes the awareness of what you are good at and what is challenging for you.[2,7]

Example: You give a presentation at work. With metacognition as a strength, you may identify the positives and negatives of your presentation and incorporate what you learned, adjusting for future presentations. As a challenge, you may not notice your strengths or challenges; instead, you may deliver the same presentation again in the same way, even though there were results that you wish were different. You may blame the audience.

Couple Challenges: It is typical to meet a couple where one person has strong metacognition but the other does not want to talk about what they did well or might need to improve. This may be rooted in shame-based perfectionism as well as EF deficits. Regardless, it results in a willing partner being vulnerable about their challenges, while the other partner agrees about their partner's weakness but they are unwilling to talk about their own challenges. This can look arrogant. In a practical way, when a partner with stronger metacognition sees a need for the couple to do things to improve, their partner is likely to disagree. This results in many mishaps at home as well as a sense of isolation and invisibility for the partner desiring mutual growth.

11. Persistence/ Self-motivation/ Perseverance: The ability to continue toward reaching a goal when obstacles arise, such as distractions, unexpected challenges and juggling multiple responsibilities.[2]

Example: The family begins a puzzle together. With perseverance as a strength, you may stick with it until it is complete. As a challenge, you may give up on a puzzle when the border is complete, and all of the pieces look too similar. You get sidetracked at something more appealing, like hanging the new plantation shutters. You never return to the puzzle, as it does not seem worth it.

Couple Challenges: Isolation and estrangement are widely reported by many ND couples.[9] Although one or both partners may stick with the marriage and even their individual goals, they may give up on reaching relationship goals like improved communication and all forms of intimacy. Commonly, one person perseveres in carrying out a great deal of the shared responsibilities of the relationship, while the other partner is putting their time into individual goals such as work and hobbies.

12. Stress Tolerance/ Resilience: This is a task of emotional regulation. It is the ability to tolerate uncomfortable, unexpected, often demanding situations.[2]

Example: On the way to the store, your 3-year-old screams that they need to pee, and you realize that you still have a ten-minute drive and there will be no bathrooms or places to pull over. The child intensely states over and over their need to pee. As you round the corner to park and think you are almost there, you accidentally hit a parked car. Stress tolerance as a strength calmly takes the child inside to pee and then returns to the car to write a note for the other driver and take responsibility for the accident. You may laugh at the situation as things begin to settle down. As a challenge, your heart rate immediately rises in the car and you yell for the child to "shut-up"; when you hit the other car, your temper flares higher, and you are again short with the three-year-old, who then pees on you. You melt into tears of frustration. As the other driver returns to their car, you may be short with them, stating that their car was parked too close to the line. They call the police.

Couple Challenges: Each person in the marriage may be worn out and stressed at managing their joint and individual EF challenges. When there are children, a couple's shared responsibilities increase, along with the demands on EF. With each need to complete one more task comes increased stress and demand on EF skills. Resilience requires a lot of self-care and balancing fun with responsibility. The EF skills needed to balance self-care and fun may be insufficient, which often results in the couple inadvertently dropping these relationally essential things from their never-ending task list. To the couple, this initially seems necessary but may later prove to be regrettable.[26]

In their book *Smart but Scattered*,[2] Dawson and Guare state that when people identify their own individual executive function strengths and challenges, they can function better in all areas of life. I have observed this to be true in my own experience as well as in my client's lives. Awareness of EF's strengths and challenges is a first step that leads to improved skills at home or work. I have been honored to witness this kind of growth in clients regardless of their neurological profile or diagnosis. In this way, EF can be a common denominator that recreates foundational balance in two ND adults. All people depend on EF skills in daily life, and this neurological process results in behavioral strengths and challenges in each partner. With a variety of combinations of neurotypes in ND couples' relationships, this mutual assessment process done formally or informally is foundational to building a strength-based team.

Once an individual client or each person on a couples team has humbly developed awareness of themselves, they are ready to set goals for growth. This may mean further individual work and/or working together as a couple to lean on each other's strengths to overcome challenges. This process helps coach every combination of neurotypes present within ND couples. Individual EF assessments done formally or informally can be foundational to building a strength-based team.

I have often been impressed that when two people invest in learning about their own and then each other's strengths and challenges, it leads to a greater display of compassion inward and then outward toward each other. Keep in mind it may be the first time that either person is aware of their strengths. Many neurodivergent adults have spent a lifetime only having their challenges identified. Identifying strengths is an important tool worth celebrating. If you are interested in developing personal awareness of EF strengths and challenges, Dawson and Guare's "Executive Skills Questionnaire" can provide this awareness. Within the context of compassion and curiosity, this assessment can be a starting point for couples in reaching their goals[2].

The Practical Impact of EF on ND Marriage - Case Studies

To illustrate a few of the many ways that Executive Function (EF) challenges can impact individuals and couples in marriage, I will present some mini-case studies. These are drawn from my life experience, education, and recurring observations in my coaching and education practice. These scenarios are not based on specific clients but are composites reflecting common EF challenges in neurodivergent (ND) couple relationships. Details of stories have been changed to protect the anonymity of the couple from the composites of similar stories. It's important to recognize that EF challenges manifest in both men and women and across all neuro-profiles. Avoiding judgment or stereotypes is important for understanding the individual you live with and/or work with.

While the most couples common dynamic in my practice involves "high-achieving", often "perfectionist" men, believed by their "neurotypical" identifying wives to be autistic, it's not the only ND couples pairing that I serve. I also work with couples where the female is suspected or diagnosed with Autism/AuDHD and the male identifies as "neuro-typical". I also work with many couples who each identify as being neurodivergent. As with all people there is diversity among ND couples. Keep in mind that EF impacts each task a person does and, therefore, each small and large expectation that a couple might have of each other. Though every possible situation will not be displayed in these case studies, I hope that they provide insight that can help you identify EF challenges within yourself, your life, and perhaps your or others' ND relationships.

EF in Couples Scenarios

My husband (Autistic) was to pick me up at the hospital, and I (NT/NA) should have asked someone else. I don't know why I didn't know better, but I wanted it to be him. Anyway, I asked him to pick me up and he agreed. I texted him when they were rolling me out in the wheelchair, and he said he was there. I was so relieved. I gathered my things and asked the nurse to take me to where he was expected to meet us; he wasn't there. I looked at my phone and there were no texts or calls. I called and he did not pick up. I felt so alone and abandoned.

EF Challenges in the Scenario: Working memory, cognitive overload (too many EF tasks at one time), planning, metacognition, and flexibility.

EF Strategies: It is essential to give compassion in the moment to yourself and your partner; acknowledge that this is a brain challenge. If necessary, say nothing so that each person can regulate. To gain support, this wife knew to call a friend as soon as she arrived home. When we met, this husband expressed a great deal of shame and embarrassment. He had done his best to arrive on time. The unexpected construction at the hospital caused unexpected EF challenges, and with the pressure of being late, he became confused and lost. He could not think about anything but finding his wife, including forgetting to call her to tell her what was happening. When he found her, from his perspective, she was mean, angry, and unhappy to see him. She stated that she perceived the request to be on time as an easy, expected task. She needed him, and when he wasn't there, she felt abandoned and invisible; having used many strategies that she expected to work, she also had a sense of hopelessness. Such meetings begin with a structured conversation that allows each person to be heard fully without judgment. This provides space to talk about the impact of actions on each partner. Once there is understanding, a structured preplanned apology to hear the impact of the event and reactions on the other person proves helpful.[2,9] During the meeting, each partner is invited to reflect on what went right and create a plan to solve problems like this in the future (i.e. would it help to do a test drive to the hospital or to leave thirty minutes earlier to plan for unexpected events?)

My wife (AuDHD) has a new minivan which she seems to like but she keeps taking the mirror off by hitting the garage every time she pulls in or backs out. I (Autistic) didn't mind it when it happened once but by the third time, I was angry. I can't even talk to her about it without her crying, swearing, and screaming at me. I do not understand what she is saying, I just want her to slow down.

EF Challenges in the Scenario: Planning, response inhibition, emotional control, organization, flexibility, metacognition, and time management

 EF Strategy: The wife agreed to meet alone. She said that she was ashamed that she kept taking the mirrors off as well as swearing and yelling at her husband. She expressed a sensation of physical pain every time the topic came up, she explained that her therapist suspected that she experiences Rejection Sensitivity Disorder (RSD).[23] She stated that it upset her to talk in front of her husband who would blame her and tell her the answer was simple: "Just slow down." She stated that she had many speeding tickets which she felt bad about. She was tired and overwhelmed from caring for two kids and organizing a home. She recognized that being a wife and mother required many EF skills that were harder than when she "had a real career." She would get the kids washed and to bed early and get the necessary chores completed. Then she would melt onto the couch, look at social media, watch movies which she loved to do, or talk with her best friend until almost 1:00 AM. She loved the house when it was quiet and there were no demands on her brain; she found it hard to go to bed even though she knew that the children would be awake early.

We discussed ways that she could plan for the next day before bed, and she stated, "That won't happen." What helped her was leaving her planning system open on their kitchen island for her to see every day, all day. She created a diaper bag that was always full and a routine of filling it as soon as they came in from their time out. Since her planner was in clear view she would look ahead and begin to visualize her next day considering any one-offs she needed to account for. She used the monthly view to plan ahead. These strategies helped enough that she was willing to meet together with her husband. He developed a better understanding of her brain and what she needed him to do that would help her when he noticed her hurrying or yelling. As a team, we came up with some ways for him to check in with her when she was feeling overloaded. They decided to invest in another set of strollers, car seats, and diaper bags so that each car was always ready to go. He also agreed to take over the bath and bedtime routine so that she could add 5 min of mindfulness and breathing to her evening and plan ahead for the next day, feeling calmer. He agreed to make sure both cars always had enough gas so that she didn't have to worry about running out or filling up. She was still staying up late when we stopped meeting, but she discussed seeing a doctor to explore ADHD medication as a possible strategy, as well as the possibility of scheduling time with friends in person. She had not yet done these when I last met with them, but they both expressed that their goal was met.

My husband (Autistic) won't come to bed with me at the same time. I (ADHD) am concerned with his sleep. I am not sure that he does sleep, we have made many agreements, but he keeps staying up all hours watching TV or gaming. We both have brains that need a lot of sleep, and I cannot sleep without him.

EF Challenge: Time management, planning, organizing and emotional regulation.

 EF Strategies: One key aspect in working to help ND couples is establishing that a person in a marriage can only control themselves and their choices, behaviors, ideas, beliefs, etc. They can influence the other by making requests, yet it is ultimately their partner's choice. This needs to be stated regularly and repeatedly until it sinks in for each party. As much as isolation displays in ND couples, so does an almost oppositional, habitual dependency or co-dependency: each partner has unintentionally come to rely on the other, and while they say they want to change this, their habits often keep their dynamic the same. I am concerned that the reader will take this to mean that we don't think husband and wife should depend on each other. What I am describing is an extreme dependence that isn't healthy interdependence (team). If the person who doesn't want to come to bed on time enjoys and prefers their routine, then all the strategies in the world won't change this. In these situations where one partner desires change that the other won't accommodate, each partner should recognize their limitations and focus on healthily meeting their own needs.[9] When each partner is willing to get involved in achieving the same goal for the sake of their partner and/or their relationship, then change is possible.

In this common relationship scenario, the root of the problem was not a lack of desire to come to bed but rather a difference in processing and managing time. Video games provide dopamine to the brain, and when they are enjoyed, they can be a stress-free place to be. Any dopamine-inducing activity runs the risk of becoming addictive. The rewarding feeling they provide even when addiction is not the problem, can prevent anyone from stopping in the time frame that a person wishes to end the activity. Addictions can steal time from other things you want to do that are healthy for you. Enjoyable activities can be a nice way to relax when pursued with boundaries. Together with their team, the couple established the use of timers (this husband needed auditory alerts). They knew that changing this habit would be hard, so they decided all chores should be completed before beginning video games. They also determined that he would need multiple alarms to stop. The first was a warning that conveyed, "You need to begin to finish up - you have 10 more minutes." With that warning came the rule that the husband could not start another game before the next alarm. The second alarm was the fire alarm that warned you must stop and leave immediately. Every step from starting to play the games to hit the target bedtime was verbally talked through (assessing for obstacles), role-played and then executed as an "experiment." Once the "experiment" was carried out, the couple came back, and we evaluated what worked and what didn't work.[9]

My wife (Autistic) has a very busy career so she is working a lot. Even though we agreed that she would help with the kids and larger projects, the bulk of the responsibilities fell on me. It seems she thinks it's enough to attend school events, even if she isn't on time. I (NT/NA) don't feel like I can count on her and am afraid to ask her to pick up the kids for fear she will forget. I have created a list of things to remind her what needs to be done each night and on the weekends, and I put it in the pantry. She never even looks at it. I work too, and I am tired and feel alone. We sleep in separate bedrooms and have not been sexually intimate for some time. I noticed that we only had sex when she initiated, and at some point, I started just to feel rejected. This made me upset. Now after the kids go to bed, I watch TV alone. After we eat, she sometimes helps clean up and then goes into her home office where she reads or writes fiction, and creates art. I wish she would spend more time with the kids and me. I wish she would help me with more of our shared responsibilities. It seems like most of the work falls on me or does not get done. Our house is a mess.

EF Challenge: Time management, organization, planning, flexibility, prioritization and working memory.

EF Strategies: When the three of us met together, the wife explained that she thought because she made more money that he would do more of the house and kid responsibilities. She wasn't angry, she just didn't see that there was a problem. The husband stated that he had asked multiple times, and she disagreed and said that he would say things like, "Do you want to go to the grocery store while I mow the yard?" She did not want to do the groceries, so she said no and took the kids to the park.

When we began meeting as a team, the first topic was "shared responsibility." The basis of shared responsibility that I teach comes with the concept that total responsibility is greater than the sum of its parts. In my practice, I have observed that many partners come into marriage and only do what they thought was "their" work. With this couple, in talking through what they deemed was their responsibility, I realized they didn't understand that when partners get to a certain place in their relationship, they might begin to share responsibilities that once regularly belonged to just one of them. It's also common to meet a couple where one person is doing all of the couple's work as well as their own, and the other person is only doing what they believe solely "belongs" to them. These debates get heated because each partner is defining what each of "their" responsibilities is differently. My definition, presented on a concrete handout, invites a couple to list "all things and people that two or more partners are *jointly* accountable to care for, create and maintain." My handout presents some agreements that also go along with this idea. 1) Partners agree to the distribution of work in an ongoing way that accounts for each person. 2) Each partner will work together for the team's good, to be flexible, cooperate, and make changes as needed.

This couple could converse and form agreements once the invisible was made concrete and the goals were defined. They quickly created a division of labor that they agreed was "fair" for each person. The whiteboard of household tasks was relocated out of the pantry to a place each partner would regularly see it. They worked on a system of identifying three tasks on the list that were priorities. She worked on using timers to come to the school functions on time (she had previously thought her timing was just fine, since her husband was already there.) She explained that she went to her office, it was to have time to decompress after work, not to avoid him or the kids. They built a schedule that included time together and the downtime she needed each evening. This gave him time to talk to and sometimes hang out with his friends. The last thing to tackle was their sleeping arrangements: She couldn't get herself to go to bed when her husband did, but she did begin to sleep in the same location. They worked out a schedule of being intimate at times when she had fewer demands, which tended to be on the weekend. She explained that when she was overwhelmed, her senses also overloaded, making sex uncomfortable. They decided to alternate who initiated it and to work on ways to make that more fun within the structure.

My wife (ADHD) just moved out, and she said that she has had it. She was overloaded by taking care of the kids, working, and by me. She had so many responsibilities that she was forgetting to eat or take care of herself. I do not even know what she was doing (besides yelling and swearing at me), as our house was always a mess. The laundry was always left in the washer and stunk. Anyway, everyone is angry. I (Autistic) work all day, so I figured that she could do everything at home like my mom did. I always read books to the kids at bedtime because that is fun, but when she would ask me to help her with chores at the end of the day or on the weekend, I would get annoyed and upset with her or leave. I mean I was exhausted. We did go to many marriage therapists, and they would side with my wife and say that I was not participating. I went to therapy —I was doing everything she asked me to do!? What else did they want from me? It is true that it is hard for me to complete things like mowing the yard, washing, showering, laundry, and cooking. And just yesterday my plans to buy out my partner at our medical practice were finalized, so I am going to need to work a lot. I know I have to take care of my children when they visit me, but I think I will need to hire people to help me. It would have been easier if she had stayed to help me.

EF Challenge: Planning/prioritization -Working memory, metacognition, organization, planning/prioritization, self-regulation, flexibility, time management, and stress tolerance.

EF Strategies: Each individual would need to build individual awareness, and self-responsibility, grieve the loss of what they thought their marriage would be, and work together to build strategies within their marriage. While I can support them in building awareness and developing strategies to reach their goals, such a couple tends to benefit from working with a team of helping professionals. Teams can be made up of a variety of helpers (ex: therapists, pastors, coaches, etc.). Couples who have a team of helpers typically each doing individual work while also meeting with someone to reach the couple's goals. Each of the helpers must have a clear role and knowledge of ND adults in relationships. In this situation, the wife had already left and was not interested in working together or being married.

At his medical practice, he already had an electronic system and staff that supported him and understood his strengths and challenges. Incorporating this degree of system-ization into his home life was not possible, and he expressed he was overwhelmed by the thought. Compartmentalizing home and work for him required separate approaches. Developing a planning system with a neurodivergent person is personal and takes time. For most autistic and ADHD people, every facet must be explored, or it will not become functional. If it's digital in nature, will it be remembered once the tab or app is closed? If it's concrete, does the paper feel okay, does it need to be a certain color, is the size an obstacle or advantage, and what variables could prevent or facilitate its use that need to be discussed? We moved through this slowly to find what worked and felt right to him. Once a system was in place, we were able to create sub-routines that included attaching new desired actions to already-in-place systems. He began exercising, doing chores, ordering his ADHD meds, and other life tasks on a regular schedule. His planner was always with him to record and remind him about one-offs. He moved through interviewing and hiring a nanny and found a laundry service. Many aspects of overseeing these people and services also demanded EF skills, yet in the long term, the planning systems we developed made managing home, children and work more manageable for him.

As he wanted to understand his mistakes in marriage, we discussed that he had learned things in his life by watching, through a "bottom-up" brain perspective (i.e., observing his parent's marriage). For him, this meant that the wife did the traditional "woman's" in-house chores, while the husband went to work to provide (and maybe did the yard work). It has been my observation that this is a common occurrence and can be mistaken in a person as narcissism by people who aren't aware of the many nuances of EF. Without realizing it, he had also blended his youthful observations of his mother with the idea that his wife would also take over all the personal care tasks his mom had done for him. He did not account for meeting his wife's emotional needs or even realize this was an expectation in most marriages. None of these things were discussed between the couple before marriage, and his wife did not have any desire to be in either of these roles. This led to him making unilateral decisions and becoming upset with her when she did not meet his expectations. Her view of marriage included a fair distribution of shared responsibilities, which might need to be redistributed if she got sick, overly tired, or was just in need of a break. She expected her husband to display empathy when she was in need, in the way that her brain recognized. She did not have the language to talk about her needs, including invisible things like fun, romance, spontaneity and connection. He, in all truth, had no idea that there was any other way to approach marriage other than what he had unilaterally determined in his mind. This caused each of them a lot of confusion, emotional dysregulation and missed opportunities to connect.

He expressed a desire to learn what went wrong in his marriage so that he could date at some point and possibly re-marry more successfully. We used concrete strategies to help him understand equal and fair male and female roles that are flexible and created by agreement. We discussed the difference between a mother-son relationship vs. a wife-husband relationship. This helped him to see that in marriage, you do things for the team, not because your partner "told you to." He stated, "I guess my wife wasn't bossing me around." He began meeting with a pastor to re-evaluate his literal view of *headship*, and he learned about *servant-leadership*, as well as concrete displays of Christ-like love in marriage. The pastor and I worked together: I consulted on the value of discussing how, when, where, and why specific homework could be scheduled, completed, and reviewed to ensure accountability for the changes he wanted to make in his life.

We defined words like *mutuality* and reviewed past scenarios where he had made unilateral decisions. In rehearsing how to make mutual decisions, he saw how he could work on this in the future. He was able to have compassion for himself, acknowledging that his natural brain had the strengths of assessing and making solid judgments, but that in relationships, he would need to receive the internal and external data of his partner to come to a mutual agreement. Without this, his judgment would only be based on a limited data set and perspective. Similarly, we covered topics of empathy, dating, and self-regulation.

We retired last year. Our children are grown and are living on their own. We've been married for 41 years, and though it has always been hard, I (NT/NA) thought that when we got to this point it would be fun. My husband does not want to travel to any new locations, visit with friends or make any plans with me. He won't even try new restaurants. He becomes irritable with me when I mention this, and he will not even talk with me; it is like I did something by asking him to just talk about it. We do not have any common interests. I would love to take a cooking class with him. Maybe he is worried about money – he gets angry when the credit card comes and doesn't talk to me for days, but we have plenty of money, and there is nothing to worry about. He spends his time watching the news, riding his bike and collecting old coins. When I ask him to help with chores, he makes loud sighs, complains and often forgets to do what I asked him to do. I think this is on purpose, as he is too smart to forget. If he does the chore, then he announces that he did it for me. Buying groceries is not for me; he eats too! Anyway, I have friends to do things with, but it is not the same. I don't want to spend the rest of my life like this, and I recently saw something about autism. I can't believe this, but I think my husband is autistic.

EF Challenges: flexibility, task initiation, emotional regulation, stress tolerance, metacognition, and planning/participation.

EF Strategies: It is common in coaching to meet unidentified ND couples who have recently transitioned to retirement and are finding things to be different than what was expected. All transitions place a demand on EF, even the ones we look forward to or that are somewhat positive. Retirement is a time of many transitions. Roles, schedules and finances change. Each person in the marriage has their own internal hopes or expectations that may not be expressed or moved into negotiated concrete plans.

This couple came to meet me together. The husband was resistant to the idea that he was autistic, but agreed for his wife's sake, and said he would like to learn about both of their brains. He came to conclude that he was autistic, "if this is what autistic is," referring to my common Autism strengths and challenges evaluation materials. They found a group for ND married couples online and enjoyed attending together. The wife also went to a group for neurotypical wives; she said it made her feel so validated and "normal."

They worked with me individually and together to redefine their roles in their retirement, including self-care, intimacy, romance, fun, the budget, and shared responsibilities. We discovered common interests they had and worked to incorporate them into a joint calendar. We scheduled times for planning, daily conversation, fun, intimacy, and weekly alone time. We also added times to resolve old conflicts, one by one. Each of these required EF strategies, plus SR skills and awareness. Travel was a huge barrier, but they began with road trips that allowed for bringing things that helped each other feel comfortable, such as the coffee pot from home. As we built strategies and reviewed what worked or did not work, they were able to pre-plan and tackle a more complex trip that involved flying and going to a completely new location. This couple agreed that they believed three of their five children were likely also autistic; they decided that her family tree had ADHD (she possibly did as well) and that this included multiple autistic relatives. Working with this couple highlighted the value of building systems to develop fun and connection, while also working toward better conflict resolution.

I hope that this chapter has enriched your understanding of EF as well as its impact on individuals and couples. My approach is rooted in my lived experiences, faith, and professional knowledge. The foundation of growth for ND couples is compassion. In writing, I am reminded of the words of Dr. Vernard Gant[28], while speaking on the topic of diversity he expressed "The answer is right there", it's in Christ's command to "Love one another as I have loved you" (John 13:34, ESV). In Christlike love, we can bridge our differences. This kind of love grows out of curiosity. It evolves by humbly sharing truthful self-awareness with our partner, receiving our partner and ourselves as we are created, and displaying an understanding of each other's brain in the form of daily practical strategies. In this foundation, we can create safe, inclusive home-based *teams*.

Working together, couples can develop EF strategies tailored to their unique personal and marital needs. Ideally, this process combines concrete, strength-based EF strategies with the SR skills and awareness needed to achieve individual and mutual goals. For those in neurodivergent (ND) marriages or those helping such couples, this chapter is meant to establish a foundation of awareness. Building and implementing these strategies in an ND marriage involves much deeper understanding, time, effort, and the incorporation of elements of mutuality, reciprocity, and freedom that consider the value of each partner's neurological makeup.[29]

This chapter has scratched the surface of a topic that needs more exploration. In writing this chapter, it became clear that I have more to write and contribute in this area. Follow me on my website as I begin my journey of writing and developing more content that helps ND couples reach their goals as a couple.

Chapter Nine
Navigating the Mazes of Diagnosis, Acceptance, Pre-Regulation, & Curiosity: Better Than Imagined or Worse Than Expected? It is up to you.

BY JEREMY ROCHFORD, BA, TI-CLC, C-MHC, C-YMC

I've been called many things in my life. Some of them are highly inappropriate, so we're not going to get into all that here. As it relates to us, though, I've found that many in my social and professional circles tend to view me as "Optimistically Positive." Which I appreciate.

But it does beg the question "Why?" Why be so optimistic and positive, when in my life I've experienced the exact opposite?

How can one have such a cheerful disposition knowing first-hand the challenges of being autistic? And how can one stay optimistic knowing the challenges of having two autistic children?

And let's not even get started on the statistics of neurodivergent marriages and relationships.

So how does someone even begin to find joy in all of this?

By the grace of John 8:32 (NIV) which states:

"Then you will know the truth, and the truth will set you free."

I don't take this verse lightly because, for the longest time, I couldn't understand why I was so good at some things in life while at the same time, I was so downright bad at others. Those "others" mainly being things that revolved around social "norms" and relationships. It's frustrating because I can still remember asking myself, on numerous occasions:

"How do I even get into this type of trouble? I'm smarter than this. I should be able to figure these types of things out...."

But for years, I simply couldn't. In fact, I would only seem to make things worse.

My life felt like one of those moments where you find yourself in a room of your house where you can hear the chirp of a dying smoke detector, but you can't figure out which one it is or what room it's in. And it bothers you because you know something's not right, but also, you can't pinpoint where the actual problem is. So, you can never really fix it. You just have to sit there, trying to go on about your life with the constant reminder that something about the situation just isn't right. But you don't have enough information to fix it. So, you and everyone around you must suffer. And, since it's your house, you're the one responsible for it all.

It's very annoying and very unsettling.

That's how my life was. For years. For decades. Until an understanding of autism entered my life.

Through the lens of autism, and my own personal ASD diagnosis, so many of my quirks, behaviors, and what some people would call "deficiencies" started to make sense. And, honestly, that's all I was ever searching for. To have the ability to look myself in the mirror and say "Ok – right or wrong, at least I know *why* that happened."

For me, autism never excused any of my behaviors, but it did start to explain them.

And that gave me the freedom to openly assess the aspects of my life that were serving me well, and the parts that were causing conflict.

It was like I was finally given the instruction manual to my personality.

Or better yet, a cheat code…

My Autism Diagnosis Became the Ultimate Cheat Code

Up-Up.

Down-Down.

Left-Right.

Left-Right.

B-A

Start....

If you know what I'm referring to above, then please allow me to give you a written "high-five."

If not, no worries, please allow me to explain.

Growing up there weren't too many things that mattered more in my life than playing Nintendo. For your childhood it might be something else: PlayStation, Xbox or even TurboGrafx-16. But I'm old-school. As such, I loved the NES as well as one game in particular, Contra. This game was my absolute favorite. Beyond its spectacular gameplay and the purely awesome graphics, there was something genuinely unique about Contra.

It had a *cheat code*.

That's right, a cheat code.

And not just any cheat code, but the most epic of cheat codes ever.

If you entered the sequence *"up, up, down, down, left, right, left, right, B, A, start,"* you would begin the game with 30 lives. Think about that: when most Nintendo games started you off with a measly three lives, finding a way to 10x your existence was pure magic.

Especially in a game where you're being shot at.

But, alas, those were simpler times.

And as my youth gave way to my 20s, which gave way to my 30s, which now has given way to my 40s, I'm not going to lie; there are times I wished for a cheat code to become a better parent, spouse, and overall adult.

Finally, I had one.

Since my diagnosis, my life has become exponentially better.

My marriage is better.

My job is better.

My parenting is better.

Legit, just about everything in my life is better.

How come?

Because I'm finally able to look at myself in the mirror and ask the question "Why" in a *curious* tone, rather than the tone of *guilt* and *shame* (that I used for far too long).

I'm now comfortable enough to question things like:

"Why do I have to wear a compression shirt under every shirt I wear (including t-shirts)?"

"Why do I have such a deep fascination with NASCAR and collecting specific die-cast cars, even though I was born in Pittsburgh, PA, (a town not necessarily known for being a NASCAR hotbed) to a family with no automotive aptitude?"

"Why can't I sit still for even a second without tapping my fingers, hands, or feet?"

"Why do I get headaches after an hour or so of being with people, and why is there a need to 'walk it off' afterward to feel better?"

"Why must I weigh my hockey sticks after taping them before every single use? And why can't I force myself to play with them if they're more than exactly 400 grams? Why do I need to rip all the tape off and start over it the stick weighs in at 401 grams?"

Being able to see these "quirks" through the lens of special interests, stimming, and dysregulation allows me to make sense of so many things in my life. And it makes me feel normal.

Maybe not typical, but normal.

More importantly, though, it helps me know that…

I'm not alone.

I'm not weird.

I'm not broken.

I belong to a tribe of like-minded people.

I have a "standard operating procedure."

And I finally have the cheat code to life that I wished for all this time. A cheat code that allows me to make sense of who I am, which can then allow me to make sense of myself to others. Beyond that, I'm now aware of how to enter situations where I can get the most favorable outcome (internally) as well as avoid situations where things might go sideways (externally).

More importantly, in either situation, I know why things happen the way they do.

Because of that, I can either encourage or prevent certain things from happening. That reality feels so empowering. So freeing. Literally, words cannot express the reduction of stress and anxiety that my family and I have experienced since we discovered my place on the spectrum. That is why I come across, to many, as "Optimistically Positive." Because

I know what it feels like to be in a place of sadness, anxiety and hopelessness, I no longer have to feel that way about myself, my marriage, or my existence. Why wouldn't I focus on the positive?

But not just that.

Why wouldn't I want to share what I've learned with others?

That is the real reason you and I are having this conversation today.

Not to validate my own happiness, but rather, to offer an insight on how you, too, can accomplish YOUR OWN version of happiness. Not only within external relationships but also, within the one you have with yourself. So, if you're ready to move forward, and you've got the ultimate cheat code of knowing who you are in this life, then let's begin by discussing the three biggest mind-shifts that have occurred that allowed my marriage to be saved. The first came by way of a conversation that we often have with couples where one is neuro-divergent and the other is not. It's based on the theme of "*HELP! My husband changed all of a sudden!*" Maybe you're familiar with this or perhaps you've experienced it yourself. Either way, a "normal" couple's experience might go something like this:

Two awesome people start dating. They find each other more and more interesting, and as time goes by, they decide to get engaged. The engagement goes well, which leads to the next logical step: marriage. Upon that joyous occasion, the couple then moves in together and the reality of sharing a life together starts to take shape. From there, perhaps a pet or plant of some sort may join the family. Then, for many couples, children enter the picture. Sometimes one, sometimes many, but with each little blessing the family grows more and more. Until, one by one, the dynamic of the family starts to change again. Pets (and plants) will go to be with the Lord. Children grow up and start to establish a life of their own. Then there's the couple. Who, after all those seasons and life changes, still have each other. Right?

Well... sort of. What we often see is that somewhere along the way, the wife in a neurodiverse marriage finds herself thinking something like:

"My husband has changed! I feel so duped. Like I've been bait-n-switched. It was like I signed up to spend the rest of my life with this amazing man and as soon as we got married, he's changed. Especially after having children. I just wish I could get back the man that I fell in love with! How'd this guy even get here?"

All the while, the husband is thinking something along the lines of:

"What in the world is going on? Why does she think that I've changed? She's the one who's changed. She used to love who I am and all the quirky things I do. She even used to call them charming and endearing. Now, it seems that all she ever does is yell at me for them. How'd we even get here?"

The good news, for the husband, is that he's right. He hasn't *really* changed at all. The bad news, for the husband, is that he should have changed. At least a little. Which seems confusing until you understand it like this. The societal norms that (rightfully so) have influenced his wife's expectations (which are that we're all supposed to grow into the person we need to become to fit the demands of the situation) are the same societal norms that most autistics don't inherently understand.

It's like the husband and wife are both playing the same game while having completely different playbooks. So, for them to make it better, they first have to understand *how they even got here.*

Let's break it down.

When the couple is dating, everything is fine. Autistic masking can start and stop as needed, there is plenty of time to self-regulate, and everything is still new and segmented. The autistic person is not doing this to be deceptive. As the relationship turns to marriage, there is less opportunity for the autistic to "comfortably" be themselves. The time they once had to decompress and regulate is now lessened. The space they had grown accustomed to has changed. And the quirks that were once endearing in small doses start to become a little annoying. It's like when you hear a new song you like on the radio: if you hear it once a day, it's awesome. If you hear it every 15 minutes, it's not.

Once you add kids, the whole dynamic shifts again. Sleep patterns are interrupted, additional income is typically (and sometimes suddenly) needed, and opportunities for sensory overwhelm go off the charts. But that's only for a little while. Because, as the needs of the kid(s) evolve over time, so do the challenges of dysregulation and sensory overwhelm for the autistic. It seems that each phase of a child's development brings a new "routine" for the autistic to have to navigate. Then finally, we get to the empty nest phase of the relationship where, once again, things change. But, at least this time, the couple has more autonomy to choose how they'd like to spend this next chapter of their lives together.

Unfortunately, many neurodiverse couples never see this final phase of their relationship, because some will drift apart, or give up, or just get tired of "dealing with him/her" and so they "just needed out." This is sad, because neither spouse is typically equipped with the tools or strategies, they ACTUALLY need to make a neurodivergent relationship work.

I had to learn the hard way (via my son's ASD diagnosis) that about 98% of what I learned to prepare myself as a parent was NT applicable, and now irrelevant because autism was involved. Meaning, that you can't raise an ND child with tools and processes that are only proven to work on NT children. Rather, I had to learn how to think differently, act differently and love differently. As my wife would attest, this requirement is as true for loving an ND spouse as it is for nurturing an ND child. From my perspective, it was amazing, because it proved that if I was able to do this for my children, why couldn't I do this for all the loved ones in my family, especially my wife?

Rather, I had to learn how to think differently.

I understand that not everybody thinks this way, but perhaps that's part of the issue. I've heard it said that to be "exceptional" at something, then you must first be the "exception." It's been said by many of our clients that "*Team Rochford doesn't do things the way they're were traditionally taught*" and "*we wish they'd have worked with us sooner because we wouldn't have had to struggle for so long.*" They feel our approach "*just seems to work.*"

But that's the trick – doing *the work*. I think it's true for any individual or couple, ND/NT or not, that those who *make the effort to grow and adapt* together are the ones who will be the most joyous and successful. The problem, again, is that many autistics don't inherently "get" this.

At least in this capacity.

For years, I know I didn't. Which, looking back, is very odd. Because I could understand the premise of change as it related to my special interests, just not my family life. Meaning, I understood the concept that the higher you wanted to go in NASCAR, the more money, time, and attention to detail you needed to invest. Likewise, I understood that the further you went in your driving development, the more adaptable you'd have to become (to different tracks, climate conditions and various race durations) to be successful. But I couldn't easily recognize the need for adaptation in my marital life.

Looking back, this is even more ironic as I examine it through the lens of Christianity. Because no one comes to the cross perfect. There's at least something we *have to change* to be more like Christ. So, if we're willing to lose, learn, or change certain behaviors for the gospel, why wouldn't we be willing to do that for those the gospel calls us to love, such as our spouse and/or children?

After I came to know how true this perspective was, I couldn't un-know it.

This led me to realize that while I can't change how the world operates around me, I can change how I respond to it. Furthermore, if I was willing to lose, learn, or change the behaviors I needed to as a love response to the cross, then why wouldn't I be open to the same mentality for my wife? And so, change, I did. This then led me to the second biggest mind shift that helped me save my marriage- how I approached self-regulation. Because, let's be honest, if we're preparing to lose, learn, or change behaviors that we've held onto for a while (either consciously or unconsciously), then we're going to need to be as level-headed as possible. Which begins with self-regulation. Choosing to self-regulate (whether neurodivergent or not) will have one of the greatest impacts on how we're able to show up as the best version of ourselves, while also saving our loved ones from seeing us suffer, shut down, or explode. While many things can help us get into a more self-regulated state, the *most important* thing is to focus on our "pre-regulation."

Pre-Regulation?

Yes, pre-regulation.

To understand this best, we must have a little fun with the old saying, *"The best time to plant a tree was 20 years ago. The second-best time is now."* In the same way, the best time to start self-regulating is 6 hours ago when your dysregulation level was at about a 4, rather than now, when it's risen to an 8. Joking aside, that's where pre-regulation comes in. Pre-regulation builds mindfulness and intentional living into your current lifestyle for a more consistent and regulated emotional existence. We can achieve this in 3 simple steps.

Step #1: Build Regulation Breaks into Your Day

Schedule a regulation break every 1-3 hours throughout the day. Ideally, every hour, but if this is a new behavior in your routine, then shoot for every 3 hours to start and then level up from there to get to every hour. Here's an example: If you work in an office setting, whether at home or in a corporate space, set a silent alarm on your phone to go off every hour. Once it does, use that as a cue to get up and walk around for 5-10 minutes. Maybe stretch. Maybe do some regulated breathing. Maybe do all three. You can even make it personal to you. My special interests include NASCAR, hockey and Star Wars. So, sometimes I'll spend 10 minutes looking at my die-cast collection. Or looking through binders of hockey cards. Sometimes I'll throw on a podcast about the new Star Wars mini-series. Regardless of what you do, what you're looking to accomplish here is breaking the patterns that can lead us to get overwhelmed in a way that leads to dysregulation.

Step #2: Actually, Want to Do This.

This might sound trivial or hurt some of us to hear this, but far too often, we'll embrace a "man-up" mentality that internally causes us to "push through" stressful things that bottle up inside and lead to dysregulation. Once we're finally done with the day and can rest from our job-based responsibilities, we tend to unload and inflict our dysregulation on the ones we're supposed to care for the most. I've done this long enough to know that someone who is reading this is saying, *"But Jeremy, you don't understand; I've got bosses. I've got deadlines. I've got this sense of urgency or ambition."* I get it. Before coaching full-time, I had sales, management, and project management jobs. I know how it feels to have someone "breathing down your neck." There will always be an "urgent" email, phone call, or meeting that needs you. But you know who else needs you? Your family. But not just a shell of you. The best of you. Realizing this sooner rather than later will not only save you a lot of heartache but also a lot of time and money. I know it's hard because you're always going to have something pulling for your attention, but assuming you're committed to becoming more regulated, we can move on to the next step.

Step #3: Make a Plan & Do the Plan.

Here's an example of how this typically happens in my daily life:

9:00-10:00 (Emails/Voxer)
10:00-12:00 (One-on-One Coaching)
12:00-1:00 (Regulation Break & Lunch)
1:00-2:30 (One-on-One Coaching)
2:30-3:00 (Regulation, then Emails)
3:00-3:45 (One on One Coaching, then Regulation Break)
4:00-4:45 (One on One Coaching, then Regulation Break)
5:00-5:45 (One on One Coaching, then Regulation Break)
5:45-6:00 (Regulation Break)
6:00 until whenever… so I can be a dad, husband, friend, son, and/or whatever else is needed of me, and do it in the best mental state possible.

In this scenario, I've built in 6 regulation breaks during the day. Therefore, when I get to the end of my work schedule, I've had 6 opportunities to hit the "release valve" so that all the pressure doesn't bottle up and render me dysregulated for the rest of the evening (like it used to for a greater part of the past 20 years). Also – there are times when 1/2 the coaching sessions are challenging, and maybe the other 1/2 are full of progress or victories. So, I may only take four regulation breaks during those days, because I'm less emotionally taxed. The goal is to be mindful, not machine-like.

Your schedule might look different, and that's OK. The point is to intentionally allow yourself "micro" breaks to alleviate stress, so it doesn't bottle up and become unmanageable. I know that this concept can seem counter-cultural, which leads me to believe at least one person is reading this with the thought "*Wow, this seems like it'll take a lot of time.*" But is it really a lot of time? In the grand scheme of things, isn't taking 5 minutes to prevent a fight worth more than 5 hours to calm down from one? Also, lest we forget, just a few years ago people wouldn't bat an eye if someone had to take a "cigarette break" just about every hour. So, if we're willing to normalize those types of behaviors, then why wouldn't we want to normalize these healthier types of behaviors?

But it must start with us. As mentioned before, if you want to have an exceptional relationship, then you have to do things that would be considered the exception. Don't you deserve to be happy? Doesn't your marriage deserve to be in the percentage of neurodiverse marriages that work? Then don't settle for what's not working. Start leaning into what does work.

If you apply this approach to self-regulation, I guarantee you'll reduce stress quickly and find regulation even faster. Not only will it improve your performance at work, but your personal life will improve significantly as well. This brings us to the third mind-shift I had that saved my marriage. It's a concept I like to refer to as *"Dumping Out – Not Dumping On."* The best way to describe it is through one of the most common scenarios I experienced in my coaching practice. It tends to play out like this:

Husband: *"Jeremy, I don't understand. There I was, minding my own business when my wife suddenly came out of nowhere and started dumping on me with ALL the things I've ever done wrong in our marriage. And then, I don't even have a chance to defend myself. She just leaves. All the while, I'm left here to feel like garbage and I'm automatically wrong because I'm the autistic one. What am I supposed to do with that?"*

Jeremy: *"Well – how does that make you feel?"*

AS/ND Husband: *"Deeply hurt and confused."*

Jeremy: *"Do you take it personally?"*

AS/ND Husband: "Yeah, how can you not?"

So glad you asked, because that's what we're going to talk about in this third mind-shift: How to receive feedback on our behaviors in such a way that it separates the facts from the feelings. This will allow us to work through the facts and the feelings separate from each other, and then bring them back together in such a way that helps the situation, rather than harms it. A tall order, you say? Perhaps. But how many times have you sat back and thought something like:

> *Dang it! Why does my spouse have to be so cryptic and confusing? If they'd just tell me what I'm doing wrong, then I could fix it, so we can finally move on and have a happy marriage.*

Well, what do you think they're doing when they "unload" on you? They're literally doing what you've been asking them to do. They're answering your question. However, the challenge as I see it, is that when those answers to "what am I doing wrong" finally arrive, they tend to do so in a tone, time, and place where we're not ready to receive those answers. So, rather than listen to the answers we've been asking for all along, we tend to get defensive and push back in self-preservation, seeking to justify our actions or behaviors instead.

And in that situation, no one wins.

But there is a better way.

It starts with this mentality: *"Dumped Out – Not Dumped On."*

The next time you feel like you're getting read the riot act of all you've ever done wrong, rather than seeing it as a personal attack (where all your transgressions are being "dumped on" you), I encourage you to imagine sitting at a table, and all the issues that have caused strife in your marriage are finally being "dumped out" on the table for you to look through and analyze. Kind of like when you were a kid, and you'd dump out all the pieces from the box before you'd start to solve the puzzle. The power in taking this stance is that you finally have the answer to the question, *"What in the world is she(he) thinking?"* Now, you can actually know. And you also have the ability to analyze the data to see what you agree with and to assess if those behaviors were intentional or simply a misunderstanding. This is how the *"Dumped Out – Not Dumped On"* concept saved my marriage.

Growing up, I was a connoisseur of sarcasm. But also, my parents were sarcastic, and my hockey friends were sarcastic. And, before I lost 200 pounds, the typical "fat kid" thing to do was to make fun of yourself sarcastically. Just about every communication in my life was rooted in sarcasm. So, when my wife entered the picture, I assumed she would also love sarcasm. Turns out no bueno. She HATED sarcasm. And it nearly ended our relationship. To her, sarcasm came across as mean, vindictive, and abusive. Which was NEVER my intent. But, also, I had never been challenged to think a different way about it. Could I have sat back and held onto my belief that my sarcasm was fantastic and that SHE was the one who needed to change? Sure. I could have. Or I could look at it in a different way. So, I started to ask myself why was I being sarcastic in the first place? For me, sarcasm was initially a way to connect with my family. To impress and fit in with my hockey friends. To seem funny in front of girls. And to protect myself from feeling made fun of due to my weight.

What was actually happening, though? My family wasn't around when I was having intimate conversations with my wife. Neither were my hockey friends. My wife was the only girl I wanted to be funny in front of, and sarcasm was doing the opposite. And I had lost 200 pounds by the time we married, which meant no one was making fun of me for my weight anymore. In short, when I thought about it, my sarcasm was doing NOTHING but hurting me. So, if that's the case, why continue it? Or at least why continue it around her? There was no good reason.

So, I stopped.

Am I still sarcastic from time to time with my hockey friends? Occasionally, because that's the time and the place for it. However, when my wife is involved, that is not the time. And that is not the place. Ironically though, as I strive to be the husband, father, and man that GOD has called me to be, I find the desire to be sarcastic becoming less and less. It's like I'm growing into a person who no longer needs to be protected by the barriers that sarcasm can create. I realized this only after I understood how powerful becoming curious about my behavior was, and how emotionally grounding the "Dumped Out – Not Dumped On" approach could be. But it wasn't just that *one* realization that was liberating: it's the combination of all three mind-shifts that have occurred since I began to lean into my neurodivergent diagnosis "cheat code."

First, by realizing that autism didn't "change me" all of a sudden, it gave me the emotional grace and freedom to accept that maybe there were some needed changes and adaptations I could make to become the *best* version of myself. Because, while I can't always control my environments, I can control how I prepare and respond to them. Does it take a little more consideration of things than I'm used to? Possibly. But in the end, I'm worth it and so are those around me.

Second, when I realized just how important self-regulation was to my own mental state, as well as to those around me, I couldn't help but want to do it. The small amount of time it took on the front end to prevent or mitigate conflicts (caused by dysregulation) paled in comparison to the hours, and sometimes days, it took to repair them. It reminded me of something I've heard from many wise people in my life, which is *"an ounce of prevention is worth a pound of cure."*

Finally, I became more aware and in control of the environmental triggers in my life. And, as I incorporated steps to staying calmer and more regulated, I was able to communicate better. Not only with my spouse, but with everybody. When I got to a place of being able to give and receive feedback with a heart of peace and understanding, all my relationships got better: my personal ones, my professional ones, and the one I have with myself. I've seen first-hand how much of a challenge being neurodivergent can be in ALL aspects of life, because I live it every day. But in a world that, more often than not, tries to paint autism and neurodivergence in a negative light, I choose to be different. I choose to embrace it. I choose to be "Optimistically Positive." Because by being so, it's made my life better.

If that sounds like something you'd like, then I highly encourage you to follow the four steps that I laid out for you in this this chapter.

1. Embrace your diagnosis. It's not a label, it's a cheat code.
2. Lean into becoming adaptable and embrace the reality of change.
3. Take control of your self-regulation.
4. Communicate with a heart of curiosity.

These four steps not only saved my marriage, but they restored joy in our very challenging neurodivergent relationship. What's nice is that they haven't just worked in my life, they've worked time and time again in the lives of the people we've been able to coach through our practice, NeuroFam. I want to leave you with a testimony from a client who just graduated from one of our programs. His marriage is the best it's been in years. He and his wife were so happy with what we were able to accomplish together, that he wanted to share it with others.

Here's what he said.

My wife and I were both told, either via podcasts or previous ASD counseling, that 'if you're living with an autistic husband, you're just going to have to deal with it because nothing is ever going to change.' This was difficult for me to accept, as a part of me thought if I was able to understand the reasoning for my behavior then there would be opportunities to learn new behaviors and react to challenges differently. This could then lead me towards becoming the husband that I knew I truly wanted to be. The husband my wife needed me to be. Jeremy helped me make those connections and understand those reasons. That's why working with him was so different. It wasn't like previous therapy and counseling where we'd spend an hour or so learning about how bad of a husband I was, or, how I could never change. Jeremy would listen to my goals, understand what I was going through, and actually give me the confidence and the tools to make it happen. He understood me, because he, too, was ND. I always felt heard, understood, encouraged and empowered. "Thank you, Jeremy, from the bottom of my heart.- William S.

If your marriage is struggling and it seems like there's no hope, please know that there *is*. A healthy, and happy neurodiverse relationship is possible. We know, because we've seen the bad, we've seen the ugly, and now, we're seeing the good. Will your neurodiverse marriage be better than imagined or worse than you expected? The choice is up to you.

Chapter Ten
Navigating the Maze of Co-Parenting and Teamwork: "Fruitful" Parenting

BY NEURODIVERSE COUPLE, TEAM ROCHFORD, JEREMY ROCHFORD & CHARITY ROCHFORD BA, TI-CLC

We've all had those moments where we'll never forget where we were, or what we were doing when we heard "the news." For some of us, it was when President John F. Kennedy was assassinated. For others, it was the tragedy of the Challenger Space Shuttle or the explosion at Chornobyl. For myself, it was the tragic events of September 11th. More recently, for everyone reading this book, it was early 2020 when the country, and most of the world, systematically shut down due to the Corona 19 pandemic. While experiences like these often blindside us on a national level, so too, can unexpected deeply personal experiences.

For me, I'll never forget the day that the realities of "neurodivergence" and "autism" were introduced into our family. I had just arrived to pick up my son (Johnathan) from pre-school and no sooner did I make it out of my car, than I was asked if I "*had a moment*" to speak with the center director. Stepping into her office, I was initially confused and had a little bit of quiet anger. Clearly, as the father of very young boy, my first thought was

"Ok, who did he hit or what did he say that's going to get him expelled?" Being a child of the 80's, I remember all the shenanigans I got into when I was his age, so I was preparing for the worst.

But as she asked me to take a seat, I noticed her face was more concerned than upset. Which naturally turned my feelings from annoyed to concerned. "*Is everything 'OK?*" I asked, wondering what I was about to hear. "*Everything's fine*" she assured me. But she then went onto explain that there were some things about Johnathan's behavior that were a little different. Not BAD, but "*different.*" And while she assured me that she was no clinician, she also went on to explain that a lot of the traits and behaviors she observed in my son were very similar to those of children who were autistic.

Autistic.

As in, *autism.*

Hmmm.

Ok.

Now, as discussed earlier. I was prepared for him punching a kid, saying something inappropriate or even peeing on the wall. But autism? Nope, this had never crossed my mind.

Because (up until this point) we'd never identified anyone in our family as autistic. At all. Like, not even a little. Not even a little "fringe spectrum" like ADHD or something. Literally nothing. Nevertheless, she concluded our conversation by suggesting, very strongly, that we have our son tested and love him the same, no matter what the test results were.

On the way home, I felt so many emotions. Confused, angry, numb. I remember, as I was speaking with my wife about this, I wanted nothing more than to fight. Not with the director, but rather, the belief (or the reality) that our son could possibly be autistic. I'd never been so sure about anything in my life as I was about that fact that the center director had to be wrong. My wife, on the other hand, was much more graceful in how she received and processed the information.

Charity's Thoughts: The message that got to me from Jeremy later that day was that the school director thought we needed to have our son evaluated. I had noticed some sensory issues and assumed that was what they also saw, which made sense since I have some sensory sensitivity of my own. We reached out to friends who recently had their child (at a different school) observed by a behavioral therapist, and we asked for their contact information. She was a very sweet woman, and we scheduled with her to observe our son in preschool, just as our friends had done. Then we would have a brief talk over the phone to get her feedback. It took only a couple of visits with him for her to determine that he did, in fact, have sensory issues. She set him up with a sensory box at the preschool and some other suggestions for making the environment more comfortable for him. This time, I was the one who got to go in and talk with the director to give her the good news that we "had it all figured out" and that it was just sensory issues. As I was starting to tell her about the box of sensory-friendly toys, she gently told me that we needed to see someone else for a full evaluation. I must have appeared confused, because she continued that she meant an evaluation with a pediatric psychiatrist, the kind that takes hours and hundreds of questions. She wasn't as blunt with me as she was with Jeremy, as I still hadn't heard the "autism" reference yet, but she was being very clear that she did not believe we had found the right thing yet. There was something more we needed to uncover.

Not knowing anyone with neurodivergent children, I called the insurance company and asked who was in the network, then took the list to our pediatrician and asked if they could recommend anyone from the list. They picked a few, and I called the first one to make an appointment. During the 4 ½ month wait for the appointment to roll around, I reached out to a friend who teaches special education. I knew the evaluation might be involved and thought she might be able to help at least prepare me for what the process would be like. She'd met our son before at events, so I figured she had a good grasp on what he was like. She asked me a few questions about what they were seeing at preschool that caused the request, and we set up an evening to chat the next week. She showed up to dinner with a binder full of information for me. A packet all about 504s and IEPs and being your child's advocate. She also brought up that it might be autism and explained how some of his traits would align with the diagnosis. The more she asked about him and if he did this or that, the more I realized that she was spot on. I had earned my psychology degree before the current version of the *Diagnostic and Statistical Manual* (DSM) had been written, and autism wasn't defined the same as it is now (back then it was called Asperger's Syndrome). Those were also years before we began having kids, so I hadn't been keeping up with the newest diagnostic criteria. But my friend had been on top of it in her role, and by working with neurodivergent students every day, she knew how autism most often presents in kids. The more we talked, the more I heard from her about the challenges these children had, as well as about the good she sees in her students because of their differences. As it settled in my mind that it could be autism, she reassured me that autism wasn't a bad thing and that a diagnosis wouldn't change our son and who he was. It wouldn't be something that would hold him back or make him lesser. She explained that the more we could find out about him (if it was autism, ADHD, sensory issues, social issues, or some other difference), the better it would enable the education system to best meet his needs. That wouldn't be possible if we didn't go through with the evaluation. I knew she was right, and I knew it didn't change who our little guy was. His charm and charisma would not be erased by a label, no matter what label it was.

Getting Jeremy on board with the evaluation and the possibility of a diagnosis like autism was not easy. He saw it as a stigma, a bad thing, something that only non-verbal children were diagnosed with. I went through a list of some famous people who either have been confirmed or have been suspected to be autistic. At this point, I understood it was a possibility and I didn't want to come home from the appointment with "bad news." If anything, I was going to treat a diagnosis as good news! I was going to use it as my flag to wave as his advocate. Everything was going to be ok.

Honestly, I (Jeremy) am very fortunate to have married such a wonderful, compassionate woman, who could think so level-headedly and act with such compassion in a time like that. Because for me, I didn't know what to think, feel, or say. I just remember the months between that conversation and our son's testing as a mixed bag of emotions that played out like the typical grieving cycle of Denial, Anger, Bargaining, Depression and finally Acceptance.

One of the things that did stand out, though, was a few days before our son's testing, we were given a "take-home evaluation." These are fairly standard in the assessment process and help the psychologist understand what types of behaviors we observed in our son at home, and in everyday life with him. What we found most fascinating as we went through the questions, was that we found ourselves saying things like, "*Well, I guess this could be Johnathan, but wow, this question really describes Corinne* (our daughter.)" We kept saying that so much that we felt it might be a good idea to get her tested once our son's evaluation was complete.

The day came, and afterward, the doctor said he knew within a few minutes that our son was on the autism spectrum. He would go on to officially diagnose him as ASD-2, and also with ADHD. These abbreviations stand for "Autism Spectrum Disorder, Level 2, with Attention Deficit Hyperactivity Disorder." And so, it was: My son was *autistic*. If I had to do it all over again, I'd like to think that I could have taken the news more gracefully, but my wife will affirm that, in fact, I didn't.

Charity's Thoughts: "Gracefully" is not the word I'd use to describe Jeremy's initial response. If it's any indication, his first question to me was to ask if we had to tell anyone.

I knew the answer was yes, we had to take this information and use it. That's why we went through the process. We wanted to know for sure and use the diagnosis to help him.

With our son officially on the spectrum, we then focused on getting our daughter tested. I mean, how could we not? She seemed to score highly on an autism evaluation that she wasn't even a part of. It is kind of mind-blowing to think that we'd go from a family with no understanding of autism to becoming a family with both kids on the spectrum. All this in just about a year. Talk about a paradigm shift! I will say this. In the time between his evaluation and hers, I really came to embrace autism and the role it would play in our lives. For me, it came by way of a realization.

First, the joke, as you may expect now from me (Jeremy).

"Well, I must have unknowingly prayed for the 'expert level' of parenting when I signed up for all of this."

But now, the reality.

"Before we had kids, I knew that I was going to have to learn how to become a father anyway, being that the whole parenting thing meant that I was going to have to learn a new skill set. What's the difference between learning how to raise 'typical' children versus how to raise autistic ones?"

Now, because of the ways I've said things before this, or in previous writings, you're probably waiting for the paragraph above to be a setup for some kind of *satirical* comment. Right? Well, honestly, I went on my first diet when I was 5 and struggled for my entire adolescence to overcome a preventable chronic disease, and then lost about 125 pounds when I was 17. There was nothing "normal" about *my* growing up, so why would I expect anything less for my kids? Now, I know my wife had high aspirations for our kids, but as for me, I just wanted to spend the next few years making sure they got fed and didn't get seriously hurt. I think is a noble goal for all parents.

Charity's Thoughts: My goals for our children were a little higher than just 'don't get hurt.' Our kids seemed so much like us, part of an older sister/younger brother family of 4, both bright and seemingly advanced for their age, and they were also creative and happy. I expected that they'd continue to be like us, being generally good kids who excelled in school but weren't out of the ordinary other than having high standardized testing scores. I assumed they'd make a plan for college, go for at least 4 years, and then head off to a career somewhere.

Although I felt prepared for my son's diagnosis, I did go through a grieving process. It wasn't long, but I had that feeling in the pit of my stomach, thinking of all the struggles he would have in school, all the bullying he would experience, and I wondered if he would need to stay at home into adulthood or be able to function in the real world on his own someday. I thought about the jobs that our son wanted when he grew up, but I worried he would never be capable of them.

Oddly, my expectations have changed for both kids, and I don't think it's a bad thing. Instead of expecting them to be like us, I now expect them to grow up and do what makes them happy. It's nice to think of their future that way. No big expectations of business careers with high salaries and demanding schedules. Instead, I'm excited to think about how they can just do what they love, and I keep my focus on what I can do to help them reach those goals.

Jeremy: Corinne (our daughter) would go on to be diagnosed with ASD-1, and so, we were well on our way to being a happy little autistic family. But then an even funnier thing happened: as we were learning more and more about autism, we discovered that men were diagnosed four times as often as women, and that when siblings are diagnosed with autism, the genetic contribution to their autism usually comes from the father....

Or, in other terms, me.

My wife can add a little more clarity on how we came to this conclusion.

Charity's Thoughts: From a certain point of view, the way Jeremy explains it is accurate, but there is a little more to the story that needs to be included. I had started to put the pieces together while preparing for our daughter's evaluation and was sending him bits of information to help him see it, too, but I was doing it very slowly. After his initial response to learning of Johnathan's diagnosis, I didn't want to just spring it on him that I saw it in him, too. So, instead, I would send a video or article to him every few days or so.

I'm glad she had these hunches because she was 100% right. Looking back, I still remember her sending me social media videos made by autistic and ADHD influencers from Australia and the UK, all the while thinking to myself, "*Well, this is cool... but I wonder what it has to do with our children since these people are so much older."* Full disclosure, there were times during this process when I "just didn't get it."

But once I did, I just couldn't look the other way. When my own neurodivergence was confirmed, we found ourselves in a place where 75% of our family was on the spectrum. Besides Charity not being able to be "celebrated" during Autism Acceptance Month (every April), we had more pressing problems to contend with – mainly that 97% of what we had learned about parenting was now irrelevant because a child's neurodivergent mind doesn't work the way most parenting books assume.

I know we've had a lot of fun in this chapter so far, but all joking aside, Charity and I found we were lost on many occasions. We genuinely needed direction, and with so few resources available on how to parent neurodivergent children from a Godly perspective, we decided it was best to go to the source: we consulted God's word.

> *For the fruit of the Spirit is love, joy, peace, patience, kindness, goodness, faithfulness, gentleness, self-control; against such things there is no law* (Galatians 5:22-23 ESV).

We knew that, if nothing else, if our hearts were in the right place, then the right strategies would surely follow. I'd like to break down each one to give some insight on how we brought this to life, with the hopes that you'll be led to do the same.

Parenting in Love

Love has many definitions that range from "an intense feeling of deep affection" to "like or enjoy very much." Regardless of how one defines love, our goal is to ensure that our children *feel* love – that they *feel* that we enjoy them very much, that they *feel* we have deep affection for them. Quite often, this means learning to do things on their terms.

I had to learn that, just because I had plans for my children, it didn't mean they were going to come to fruition. In my mind, we were going to bond over amazing things like watching hockey and discussing NASCAR. Instead, they developed their own personalities, likes, and dislikes, as they should.

My son LOVES Legos. So, part of my parenting him with love is to take an interest in *his* special interests. To ask him about his "builds" and to learn about his likes. For my daughter, she loves theatre. Part of the way I parent her with love is by animating her stuffed animals with characters and voices. Every night before we go to bed, I tuck her in and while we're saying prayers, she normally prefers that I voice out one of her stuffed animal characters. Is it something I ever thought I'd be doing? No, but it's a way to connect with her on *her* level. I want my kids' childhoods to be filled with memories of doing things *they* liked, instead of having been forced to do what "dad wanted to do" (often veiled as "quality time").

Charity's Thoughts: I think expressing some kinds of love comes a bit more naturally for me, in that I am a mom, so I get to give hugs and kisses, to be the one who snuggles with them to watch a movie, who makes crafts with them, who receives the pictures of walruses drawn in art class, sews costumes, attends Comicon and is the one who practices lines for their school plays. What makes them happy makes me happy. I get to hear the same song sung over and over and over again at a decibel that gives Jeremy an immediate migraine, but for me, it's not bothersome. To me, it's another way that I can show them love.

Parent Growth Tips and Coaching Questions

What are some ways you parent your kids with ***love,*** and what are some ways you haven't tried, but should consider? What mindset shift do you need to make about parenting in love?

Parenting in Joy

It's ironic that *joy* is so foundational to the Christian faith but, for many of us, it's so hard to experience or express. Joy is defined as "a feeling of great pleasure and happiness," so I've put a lot of effort into making sure that my body language and tone of voice reflect the *joy* that my kids bring to our lives. Now, I'll be honest, there are times when they're super annoying and choose the worst time to ask for something. But overall, I want to be very intentional about making sure that they grow up in a household where they feel like their existence is a joy and not a burden.

Charity's Thoughts: My thought of parenting in joy is different: I try to emulate joy for the kids. Yes, I'm a kid at heart and one of those "Disney adults," in that I love Disney movies, visiting the theme parks, hugging the characters, and sleeping with a stuffed animal. And do you know what? That's OK! It's OK to be an adult who finds joy in things that other adults don't. It's OK to collect toys, color pictures for friends, sing at the top of our voices during carpool karaoke and dress up like our favorite characters. I decorate with what brings me joy. Our house doesn't look like the houses of other families in the neighborhood. Who else has a Star Wars rug in the living room and one with Mickey heads in the room in front of the bookshelves? I'm sure we're the only house with a giant painting of Kermit the Frog overlooking the Nashville skyline above their dining room table. I wear bows in my hair and a smile on my face. So, what am I really trying to show my kids? I'm showing them that I find joy in my life. I show them that it doesn't matter what others think.

Parent Growth Tips and Coaching Questions

What are some ways you can parent with *joy* and what are some ways you haven't tried but should consider? Is your home low joy or high joy? Are you as a parent approachable? (Refer back to the neuroplasticity chapter for a refresher on relational joy).

Parenting in Peace

I'm not going to lie, living with two autistic children can be the opposite of peaceful. As a part of my son's autism, he doesn't recognize the volume of his voice and is very loud quite often. Also, my daughter loves singing and (as she should for proper vocal support) projects her voice very loud as well. In addition to that, both kids are under 12, so, you've also got the inherent tension of kids developmentally pushing boundaries and testing patience. In short, there's the potential for a whole lot of unrest. I've responded to this in two ways.

1. I've really started to take my self-regulation seriously: if I'm going to need to diffuse potentially stressful situations, then I'm going to need to be coming at things from a place of peace and balance.
2. I've gotten curious about their behaviors. Meaning, instead of jumping right into "anger" or "punishment" mode for what they're doing, I've started to ask myself, *"Why are they doing this?"* By getting curious about the cause of their behaviors, I've been able to keep our interactions a lot calmer and more peaceful.

Charity's Thoughts: Because I get to spend more time during the day with the kids, I get to have peaceful times with them, too. When it's time to get 'regulated' or go to sleep, we have set up song playlists together. For our son, it's his Peaceful Disney Piano Music playlist. For our daughter, it's the combined sounds of light rain and ukulele. Sometimes bringing peace is about co-regulating with them and giving a long, firm hug in the midst of a moment of big emotions.

Parent Growth Tips and Coaching Questions

What are some ways you parent with *peace* and what are some ways you haven't tried but should consider? Peace is about shalom in the home. Dr. Wilder and others who have written about joy and shalom share that both joy and shalom and inter-active quieting are essential to relationship building. Do you know how to quiet yourself? Do you know how to bring peace to a challenging situation?

Parenting in Patience

When it came to growing my capacity to tolerate trouble or delays without getting angry or upset (the definition of patience), I will say it has taken some work on my part. Being autistic myself, I have a tendency to jump to conclusions or react emotionally, based on things I've assumed (mind-reading) without asking if what I am reacting to is true. This has been both a challenge and a blessing as a parent.

It's been a challenge because it's forced me outside of my comfort zone and pushed me to modify a lot of behaviors that I felt were working (although they weren't) before children. So, having to learn these new skills has definitely made me a better person for everyone. The blessing is that knowing how much I struggle with some of the things that don't come "factory installed" gives me a unique perspective on how my kids are struggling in their autistic lives. The combination of having to do my own self-work as well as my understanding of autism has improved my parenting and my ability to practice patience.

Charity's Thoughts: This is where I have to check my expectations on a regular basis. At times, I feel like I'm rocking "patient" parenting! I have a planned trip to the store with a child and we treat it like a math excursion: I teach them how to figure out the sale price of each item when the sign just says that the section has a % discount (the clearance fabric section at JoAnn's provides excellent opportunities for this!)

Other trips are intended to be quick: Let's get ready to leave quickly, come on let's get to the car quickly, oh my, can we manage to get buckled up at least without an issue? Why did we all of a sudden forget how van doors work and where the seatbelt is? And where did our shoe go while on the drive to the store? Why did we have to spend so much time talking to the cashier and why are we having a meltdown now when this was supposed to just be a quick trip?

I'm still learning to check my expectations on a daily basis. Just because some-thing has happened once, doesn't mean I should expect that it will happen without issue a second time. It still doesn't always make sense in the moment, but I learn over and over again that my expectations greatly affect the amount of patience I have in the moment.

Parent Growth Tips and Coaching Questions

What are some ways you parent with *patience* and what are some ways you haven't tried but should consider? Do you have work to do in cultivating your patience? Part of parenting with patience is learning to be patient with yourself as you learn new skills, patience with your parenting partner, and patience with your children.

Parenting in Kindness

Living in kindness, and parenting through it, is not something that came naturally to me. Not because I'm an angry curmudgeon by choice, but because many autistics struggle with "theory of mind" (the ability to correctly surmise another's thoughts, feelings or perspective). However, in the same way that running a 5K or beating Super Mario Brothers can be a struggle, one can also learn and adapt the skills needed to accomplish things *kindly*. Likewise, one can improve their "theory of mind."

In doing so, my ability to gain insight into others' beliefs, desires, intentions, emotions, and thoughts has greatly increased my ability and capacity to be friendly, generous, and considerate, with not only my children but with almost everyone I now meet. Working to stretch my understanding allows me to have that much more compassion for my children's struggles, which moves me to want to be even kinder to them.

Charity's Thoughts: Kindness is hard to think of on its own. We're all "kind" to our families, right? To extend kindness beyond just being kind, I relate it to being empathetic. Am I empathizing with my children? Do I really understand where they are coming from? This is one thing that I've always had a knack for. In my two decades working in Human Resources/ Employee Benefits roles (wow, that hurts to type out,) I did a lot of putting myself in others' shoes. Mostly, I would try to find a 'good' reason why someone may have done something and not always assume the most negative reason. Sure, it might be the most negative reason, but it might not be. So, it was always a best practice to treat them as if they didn't do anything wrong intentionally, maybe they were confused, didn't have the right info, etc. Jeremy points out that I do the same thing with the kids. I'm always looking for the 'why' to explain their action or words. When they were younger it was often because they were mimicking a show, they saw on PBS or Disney.

Like the time our son mooned our Bible study group... it took a lot of kindness to realize he wasn't trying to be bad. We had recently watched the movie Brave, and Merida's cute little brothers were quite fond of showing others their tiny, animated bums. (And with that, I hope you don't giggle too loudly the next time your pastor preaches a sermon on "kindness," and you're reminded of the Rochford's kid mooning their Bible study!)

Parent Growth Tips and Coaching Questions

What are some ways you parent with **kindness** and what are some ways you haven't tried but should consider? Are you open to hearing from your children about what kindness looks and feels like to them? Sometimes doing the hard thing is the kind thing, but your approach, tone and method should reflect loving kindness.

Parenting in Goodness

As someone who's been involved in ministry for over 20 years, I think we had a pretty good handle on raising our children with a morally *good* or "virtuous" foundation. And, at a surface level, we have. We're not a house that swears. We don't push the boundaries with what's "child-appropriate" and we're always complimented on how well our children behave (the Bible study episode aside).

That said, my parenting really took an upswing when I realized how important *modeling* good behavior was for my children. The more I learned how to show joy, peace, patience, etc., the more they experienced it from me. The more they saw good behavior in me, the more I could see them trying to mimic those behaviors when relating to others.

Charity's Thoughts: Because our children are autistic, it means that sometimes things come out sounding more blunt than helpful. Instead of yelling at them for their hurtful words, we try to help them recognize how their words make others feel and find ways to help them prevent being hurtful in the first place.

We have an interesting list of vocabulary words that aren't allowed in our house. For example, the word "actually" had to be removed from the accepted list in our household. That was our daughter's favorite word for a few months around age 10. It seemed like she'd follow up anyone else's statements with an "Actually…" {then insert her opinion about how they were wrong}. It was an odd step to take but banning "actually" is what helped her. It makes her pause and think before she utters a critical remark. Now, because she has to think before she shares her criticism, she doesn't end up making the mean statement most of the time. That's just one of those things that we handle differently because of the way their minds work.

Parent Growth Tips and Coaching Questions

What are some ways you parent with *goodness* and what are some ways you haven't tried but should consider? In your anger or frustration do you withhold goodness or the best of yourself? While discipline may require consequences, do you discipline in a way your child feels and believes hesed from you? (Reminder: Hesed is an attachment that indicates you are for someone's good, and they can rely on you to do what is good and right on their behalf out of goodness and loving kindness).

Parenting in Faithfulness

Simply put, the better I am at showing my children the value of following through on my word, the better they understand faithfulness. This isn't always easy with such a busy schedule, as I'm sure you can relate. But I've come to realize that there are some things money can't buy and when there are core memories involved (things such as championship sporting events or starring roles in theatre performances), showing up and being there is what's most important.

Beyond the big stuff, though, making sure that your "yes" is yes and your "no" is no is very important. The more your children can learn to trust in your faithfulness, the more they're going to be open to trusting God's faithfulness. If you have a habit of not showing up and keeping your word, how do you think they're perceiving God? It's easy to forget sometimes but we're not just parenting, we're also ministering to our kids on a daily basis. What they learn from and perceive in us is also how they're going to perceive God and Jesus.

Charity's Thoughts: We both feel strongly about making sure that your "yes" means yes and our "no" means no. This not only goes for setting boundaries and making rules clear for them (unlike the lyrics of the "Be Our Guest" song, the "grey stuff is" NOT "delicious," which isn't helpful when your children are black-and-white thinkers) but also for offering rewards and things they are looking forward to. Our children will remind us constantly of a good consequence that they are waiting for, but they are also paying attention to whether a negative consequence is actually going to happen or not. It's hard sometimes to stick to exactly what we said, but it's important for us to show them consistency.

Parent Growth Tips and Coaching Questions

What are some ways you parent with *faithfulness* and what are some ways you haven't tried but should consider? You are probably seeing a theme from the previous chapter that aligns with Dr. Wilder's materials. The fruit of the spirit works together in cultivating the four soils of joy, hesed, group identity, and healthy correction. Do you model faithfulness by keeping your word and following through?

Parenting in Gentleness

If we're being honest, you've probably noticed a theme in this chapter. It revolves around how the more I understand and lean into my own diagnosis of autism, the more I can understand and respond positively to my autistic children's behaviors. And honestly, it might not just be understanding myself better that's helped, but rather, understanding autism better. Once I learned about and experienced the challenges of living as an autistic in a world that's not designed for autistics, I had a greater appreciation for the things all autistics go through.

Much in the same way, when one understands the Cross and what it took to get there, many respond to the gospel with love and appreciation, out of respect and reverence for what Christ suffered. So too, I sympathize with and appreciate my children growing up in today's world. There is sensory overload everywhere, and, unlike me, they don't understand most of it. Knowing how much of a struggle I had in my own youth makes me want to be even more kind, tender, and mild-mannered with my children, because I know what they're going through. I always want them to know that I'm a safe place in the same way I know that the Lord is a safe place.

Charity's Thoughts: How many times have I said the words "be gentle" when my bigger children are around a baby or pet smaller than them? Probably not quite as many times as I've asked them to be safe, but it's pretty close. I can be gentle by remembering that what they think of as "gentle" is different than other children. Our kids' feelings are so strong! There is much debate over how autistic individuals either have 'no emotions' or 'feel emotions stronger than neurotypicals.' I don't think it's one way or the other. I think it's confusing because they show their feelings differently, so it's harder to gauge. What my kids respond to, and how they respond, will be different, just like no two children will react to the same thing in the same way. None of us do. The best practice is to be gentle and learn their tolerances and boundaries, instead of trying to conform them to what we think they should be.

Parent Growth Tips and Coaching Questions

What are some ways you parent with *gentleness* and what are some ways you haven't tried but should consider? Sometimes what may seem gentle to you may not be gentle to others. Are you open to feedback if you desire to work on gentleness?

Parenting in Self-Control

After losing a bunch of weight earlier in my life, I thought I was really good at self-control. To some degree I was. But having kids brought a new level of "patience-testing" that I'd never experienced. Don't get me wrong, I am a huge believer in *delayed gratification*, but I don't think children know what those words mean.

The increased challenges in my life meant I had to step up my own ability to self-regulate. I learned that if I was going to model what "good Christian living" meant, then I had to do it in my own life. Whether it's breath-work, prayer, meditation or just taking 5 minutes to calm yourself, paying attention to your own regulation makes all the difference in having the self-control you need to parent your children in the way they deserve.

Charity's Thoughts: One lesson I had to learn was that although I'm not neurodivergent, it doesn't mean I'm not dysregulated at times. There is one specific scenario that, 9 times out of 10, I just can't handle: when I'm cooking at the stove, chopping vegetables (including onions that make me cry) with a sharp knife, while two or three pots and pans are on the gas burners sizzling or boiling away, and the above-stove fan is venting while making its own loud noises....and in this moment one of the kids inevitably comes to ask me a question about something that has no urgency whatsoever or to complain about their sibling. It's been hard to keep my cool in this exact situation on more than one occasion. This helps me to see what challenges the kids have when they are feeling dysregulated. It's so hard to pull back in that moment. It's so hard to have self-control. As I work on it, they get to see that we're in this together, and others struggle, too.

Parent Growth Tips and Coaching Questions

What are some ways you parent with *self-control* and what are some ways you haven't tried but should consider? The book *Emotional Intelligence in Christ*[1] states that self-control is the anchor to all the other fruits of the spirit. If you struggle with self-control and regulation, we have made the point in a previous chapter that being intentional in pre-regulated is critical. Both parents need to be regulated and operate in self-control so that your parenting can more accurately reflect our loving, heavenly Father.

So, as I'm sure you've learned from reading this chapter, our family is not perfect. In fact, we're far from it. But that doesn't stop us from trying or from seeing the best in each other. Does it look different than we expected? Yes.

But has that difference led to experiences that we would never have had otherwise? Yes. And that's the story God's given us to co-author.

If you're struggling because one of your children is on the spectrum, or it's been suggested they are, then we'd love to connect. Or, if you're struggling with your own potential autism diagnosis, we'd love to connect as well.

What we're saying is that if you'd like to speak with us about what you've read today, or anything in general, please contact us at NeuroFam.

Chapter Eleven
Navigating The Additional Challenges and Maze of Race in Autism Diagnosis: Bias & Stigma in Diagnosis

BY DR. MARY H. JONES, PEDIATRICIAN, ASD CLINICAL SPECIALIST & LIFE COACH

When I finished my pediatric residency almost 20 years ago, I thought I had life all figured out. I was going to be an amazing pediatrician and start a family soon with my amazing boyfriend, who was also a doctor. I felt like this was the culmination of hard work and the grace of God. It was the perfect fairytale story for this black girl from the South. I had made my mama proud and had realized a lifelong dream of becoming the first doctor ever in my family. I indeed went on to get married, start a family, and begin a rewarding career in pediatric medicine.

As a pediatrician, I have had years of professional experience being the first line in helping to get children diagnosed with various simple and more complex health and other issues. This includes autism. Over the course of my career, I have seen a troubling difference in how race can affect how early some children are diagnosed with autism compared to others. And, how readily they and their families can access necessary services in the community and in schools. I can't say that I noticed this trend right away or even before midway through my almost 20-year career. Possibly this is because in residency I was in a large university environment where we really were very conscious of treating each patient the same. I'm sure there were missed cases of autism due to patient volume and human error. But in "real world" community pediatrics, I'm certain that the diagnosis disparity is large. Numerous studies show that black and Latinx children are diagnosed with autism at lower rates and later ages than white children. This has been shown to lead to later access to care and services. Such care and services are proven to be vital to lifelong success and quality of life for those with autism. It has long been known that access to early intervention before age three can and does make a substantial impact on the quality of life in children diagnosed with autism. The Autism and Developmental Disabilities Monitoring Network states that "By age 2, diagnosis by a professional can be very reliable." However, the average age at diagnosis in the US is about 5 years old.[1] Black children, however, are on average 5½ years old before they are diagnosed with autism.[2]

This delay, when combined with the fact that it takes black children 3 years from the time of voiced parental concern to an autism diagnosis, means a significant delay in services for these children. Also, many of these children are likely to have carried one or multiple other diagnoses before being diagnosed with autism—often incorrect diagnoses. In addition, black children and their families have known disparities in acquisition and quality of services once a diagnosis has been made. This means it could be years after diagnosis before they receive necessary and effective services.[3]

This is especially concerning because black children have a higher proportion of intellectual disability associated with autism.[3] A study in *DisabilityScoop* offered no clear explanation for why black children with autism are twice as likely as white kids to have intellectual disability; autism prevalence is largely consistent across racial groups. "Remarkably, among the African American children with autism in the new study, intellectual disability was not related to the factors that usually predict cognitive strengths and weaknesses," Constantino said. "Household income, the IQ levels of blood relatives and preterm birth often are linked to cognitive outcomes, but those factors did not explain the disproportionate burden of intellectual disability suffered by African American children with autism. There is an ethical imperative to determine whether leveling the playing field for the timing of diagnosis and the quality and quantity of developmental therapy might resolve this disparity."[4]

As we in the medical community have started to become more aware of these deficits in the care of black and other minority children, there has been a gradual positive shift in diagnosing black children with autism earlier. We still have a long way to go. The earlier the diagnosis, the more likely these children are to receive necessary services. Literally every minute counts. Delays in diagnosis and access to services affect these children's ability to live life to their fullest potential.

I have always been a fierce advocate for my patients and their families—especially those with children who have differences and unique challenges. Professionally I have seen the difficulties that children with autism and their families face. Moreover, about 4 years ago one of our children was diagnosed with autism, and I now am experiencing firsthand what the families I have served experience.

I have watched my black child experience some of the same disparities and delays as some of the patients I care for. My son was diagnosed at age 11. We had known something was different about him since he was about 2 or 3. In kindergarten, he was held back because he wasn't adapting "socially". He cried at school most days. The teachers thought giving him an extra year in kindergarten to mature would help him. We talked to his pediatrician and decided to let him repeat the grade. This seemed to take care of his social issues. He also did well on his schoolwork and didn't have any behavioral issues, so we were satisfied. Later he began to have difficulty in the classroom setting. His teacher told me that he would just sit in class and not do his work and not interact with the other students. They said that he seemed unable to focus and uninterested in doing his work. They even implied that he was lazy. This didn't add up to me because he had never had these issues before. He has always been very obedient to me and his father, teachers, and everyone else. But as a concerned parent, I scolded him and insisted that he do his work. It is difficult for me to write this even now. I feel this sense of guilt that I should have known what was going on with my child. After all, I am an "expert" on autism. I help diagnose and treat children for my job. And I couldn't help my own child. He was struggling and I didn't know why. We did eventually get his diagnosis, and what a relief that was!

Now that we knew what was going on with him, we could get him the support that he needed. For us, that wasn't as difficult as for most. My husband and I are both physicians. We not only had the means, but also the language and expertise to get our child what he needed. I don't know at what point during this whirlwind I began to see our story in the context of what my patients go through--especially my black and other underrepresented patients and their families. If this happened in my family, how much more likely is it to happen in theirs? I am determined to use my story and the stories of others to address this issue. First, I want to educate black parents and caregivers on how to advocate for their loved ones with autism. Of equal importance is educating those in positions to help these families. Those in the medical community and in the educational system need to be challenged to begin to understand the obstacles black and other underrepresented populations face in getting diagnosed. They should be taught how to recognize autism in these children and to see it through a culturally informed and culturally competent lens. They need to understand what black people and other minorities go through to get the diagnosis of autism and the services they need. This understanding is crucial to them becoming advocates for this population in order to provide them with equal access to services as white children have. One of the most crucial pieces to this education is to understand how autism is viewed in the black community, as well as the long-standing mistrust and suspicion we have for the medical establishment and educational system in this country. The Tuskegee Study of Untreated Syphilis in the Negro Male is a well-known and often pointed to reason for not trusting "white" medicine for black people. In this study, black men with known syphilis were told they were being treated for "bad blood" when many were actually not receiving treatment, even though penicillin was the known treatment for syphilis. This went on for 40 years, from 1932-1972[5]! This is probably the most famous example of how blacks were lied to and not given the standard of care by the medical community. The educational system has also been a place of racial prejudice and pain, from barring slaves from learning to read and write, to segregation of the school system. The effects of this discrimination can still be felt today. Is it any wonder that black families who note that something is different about their child are hesitant to seek help from these systems that have not been a friend to them in the past? And when we do, we still are not afforded the same level of care as white families.

Is it any wonder that black families who note that something is different about their child are hesitant to seek help from these systems that have not been a friend to them in the past?

Constantino and fellow researchers in *Pediatrics,* state that "variation in cognitive outcome was not explained by sociodemographic or familial factors that have been associated with variation in IQ, suggesting that excess ID *(intellectual disability)* in AA *(African American)* children with autism cannot straightforwardly be accounted for by these factors, or by over-classification of ID (which in and of itself would constitute a problematic disparity)."[4] A recent analysis of outcomes of young children receiving therapy based on applied behavior analysis demonstrated that greater intensity and duration of service were associated with clinically and statistically significant gains in cognitive capacity and executive skills.[6] An immediate public health and research priority is to explore the extent to which resolution of health disparities that compromise timely access to effective intervention can reduce deleterious effects on cognition that disproportionately accompany autism among AA youth.

The medical community and the education system are supposed to make it possible for every child with autism to thrive at their fullest potential no matter their race or socioeconomic status. Until everyone is united in this effort, it will be difficult to accomplish. The first step is the acknowledgement by the majority that there is a problem. Then we must all work together to close the gap for all children in this country by making the medical community and the educational system safe and welcoming spaces for people of all races.

My experience with autism does not stop with my career or as a parent of a child on the spectrum. About 4 years ago I began to suspect that my husband may be on the autism spectrum. In fact, my husband's diagnosis is what led to my child being diagnosed. We had been married almost 15 years at the time. To say that our marriage was challenging from the start doesn't begin to describe the situation. I was at my wit's end and by the time the diagnosis came, I felt like I was living in a nightmare from which I couldn't awake. I had been crying out to the Lord to give me answers as to why our marriage was so hard. And not just our marriage, but our lives in general.

> By the time the diagnosis came, I felt like I was living in a nightmare from which I couldn't awake.

We had been in counseling on and off throughout our whole marriage, mostly going to multiple Christian marriage counselors who all instructed us to do the same things: date more, pray together, have more sex, etc. We diligently tried to do the things we were told to do. But inevitably after a while they fell by the wayside because they weren't working. My husband would go back to focusing on his career as an emergency medicine physician and his "hobby of the moment." And I would throw myself into caring for our children and my work as well. We were living parallel lives. The children and I were on one path, and my husband was on his own. Sometimes, when his schedule permitted, he would spend a few hours with the kids or take me on a date. But mostly he was unavailable except for those short periods of time. He seemed to be content with this pattern. I was left to navigate life in a state of confusion, extreme loneliness, and pain. By the time I cried out to God to help me know what I wasn't seeing in our marriage, I was as desperate as I had ever been in my life. I was living in a constant state of misery. I was almost suicidal at times. I had begun to isolate myself from friends and family. When I tried to articulate what I was going through, no one would understand or believe me. On the surface, we seemed to have this amazing life: we were both successful in our careers, our kids were healthy and happy, and we were doing well financially. Inevitably, I would be chastised for not seeing how awesome my life was. I was made to feel like I was complaining and ungrateful. This led to me becoming more and more quiet and withdrawn until eventually I surrendered my voice altogether. I lost myself in the stress and pain of what I had been going through. Though I lacked the understanding or language for any of this, I finally got the revelation from the Holy Spirit that my husband was autistic. That's right, I got a literal audible revelation that my husband was autistic. It wasn't from all my years of training or working as a pediatrician. I asked God for the answer, and he provided it one particularly brutal evening as I sat on my couch licking my wounds after another circular argument with my husband. I just heard *"he's autistic"* in my head. When those words came into my mind, they immediately made sense. Even though I didn't really know any adult that I could think of with autism. I knew that the diagnosis fit. So, like a true scientist, I started reading and researching and became more and more convinced that I had the answer. However, this only led to more questions. How had my husband not known this before now? What would this mean for our marriage? What about our children? What were the next steps from here? Could anything "fix" him or make him normal? Would he believe me when I told him what I thought?

I got the answer to the last question quickly. When I brought my suspicions that he might be autistic to him, he looked at me like I was off my rocker. He was not willing to consider that this diagnosis could even possibly describe some of his differences. I was convinced that autism was at least part of the reason for our difficulties in communication and marriage. So instead of letting my husband's opposition to the diagnosis deter me, I continued to research autism in adults. The more I learned, the more I was convinced that my husband was autistic. My brilliant, high achieving husband was on the autism spectrum. However, this assurance gave me far more questions than it answered.

My biggest question to start was, how do I get my husband to at least consider that he could be autistic? And where do we go from there? I knew where to start with a child. But my husband was 46 at the time! He obviously had never had any services because he was undiagnosed. What do adults on the spectrum need? Was there even anything to be done? How and where could we find help for my husband? If he truly had autism, what would this mean for our marriage and family? I also wanted to know how this was missed for 46 years and how I could not have seen it while we were dating or in 15 years of marriage. My mind was flooded with questions for a few weeks. Even though I was overwhelmed I was certain that I was on the right track. I just kept praying and asking the Lord to show me the path to take for answers, and He was faithful to do so. One evening I was again searching for resources online and I found a website for Dr. Stephanie Holmes. It said that she was a counselor who specialized in neurodiverse marriages. I had never heard that term before and had no idea what it meant. I was intrigued so I clicked the link. This was the first time I began to think that maybe I wasn't crazy, an unreasonable wife, or possessing some personality disorder. It was also the first time in a long time that I began to feel that I wasn't alone. There was language for what I was going through and possibly some help for me and my husband. So, I contacted Dr. Stephanie. This was the beginning of my healing and finding my voice again. For this I will be forever grateful. I know that it was the Holy Spirit who led me to Dr. Stephanie. A verse that has been a great comfort to me is Psalm 40:2, *"He lifted me out of the pit of despair, out of the mud and mire. He set my feet on solid ground and steadied me as I walked along"* (NLT).[7]

This is what I felt like when I was able to talk to Dr. Stephanie and see the understanding in her eyes and hear it in her voice. This was the first time I had felt validated, seen, and heard by another human being about what was happening to me in my marriage. It was like a breath of fresh air. I felt like God had personally put us together to let me know that I was not alone and that He saw me. I am by no means saying that all was rectified after this. It was just the opposite, as everything in my marriage seemed to get worse and become more difficult. But now I had an ally and was being given the tools to see and understand how to begin to navigate this new path that I found myself on. I can't say it was the path that "we" found ourselves on because my husband was not on board with the diagnosis or working with a counselor who specialized in autism in marriage. Eventually though he agreed to give it a try. We had been to plenty of Christian marriage counselors over the years. Most of the time my husband, who I now know was extremely good at masking and keeping up his image, would win them over. I would end up being portrayed as the "angry black woman" by him and would end up being blamed for the issues we were having. We would then be told to do the "date nights and more sex" regimen, and that I would need to be a more submissive wife. Back at home, things would change for maybe a couple of weeks. Then my husband went right back to his patterns of focusing on his career and special interests 90% of the time and gaslighting me when I would bring up the fact that the children and I were suffering. I became very angry, resentful, and manipulative as a coping strategy for not getting my needs acknowledged or met. Of course, I didn't have this language for what was going on then. So, I convinced myself that *I* was ungrateful and hard to please, and that my husband *really was* what he presented to everyone outside of our home: a devoted, hard-working man who lived for his family. The trouble with this version of reality was that I was the one who was always at fault. I was the one who needed to change. There was something wrong with *me*. So, I was constantly trying to "fix" myself, to make myself into this perfect, biblical wife that would be worthy of the "perfect man" that others believed my husband to be... in fact, as *he* thought he was. He told me on more than one occasion that I had "won the husband lottery." These words excoriated and demoralized my soul. I know that he didn't mean the phrase to be harmful, but he made me feel so unworthy and flawed. I secretly felt that I could never deserve him, and I despised myself for it. I cannot tell you how damaging this was then, and in some ways has continued to be even now, despite all of the therapy I have done. I have experienced a great deal of healing and freedom over the last 5 years. And I am still working on becoming the best version of myself every day. I'm not trying to portray my husband as a monster, but I want to be as real and honest with you, the reader, as I can be. I promised the Lord that if He would help me, I would use my story as a testimony to help as many others as possible. That is why I am telling a part of my family's story in this book. I am passionate about showing women who find themselves in the same position that there is freedom available. It will probably be hard and messy. It will probably become worse in some ways before it gets better. But the freedom and healing are there to be had! You are strong enough to do what you need to do for yourself. It may seem daunting and impossible at times, but there is a way! I am a living witness to that. My story did get worse before it got better. That is a topic for another book though. I will say that I still don't regret finding out about my husband's autism diagnosis. Being able to view the past, present, and future through this lens has helped me to make many decisions for the safety of myself and my children which I might not have been as sure about otherwise. My husband has since come to fully accept his autism diagnosis (about 4 years after it was made). He is now on his own healing journey. We are also continuing to work to heal and repair our marriage while healing ourselves. This healing has also begun an ongoing grieving process for what I thought our marriage was and what I now know it will never be. I am coming to terms with what I can expect as I navigate living in a neurodiverse marriage and family. While this is not what I envisioned my life would be almost 20 years into marriage, I know that God is faithful and there are no surprises for Him. I also know that He has good plans for me, my husband, our children, and our family. I trust Him wholeheartedly.

> *"For I know the plans I have for you," says the Lord. "They are plans for good and not disaster, to give you a future and a hope" (Jeremiah 29:11, NLT)[7]*

Dr. Mary Jones is a life coach and works to help people of color navigate the maze of an autism diagnosis.

Dr. Holmes' Interviews & Unmasking Racism in the Autism Diagnosis

For the research survey that formed the research basis of this book on neuro-diverse marriage, Dan and I (Dr. Stephanie) advertised the research far and wide on social media and through providers who work in this field. We had over 300 unique participants and out of the data less than 5% of the individuals identified as black/African American.

As we went deeper into research, I had one couple of color who were able to be interviewed to represent the ND population's minority, people of color. It was these quotes from these two respondents that made me stop and pause and ask Nicole Mar, a woman of color, her thoughts on joining me in writing about autism and race for a blog post.

Respondent's Responses to: *What do you want to share about your experience with autism and race or autism and neurodiversity?*

Interviewee 1 *(AS/ND African American Husband):*

Neurotypical behavior in the black community is a necessity because there's a lot of trauma. Knowing what I know now about genograms and the generational impact, I, personally, am only four generations removed from slavery.

I am imagining my great, great, great grandmother, born into slavery, who was an infant when slavery ended. The values she learned as a result of her parents' upbringing were passed all the way down to me. Now, I'm trying to deal with my trauma and not pass on that trauma to my kids. For example, there's a huge stigma about how we have to be two or three times better than our non-minority counterparts. This adds a lot of pressure, competition, and unwillingness to support each other.

With that being said, neurotypical behavior and mental health are not spoken of because that pushes people a step back from everyone else. That's where a lot of the avoidance and denial comes from. It also makes Black people avoid soft emotions. Showing that means the person has an issue — unlike our non-minority counterparts.

Hopefully, these facts bring some awareness to minority neurodiverse couples or neuro-diverse individuals out there to help them live with neurodiversity.

Interviewee 2 *(NT/NA African American Wife):*

There is not a lot of support for neurodiversity, especially with blacks in the black community. We have not told anyone about my husband's diagnosis yet, and it's not out of shame, it's really because we just need time to process it, and I don't want well-intentioned family trying to diagnose my children and point to them instead of letting us do our job as parents and go through testing.

It can be isolating, and there isn't a lot of information out there about neurodiversity in the Black community, obviously. I think we found our neurodiverse coach through a search online. Thankfully, we lived in the same state, and we were able to reach out and visit.

Unmasking Racism in Autism (By Nicole Mar)[8]

The following is taken from a blog collaboration by *Nicole Mar* (pseudonym), NT/NA woman of color.

Your child has autism: It is a statement that sends shock waves of fear into the minds of many parents.

- Will my child be treated kindly?
- Will my child receive a good education?
- Will my child have a bright, adult future?

While much has been done to quell the fear around autism and eliminate the idea that it needs to be cured, some affected families are still outliers, silently on the sidelines, choosing not to enter the conversation. Why? Because as a marginalized people group who have been prone to degrading isolation and stereotypes, they can't risk another strike against them. Who are these people, you ask? African Americans.

I can imagine you might be rolling your eyes—yet another writer arguing that Blacks are mistreated, and that systemic racism is a source of great pain. Blah blah blah. Here is the reality: it's the absolute truth.

As true as it was during the days of slavery, it remains true in 2024.

Black people, and, in particular, Black males, are seen as a source of imminent danger. They are not to be trusted. They are not to be extended grace, opportunities, favor, respect, or dignity. So, when this visible identification is combined with the invisible condition of autism—which impacts one's ability to communicate—silence about the condition or symptoms is often the preferred method of choice. For those with low-support needs, also known as Level 1 autism, the go-to method is to blend in, deny differences, refuse academic and/or employer support, and stay away from doctors.

So, when this visible identification is combined with the invisible condition of autism—which impacts one's ability to communicate—silence about the condition or symptoms is often the preferred method of choice. For those with low-support needs, also known as Level 1 autism, this means that Black male children in school who have less noticeable signs of autism will often slip through the proverbial cracks since their parents, in an effort to keep them safe, will not reach out for support. After all, this heightens their risk of child protective services removing the child. These parents will not share that a child has meltdowns at home. This, after all, increases the likelihood of the child being suspended, or, worse, expelled. The same holds true for adult men with autism signs and symptoms. They will not seek accommodations at work because this increases their risk of being fired since employers may seek out opportunities to catch them making errors or will ostracize and belittle them right out of their jobs.

If the desire is for systematized, fair treatment for all, then leaders within education, the medical field, government, prison systems, housing, and pharmacy will need to accept that they are likely showing overt racism against Black people, or they will have to admit that there is a chance they are doing it unknowingly. Humans who sit in board rooms making policies and exacting rules of law will need to humble themselves, acknowledge an American history fraught with injustice, and take measures to intentionally act differently, question their assumptions, dig into their motives, and seek a different path.

If that would happen, Black people would be able to freely share their challenges. They would be able to move in this country, their cities, their neighborhoods, their schools, and workplaces with a sense of safety. They would lay down the heavy and burdensome mask of pretense and access the resources they so richly deserve. Parents would not feel forced to threaten their sons into perfect behavior in order to keep them safe from dangerous school leaders. Black people, especially those twice exceptional—males with autism—need the opportunities that would be afforded to them if only they were treated with kindness and fairness. It would make our country a better place. It would make us, as individuals, better people. We have recently found this resource in my search for support for the black/African American community. Look up: Autism in Black.

 Section 3

When Things Do Not Go as Planned

Introduction
What Happened to My Happily Ever After?
REV. DR. STEPHANIE C. HOLMES

Writing the last section of this book was challenging, as all contributing authors, including myself, advocate for covenant marriage within Christianity. Yet, we recognize that religious doctrine, when misapplied in marriage, can lead to abuse. This section delves into the complexities of neurodiverse Christian marriages, highlighting the unique communication challenges and potential for misinterpretation of roles and rules by the neurodivergent spouse. Notably, strict adherence to certain beliefs, such as divorce being permissible only in cases of adultery, can trap individuals in abusive marriages. My mentor, Leslie Vernick, emphasizes valuing marriage without compromising individual safety and sanity. This reflects the principle that marriage should mirror Christ's sacrificial love, not harbor abuse or trauma. In this next section, we will explore how religious rules and autism intersect in marriage, leading to misapplications that result in abuse. Rev. Iris Knapp will share stories and discuss types of abuse experienced by women who have left their neurodivergent spouses due to unaddressed and persistent neglect, trauma, or abuse.

We of course want to state that most Christian men on the spectrum do not hold to abusive rules and roles in their interpretation of religious truth; however, when there are years and sometimes decades of undiagnosed autism, unintentional abuse, unchecked dysregulation, or emotional neglect, these all lead to trauma and unhealthy dynamics in the relationship. In an interview with David Glick, EdM, LCSW, who identifies as on the spectrum, he stated that those on the spectrum can at times weaponize their dysregulation or use their autism diagnosis as an excuse or pass to behave the way they want because the unhealthy strategy works.[1] He continued to say if the dysregulated autistic spouse uses the dysregulation to get out of tasks or finds this strategy works, they will continue to use whatever strategy has been working.

The first two sections of this book have outlined what autism is and is not and given hope that with proper diagnosis, support, and each spouse taking responsibility for their role in the marital cycle be it abuse or codependency or co-occurring trauma, marital satisfaction can be found in a neurodiverse Christian marriage. However, no matter how strong someone is or how good their boundaries are, boundaries and guidelines do not change people. A desire to be transformed into Christ's likeness, motivation to change, humility and teachability are the key ingredients to a God-honoring, healthy marriage.[2]

These chapters will focus on how autism and faith can impact a neurodiverse marriage. We want to clarify that all the authors of this book understand that both neurodivergent and neurotypical spouses can develop patterns of abusive behaviors. That said, Chapter 13 will contain narratives that exemplify the types of abuse that can occur when the husband is on the spectrum and his religious or traditional beliefs are used as a license for abusive behaviors. We hope this serves to help illuminate the need for greater understanding and support for any abused spouse in a neurodiverse marriage.

Chapter Twelve

Escaping the Maze of Religion & Roles and Weaponized Scripture

BY REV. DR. STEPHANIE C. HOLMES & REV. DAN HOLMES, MS

I n our discussion of neurodiverse (ND) couples, we have yet to consider the influence of faith or religious beliefs. It's crucial to acknowledge that Christian couples do not uniformly interpret Scripture, leading to the diversity of denominations; faith can either be a guiding force in navigating ND relationships or a source of barriers and complications if rigid or inflexible interpretations of biblical texts are applied. This chapter aims to explore cognitive inflexibility and its impact on couples, along with common Scriptures that underpin what is often referred to as marriage theology. We will also examine how well-intentioned but untrained Christian marriage helpers (clergy, coaches, counselors, and chaplains) can inadvertently cause harm and enable abusive behaviors. This chapter does not delve into the impact of cultural beliefs on gender roles in ND relationships, but readers may infer how these beliefs might exacerbate complexities for women in such couples.

Reviewing the *DSM-5*'s criteria for autism spectrum disorder (ASD), we find that restricted or passionate interests, cognitive inflexibility, and a preference for rules and consistency are common traits.[1] Hollander and Ferretti began their 2023 research article[2] by highlighting the public health implications of inflexible thinking, noting its adverse effects on adaptability in an ever-changing world, along with the resulting challenges in the workplace and relationships. They reference American historian Daniel J. Boornstin's observation: "The greatest obstacle to discovery is not ignorance- it is the illusion of knowledge." We will revisit the concepts of knowledge and perceived knowledge later.

Autism is not the only diagnosis characterized by struggles with inflexible thinking. Such cognitive rigidity can also be a feature of other diagnoses, complicating the marital dynamics for ND couples where the non-autistic spouse might have one of these conditions. Hollander has noted that, in addition to ASD, conditions like obsessive-compulsive disorder (OCD), obsessive-compulsive personality disorder (OCPD), anorexia, body dysmorphic disorder, problematic internet use, as well as anxiety, and depressive disorders all exhibit cognitive inflexibility. Hollander and Ferretti define cognitive inflexibility or rigid thinking as an executive function issue. This issue manifests as a persistent need for sameness, adherence to rituals or patterns of behavior, and a tendency to be entrenched in one's own thoughts, beliefs, and perceptions of reality, often at the expense of considering others' perspectives. This concept ties in with the observation that people with ASD struggle with the theory of mind (ToM). ToM refers to the ability or challenge to understand the intentions and thoughts of others and recognize that others may have perspectives and thoughts different from one's own. Challenges in ToM include difficulties in appreciating these differences in viewpoints and intentions.[3,4]

Autism researcher, Dr. Peter Vermeulen stated that our brains are predictive brains, meaning that our brains are not simply passive in receiving information but an active processor which is seeking to predict what will happen so we can better plan and react. He argues that the "brain does not like surprises and wants to anticipate what will happen to the maximum possible extent."[5] Vermeulen's research shows that the autistic brain's capacity is quite different and may have what he refers to as predictive coding errors, especially in relational or social contexts. What might some of these differences in predictive coding be, according to Dr. Vermeulen and other researchers?

1. Those on the autism spectrum may pay attention to different details than non-autistic individuals. (Dr. Tony Attwood and Michelle Garnette note the positive in this feature that those on the spectrum can think creatively and be out-of-the-box problem-solvers.[5])

2. Those on the spectrum may find it difficult to generalize new information or new learning to broader contexts and social contexts.

3. They may struggle in learning information that is not very context-dependent, as the autistic brain needs highly specific contexts.

4. Prediction errors in the autistic brain can impair the ability to adapt quickly in an ever-changing socio-relational and emotional world.

5. Precision weighting in autism "could be aberrant in several ways, each resulting in context-insensitive perceptions and actions."[6]

6. "The process of predicting the world and dealing with prediction errors is much less context-sensitive in people with autism than in people without autism."[6]

7. "The models used by the autistic brain to predict the world are absolute and therefore, insufficiently contextual."[6]

When Dr. Vermeulen was interviewed on our podcast about the predictive brain and predictive brain errors, he listed many jobs or career contexts that those on the spectrum will excel because of how they see the world and notice various details. At the same time, he noted those prediction errors can be most problematic in the sphere of social navigation since in an open system (such as predicting the behaviors and intentions of others) there is no one fixed method, rule, algorithm, formula, or law to predict people's behaviors or feelings, which requires context-sensitive guessing and assumptions.

At this point, you may be wondering what the connection to faith, autism, and marriage is. Faith is very personal and how one lives and acts upon faith is also very personal. It is founded on one's values and belief system. Understanding such differences in neurodiverse and neurotypical processing and predicting is crucial for both the ND Christian couple (NDCC) and those trying to support or help them.

Another recent study unpacked the ways cognitive rigidity can be problematic when an ASD person's interest becomes increasingly inflexible or fixed. This often results in the need for sameness and predictability, or a *rule* to follow. An intolerance for ambiguities plus black-and-white thinking can present as *literalism*, which can be problematic for any relationship. The addition of a religious tradition with prescribed rules and roles only increases the complexities and issues for NDCCs. In the study, literalism was defined as "observed bias toward understanding metaphors, idiomatic expressions, implications, irony and other figurative language in a literal way."[7]

NDCCs represent a specific subset of neurodiverse relationships. To understand them better, let's examine the AS/ND profile as outlined in both the *DSM-IV*[8] and *DSM-*

5,[1] supplemented by clinical research. Over the years, the ASD profile has broadened to include several possible characteristics: challenges in theory of mind, social-pragmatic language differences in communication, emotional dysregulation, a need for predictability or sameness, restrictive or passionate interests, a preference for solitary time to decompress, hypersensitivity to criticism or perceived criticism (anything not seen as appreciation or gratitude), fear of making mistakes or failing, work-life balance struggles, difficulty applying new learning in broader contexts, lack of emotional support or reciprocity with a life partner, inadequate compassionate care, avoidance of conflict or disagreement, and specific sensory needs or aversions[2,6,7,9,10,11,12,13,14,15,16,17]

It's important to note that communication dynamics can vary between mixed neurotype marriages (involving one neurodivergent and one neurotypical partner) and marriages where both partners are neurodivergent. A 2022 study[18] found that communication between autistic individuals was as effective as that between non-autistic individuals most of the time. However, the most significant differences in social-pragmatic language occur in mixed neurotype communication (between ND/AS and NT/NA).

It has been a popularly held opinion by researchers (and online comments made in anecdotal stories or blog posts) that those on the spectrum are analytical and logical, and so, are more likely to not believe in God or to not have the capacity to relate to a personal God.[15,18,19] This simply is not true. Over 85% of those who responded to our survey noted they had a strong belief or faith, and all but a few shared that faith was in some tradition of Christianity.

One study noted that the more autistic traits a person had, the more likely they were to be atheistic or agnostic than the general population.[19] Another study reported that there is much still to learn about faith and how it is expressed in any person with developmental disabilities and differences.[20] A still later study contended that research had not considered the lived experiences of those on the autism spectrum and how they experience faith or religion.[21]

Consider the implications for a marriage if theology, marriage doctrine, and societal roles for men and women are interpreted through the lens of cognitive inflexibility and black-and-white thinking. What if a person believes that rigid adherence to daily Scripture reading or other spiritual activities are essential for themselves and their family? What are the consequences when suggestions by Christian self-help and marriage books – designed for more cognitively flexible neurotypical (NT/NA) marriages – are misappropriated when applied to neurodiverse relationships? I (Dr. Stephanie) have these critical questions in a study I published in 2023.[15] While other research has already found that non-autistic women in ND relationships experience physical and psychological abuse at higher rates than those in NT-to-NT relationships,[9] they did not consider the influence of faith and spiritual abuse. While laws exist against domestic violence, often counseling professionals or clergy do not take the psychological, emotional and spiritual abuse prevalent in ND relationships as seriously. Yet, such abuse can have more severe and damaging effects on individuals and relationships than physical abuse.[9,22,23,24] As a Christian counselor with over 25 years of experience, I (Dr. Stephanie) have observed that the Christian church often does not treat abuse with the gravity it deserves. When Christian marriage helpers cite "God hates divorce" (which is a mistranslation of Malachi 2:16),[25] and the legalistic teaching that adultery is the only valid ground for divorce, they effectively manipulate and guilt-trip women into staying in abusive relationships.

A 2017 study interviewed 29 neurotypical (NT/NA) partners and discovered they experience heightened distress and trauma in their daily lives.[26] This distress stems from unmet emotional and relational needs, coupled with unintentional yet harmful behaviors such as explosive anger outbursts, harsh discipline, child abuse, withholding sex or physical touch, dismissing or demeaning needs, and casting blame for not meeting the needs of their autistic partner. Additionally, the study found that the absence of a diagnosis, denial of a diagnosis, refusal to engage with an autism-trained therapist, and the expectation for the NT/NA spouse to accommodate the autistic partner's needs led to significant distress for the NT/NA spouse.[26] The scarcity of professionals trained to support ND adults and ND marriages, particularly Christian ND couples, exacerbates these issues.

A recent case study[27] emphasizes not just the shortage of qualified professionals but also a lack of understanding of the cultural nuances essential for effectively working with ND individuals and their marriages. This research did not specifically address the nuances of Christian faith and beliefs, which can intensify abuse, including spiritual or religious abuse. One study defines *religious abuse* as misconduct by a religious leader or organization, encompassing verbal, physical, social, psychological, economic, cognitive, religious, or spiritual abuse, exploiting God-given power to take advantage of another.[28] They define *spiritual abuse* as denying "one's most precious pillar doctrines of Protestant Christianity – namely the priesthood of all believers,"[28] which affirms an individual's ability and right to discern God's Word. However, when examining the following verses (which are often used to formulate marriage theology and doctrine), it becomes evident how these can be misinterpreted and lead to spiritual, emotional, and psychological abuse, especially towards women in ND relationships, whether they are autistic or non-autistic.

Core Verses on Marriage and Family:

Genesis 2:18 (NIV): *"The Lord God said, 'It is not good for the man to be alone. I will make a helper suitable for him'."*

Genesis 2:16-18 (NIV): *"To the woman he said, 'I will make your pains in childbearing very severe with painful labor you will give birth to children. Your desires will be for your husband, and he will rule over you. To Adam he said, 'Because you listened to your wife and ate the fruit from the tree about which I commanded you not to eat from it, cursed is the ground because of you; and through painful toil you will eat from it all the days of your life'."*

Proverbs 13:24 (NKJV): *"He who spares his rod hates his son, But he who loves him disciplines him promptly."*

Proverbs 13:24 (KJV): *"He that spareth his rod hateth his son"*

Malachi 2:16 (KJV): *"For the Lord God of Israel says that he hates divorce, for it covers one's garment with violence."*

Matthew 18:21-22 (NIV): *"Then Peter said, 'Lord, how many times shall I forgive my brother or sister who sins against me? Up to seven times?' Jesus answered, 'I tell you, not seven times, but seventy times seven'."*

Matthew 19: 4-9 (KJV): *"And he [Jesus] answered them, 'Have ye not read, that which he made them at the beginning made them male and female'; and said, 'For this cause shall a man leave father and mother, and shall cleave to his wife: and they twain shall be one flesh? Wherefore they are no more twain, but one flesh. What therefore God hath joined together, let no man put asunder'. They said unto him, 'Why did Moses then command to giving a writing a divorcement and to put her away? He saith unto them, 'Moses because of the hardness of your hearts suffered you to put away your wives; but from the beginning it was not so. And I say unto you whosoever shall put away his wife, except it be for fornication [adultery or sexual sins], and shall marry another, committeth adultery; and whoever marrieth her which is put away doth also commit adultery'."*

I Corinthians 7: 3-5 (NIV): *"The husband should fulfill his marital duty to his wife, and likewise the wife to her husband. The wife does not have authority over her own body but yields it to her husband. In the same way, the husband does not have authority over his own body but* *yields it to his wife. Do not deprive each other perhaps by mutual consent and for a time, so that you may devote yourself to prayer. Then come together again so that Satan will not tempt you because of your lack of self-control."*

Colossians 3:18-20 (NIV): *"Wives submit yourselves to your husbands, as is fitting in the Lord. Husbands, love your wives and do not be harsh with them. Children obey your parents in everything, for this pleases the Lord."*

Ephesians 5:22-26 (KJV): *Wives, submit yourselves unto your own husbands, as unto the Lord. For the husband is the head of the wife, even as Christ is the head of the church: and he is the savior of the body. Therefore, as the church is subject unto Christ, so let the wives be to their own husbands in everything. Husbands love your wives, even as Christ also loved the church, and gave himself for it; that he might sanctify and cleanse it with the washing of water by the word.*

I Timothy 2: 9-15 (KJV): *"In like manner also, that women adorn themselves in modest apparel, with shamefacedness and sobriety; not with braided hair, or gold, or pearls, or costly array; But (which becometh women professing godliness) with good works. Let the woman learn in silence with all subjection. But I suffer not a woman to teach, nor to usurp authority over the man, but to be in silence. For Adam was first formed, then Eve. And Adam was not deceived, but the woman being deceived was in the transgression. Notwithstanding, she shall be saved in childbearing, if they continue in faith and charity and holiness with sobriety.*

I Peter 3: 1-7 (NIV): *"Wives, in the same way, submit yourselves to your own husbands so that, if any of them do not believe in the word, they may be won over without words by the behavior of their wives when they see the purity and reverence of your lives. Your beauty should not come from outward adornment, such as elaborate hairstyles and the wearing of gold jewelry and fine clothes. Rather, it should be that of your inner self, the unfading beauty of a gentle and quiet spirit, which is of great worth in God's sight. For this is the way the holy women of the past who put their hope in God used to adorn themselves. They submitted to their own husbands [KJV being in subjection unto their own husband]: Like Sara, who obeyed Abraham and called him her lord. You are her daughters if you do what is right and do not give way to fear. Husbands, in the same way be considerate as you live with your wives and treat them with respect as the weaker partner and as heirs with you in the gracious gift of life, so that nothing will hinder your prayers."*

Now that you've seen these verses, can you see how applying them in narrow, black-and-white thinking without context and without filtering in other Scripture could be problematic for women in a neurodiverse Christian marriage? The American Association of Christian Counselors (AACC) published a book for Christian leaders and pastors which was written by Christian professionals who had expertise in various fields. The book was meant to help these leaders understand the issues Christians face in getting competent (and faith-positive) mental health and relational care.[29] One author stated that, in general, people of faith tend to feel more ashamed or guilty about mental or relational health issues and may not risk sharing their struggles or seeking help[30]; many Christians have reported that their pastors or congregants do not believe in "labeling" with a diagnosis, and even preach against psychiatric issues.[29] Because Malachi 2:16 is mistranslated, misused and preached out of context,[25,30] many Christians may stay in abusive marriages out of fear of rejection or persecution by their faith community. Many Christian wives have been taught that submission is submission to their husbands at any cost.[24,25,32] As a researcher, I (Dr. Stephanie) contributed to that AACC manual on the topic of autism, and I shared from personal and client experiences that when pastors spiritualize or dismiss concerns about autism or ADHD, it can lead to the ND person, couple or family experiencing isolation and misunderstanding in their faith communities.[33]

As mentioned earlier, while previous studies have highlighted psychological and emotional abuse in ND marriages, in NDCCs there is also the risk of spiritual abuse. In 2021, three Christian researchers conducted a study involving 20,000 Christian women, to examine harmful and abusive themes prevalent in popular Christian self-help marriage books.[34] These themes included notions such as: sex is primarily for men; a wife is to blame for her husband's pornography use (due to his sexual dissatisfaction or her unattractive appearance); wives are expected to perform sexual favors (sometimes specified as thrice weekly); there is no such thing as "marital rape"; and the belief that married women cannot refuse sex.

In their 2023 review of various Christian marriage resources (which included tweets, sermons, and blogs), Sheila Gregoire identified recurring themes such as: husbands have the final say in disagreements; it is necessary to maintain a hierarchical chain of authority; enduring abuse or suffering is a part of marriage; verbal abuse is tolerable if there is no physical harm; and wives were advised against seeking external help without their husband's consent.[34] Their research also revealed messages communicated in Christian teachings, such as: women are expected to remain silent; women should confine their work to the home; women should dress responsibly so as not to inflame a man's lust; and women should be excluded from leadership roles in the church setting.[34]

Christian self-help books, often based on personal narratives or doctrinal beliefs, are frequently regarded as gospel truth and used in various church settings, reinforcing potentially negative or harmful messages. My (Dr. Stephanie's) therapeutic experiences with Christian women, whether in neurotypical (NA/NT) or ND relationships, often reveal an emphasis on being a 'godly wife' and having a 'good Christian marriage.' These women perceive that responsibility for the success of the marriage lies with them, and that a successful marriage is seen as a reflection of their faith and spirituality. When Christian literature and sermons advocate submission at all costs and downplay concerns about abuse or neglect, it becomes particularly problematic for women in NDCCs who are seeking appropriate help.

Christian self-help books, often based on personal narratives or doctrinal beliefs, are frequently regarded as gospel truth and used in various church settings, reinforcing potentially negative or harmful messages.

Personal Story from an NT/NA Christian wife: *My Asperger's husband took very seriously washing his wife with the Word. He first required hours of uninterrupted time to read and study his Bible and the children and I were not to disrupt him, even though I homeschooled, and he worked from home the house was to be quiet. He was not to be asked to do anything to help with the home or with the children, and in washing us with the Word, this meant sitting us down almost daily and being told how we failed or sinned using Scripture against us. We were not to point out any of his mistakes or sins as he is the head of the household.*

(This spouse would eventually receive a PTSD diagnosis from the ongoing stress in her marriage.)

Personal Story from an NT/NA Christian wife: *My husband required sex almost nightly, even when I was on my period. He said that the verse in Corinthians said we must both agree not to have sex, and he is fine with having sex when I am on my period. If I had a baby or was recovering from surgery, he required a doctor's note stating that I was physically unable to have sex and for how long.*

Personal Story from an NT Christian wife: If my husband does something that hurts me or I tell him something he did was abusive to me or harsh to the children, he does not apologize – he reminds me that I need to forgive him 70 times 7.

Within the context of ND Christian marriages, marriage doctrine can be taken out of context. But what about Christian marriage helpers and clergy and their role in the neuro-diverse Christian marriage? Have schools and educators who train marriage therapists and diagnosing clinicians updated their curriculum to provide knowledge about neurodiversity? Or have seminaries begun to train their future pastors with the knowledge of autism in adulthood and how to help them and their future marriage partners?

Why are pastors included with counselors and clinicians and counted among those who need to update their knowledge and skill set? Current research verifies that Christian couples will typically first seek pastoral or ministerial support for marriage issues before contacting a licensed professional counselor.[31] The late Rev. H. B. London is quoted in *The Struggle is Real.*[31]

> *Bible schools and seminaries do a good job of teaching us hermeneutics, exegetics, and homiletics. Practical ministry to hurting people and relationships are rarely, if ever, addressed. There have always been people with mental and relational health problems in the church historically. We just haven't been properly trained and equipped to know how to minister effectively to their needs.*

It seems plausible to assume seminaries and pastoral counselors are also untrained in autism based on the above statement. The AACC (which is the world's largest Christian counseling organization), put out a call-to-action exhorting Christians, churches, clergy, and those who care for hurting people and relationships to be better informed about mental health issues and complex relationship issues.31 To this we would add that there needs to be a call-to-action to understand adult autism and ND marriage.

Few academic peer-reviewed studies exist that examine issues surrounding adult ASD adults in general, and even fewer examine issues that may arise in ASD and romantic relationships [9,15,35]; however, none have been found that examine ASD and marriage when the couple also holds to the Christian faith. I hope to have painted a clear picture that ND couples have complex issues. The many facets of undiagnosed individuals, untrained clinicians and clergy, and unintentional abuse create a labyrinth of challenges for NDCCs. (What these couples want Christian coaches, clinicians, chaplains, and clergy to know about working with them could be a chapter unto itself.) After the following section, where Dan adds his hindsight learning and insights, you will read more stories from NT/NA wives and their experience in ND Christian marriage. These will witness the marital advice given them by untrained and ignorant individuals.

Going back to our earlier quote, "The greatest obstacle to discovery is not ignorance - *it is the illusion of knowledge….*" Ignorance *can* be cured with education, insight, and humility; however, the belief or perception that one already possesses knowledge and does need additional insight or education can be far more detrimental than ignorance alone.

Expectations from Some Rigid Christian AS/ND Husbands

When a couple has been in duress and long periods of negative cycles, especially when the neurotypical (NA/NT) wife has distanced herself by moving out of the bedroom or separating into another space, an autistic/neurodivergent (AS/ND) Christian husband with strict gender role beliefs may react with anger. Rather than recognizing her actions as a response to his neglectful or abusive behavior, he might frame it as causing *him* harm or emotional distress, positioning himself as the victim in the marriage. According to the Asperger/Autism Network's (AANE) Neurology Matters in Couples: Training 101 material, individuals on the spectrum often strive for fairness or equal responsibility, without fully grasping the consequences of their actions. The course explains, "Fairness and equality are two concepts that can cause issues in ND couples. Many partners with AS profiles are sensitive to feeling that things are not fair, particularly if they engage in all-or-nothing thinking. Helping them understand that fair and equal aren't always synonymous, and sometimes achieving fairness requires unequal measures, is crucial."[36] The course also highlights that men on the spectrum might misconstrue a boundary as retaliatory, rather than a healthy limit, and may react reciprocally. In my (Dr. Stephanie's) recently published qualitative study,[15] many men interviewed did not believe that boundaries were biblically permissible within marriage.

When interviewing men rigid in their scriptural and gender role views, either in coaching sessions or for research, strict fundamentalist beliefs emerged among them. These included the idea that the man is the head (authority) and the woman should obey even in disagreement, the belief that the wife's role is in domestic and childcare duties, expectations of frequent sexual relations to satisfy the husband's needs, a policy of non-interference (by the wife) in the husband's discipline of children, discouragement of the wife's outside employment if it hinders domestic responsibilities, a prohibition of marital boundaries, and the husband's exemption from chores and accountability for his commitments. It is essential to recognize that not all Christian AS/ND men subscribe to such authoritarian beliefs. However, this chapter addresses how men on the spectrum who do hold these views might misuse biblical teachings as a sword against their spouses, rather than embracing them as the 'sword of truth' (Ephesians 6) in *their own lives* for growth.

The book *Love & Respect*[37] teaches that the Christian man is to be always respected, and this book was mentioned by many couples interviewed as a book that made their ND marriage worse. Two NA/NT participants said it led to empowering their AS/ND husbands' abusive behavior under the guise that she must always respect him. Disagreements or differences of opinion or points of view are viewed as disrespectful by the AS/ND Christian husband.

Anything less than agreement, affirmation or appreciation can be viewed as disrespectful and thus sinful. The narrative that the man of the house or any man in the woman's sphere is to be revered and respected leads to such narratives as one man I interviewed stated, "to be more of a lord almost dictator" of the home. This can happen in the NT-to-NT marriage, but applying scripture with cognitive inflexibility is likely to result in "the illusion of knowledge." We hope that those reading who are pastors or biblical counselors will begin to understand how their advice or use of scripture use may be taken and weaponized, even if that was not the intent.

Escaping the Maze: Rev. Dan's Insights and Hindsight Learning

There's a song we sang in church a few decades ago, "Blow the Trumpet in Zion[41]" about being in an army that rushes the cities and walls to carry out God's word. We sang it with great jubilation. That song is about locusts that are going to devour the crops of Israel because of their disobedience. It is taken from Joel 2 and is part of a prophecy indicating the fate of the nation unless they turn away from their wickedness. Singing this as we did, excited that the Lord would decimate our enemies, was well out of context. That is a good thing to sing but not based on this passage of Joel 2.

Context is vital in scripture. When reading, it is important to understand who the author is speaking to, when the author is writing, the style of the literature, and what topics the author is addressing. It is also important to understand the limits of the words in use. For instance, the word "forgive" doesn't imply to also *forget*. The author would use both words if that was the intention. Remember the text was written *to* a specific audience and it has applications *for* you. Jeremiah 29:11 is a good example. "I know the plans I have for you…" That was written to the Jewish community that was exiled to Babylon. It was not written to you. God had very concrete plans for them. He would return them to their homeland and restore their city and temple. What that means for us today, can be interpreted through New Testament scripture, that God has plans for all of us as he is 'no respecter persons,' but we can't apply the direct meaning in that passage to us.

Jesus modeled how we should use scripture through his interactions with those around him. Consider the story of the woman caught in adultery. He didn't force Old Testament law on her. He showed her mercy. His corrective action was "go and sin no more". His approach was full of compassion. He saw *her first,* then he addressed sin. And he addressed it without condemnation. He called her to a higher way instead of reminding her of her failure. The Samaritan woman at the well is in a similar situation. Jesus again led with compassion simply by being there. He talked with her, not *at* her. He didn't demand anything; he asked and then followed up with questions that invited her to self-revelation. He led that interaction as someone interested in whom the image-bearer of God was: She bore his likeness as a child of God, and he treated her that way. Again, he didn't use Scripture in a condemning way. He called her to something greater. The two crucified with him is another great example. He showed compassion to both in two different ways. To one he granted forgiveness and to the other, silence. There was plenty of Scripture that could have applied in that situation, yet he held his tongue. He spoke simply and gave only what would benefit the hearer.

What was true of us (Stephanie and I), was that I wasn't that way. Stephanie and I experience emotions differently. For her, they are an everyday part of her life. What I perceived as emotional extremes and quick frequency to which her sadness, anger, happiness, and other feelings could surface, ebb and flow, wasn't anything like my experience. We saw the same things occur, yet I showed barely a blip on the emotional register. As an example, our youngest daughter recently married. For Stephanie, this was a grand event full of simultaneous happiness and sadness. Her face was true to how she felt. It was evident. For me, I smiled. I didn't cry nor have a significant change in countenance. I processed the day and those leading up to it in a matter-of-fact way. I was glad for our daughter, but my feelings weren't on display in the same way Stephanie expressed gladness. My emotions, if they surfaced, would have been saved for a quiet moment alone.

Our oldest daughter's primary school experiences were challenging. Additionally, those were very lean years financially. During times of high emotion, especially sadness, disappointment and anger, there was rarely anything that could be done to make the situation right. The cause and the effect were out of our control. We had to deal with it. What I saw then, was no logical reason to be emotional because that interfered with thinking about the problem. I would summarize and quote Paul: "I have learned to be content in all things" (Philippians 4:11) and "All things work together for good…" (Romans 8:28). What I was missing, beyond the one-dimensional interpretation, was her. I didn't *see her* as Jesus did. There is a full humanity in all of us. Jesus grew the same way (Luke 2:52). Ignoring the person and dealing only with their expression, says *"who* you are isn't as important as *how* you are dealing with this." This way of responding makes the *problem* larger than the *person(s)* involved.

In retrospect, the other true thing is that I wasn't living up to my potential. To do that you need to aspire to something beyond who you are right now. I didn't. I was "content". The pain that should have inspired change, I was numb to. Those times were a call-to-action that I didn't heed because I didn't hear the call. I didn't hear the call because I didn't share in her pain. The two of us would have been better than one, but one of us didn't see the opportunity for what it was. It was a chance for us to be stronger together. It was an opportunity for me to support her. She was stronger in the areas of our family struggles than I was. I let her deal with it because I knew that; I was a passive participant at best and an abdicator at worst. She felt alone and that was on me. In those times, had both of us been engaged and operating in a healthy union, our creativity would have been higher. Our collective endurance would have been stronger, making those times less of a burden on either of us. Again, we were *one* but, in this case, I was pulling us towards being *zero*.

In 2 Corinthians 9, Paul talks about his "thorn in the flesh". Paul acknowledges this experience is unpleasant. He isn't denying the feelings. He is saying, it is worth the pain because Christ is glorified because of it. That is a very different way to view discontent. The former is a stoic-like perspective to suppress the emotion and deny some part of you. The latter is a fully human experience to know the emotion and make a conscious effort to see God's glory through it. It requires more courage to accept the discontent, work through it, and trust God than it does to deny its existence and walk on as if nothing has happened. I choose the stoic path.

Genesis 1 says we (as a married couple) are one flesh. Therefore, what affects one of you affects both of you. We know this intuitively as well. In a natural context, when one person is sick it creates the possibility that the other will become ill. If one person loses a job, that affects both of you. It is therefore reasonable that when an aspect of one of you is discounted, the whole of you is less than it was. The union is less capable and viewed as less than who we were created to be and less than the image we bear.

What I had to learn was to allow and give respect to all of Stephanie. This meant letting her feel in ways I didn't (and couldn't understand) and not considering that a 'less than.' That is how I saw it. I intended to be helpful – "If you would just be this way…," yet what I said (from her perspective) was you are 'less than' and I am 'more than': be like me and you will experience life in a better way. What she understood was that I was not for her, I didn't see her, I was not interested in her feelings or anything else. *She* was a problem to solve and no more. Then I would make it worse by standing on a scriptural high ground, declaring that not only did I think that, but God did as well. That was demeaning and ignorantly arrogant. The impact of this over the years would erode her right perspective of God and cause her to see me only as a threat. I was only someone she needed (as opposed to wanted) to make the house function. I was not someone to enjoy life with. Undoing this took a very long time.

Let's look at one of the scriptures mentioned earlier. The goal is to re-read them in context. Malachi 2:16 is commonly rendered and remembered as "God hates divorce" (KJV). The full text in the NIV translation says:

> "The man who hates and divorces his wife," says the LORD, the God of Israel, "does violence to the one he should protect," says the LORD Almighty. So be on your guard, and do not be unfaithful.

The ESV translation of Malachi 2:15-17 is:

> Did he not make them one, with a portion of the Spirit in their union? And what was the one God seeking? Godly offspring. So guard yourselves in your spirit, and let none of you be faithless to the wife of your youth. "For the man who does not love his wife but divorces her, says the LORD, the God of Israel, covers his garment with violence, says the LORD of hosts. So guard yourselves in your spirit, and do not be faithless." You have wearied the LORD with your words. But you say, "How have we wearied him?" By saying, "Everyone who does evil is good in the sight of the LORD, and he delights in them." Or by asking, "Where is the God of justice?"

The book of Malachi starts with an admonition to the priests who were offering blemished animals as sacrifices and doing other abominable things. That continues into chapter two. Then in verse 10 of chapter 2, it turns to relationships. In verse 11 it speaks directly to the men of Judah that were marrying wives that worshipped other gods. Then it moves on to those men who were 'unfaithful' to their wives and still expecting a blessing while doing so. The chapter ends with a statement that Judah is calling evil good. This verse in context isn't about the simple act of divorce. It is about the hearts of the men of Judah who believe they can live however they want and be blessed by God while doing so. Using the phrase "God hates divorce" as a weapon is acting in the way verse 16 describes: "doing violence to the one he should protect".

Let's return to the word 'unfaithful.' It is used 5 times from verse 10 to the end of the chapter. The Hebrew word is דָּגַב (bagad). The meaning is more than adulterous. From the Enhanced Brown-Driver-Briggs Hebrew English Lexicon,38 it means to "act or deal treacherously, faithlessly, deceitfully, in the marriage relation, in matters of property or right, in covenants, in word, and in general conduct". The Dictionary of Biblical Languages with Semitic Domains: Hebrew (Old Testament)39: "be unfaithful, be faithless, break faith, i.e., not trustworthy or reliable to a person or standard". In both of those definitions, adultery, which was clearly indicated in the text, is an outflow of a heart condition and only part of the definition. This is a word that describes acts in any relationship. The opening verse of this section sets the tone. Verse 10 (NIV) says:

> *Do we not all have one Father? Did not one God create us? Why do we profane the covenant of our ancestors by being unfaithful to one another?*

The same word for unfaithful is used: דָּגַב (bagad). This is not a statement about marital infidelity but about how one treats one's brother. The men of Judah are dealing wrongly with each other. This isn't a community acting like a family; they are acting like enemies. The passage continues and it shows how treachery is displayed between a husband and wife. By the time you get to verse 14, the men are rebuked with the same phrase that the community is exhorted within verse 10.

While we're here, let's look at one more word: divorce. That is the Hebrew שָׁלַח (shalach). It means "to send away." It gets translated as "divorce" in this context but let's consider the literal (and then figurative) meaning. "To send away" is an intentional rejection and to put someone in a position of being alone and unguarded. For the women in those days, this would have been a devasting change to their daily lives. It could have turned into homelessness and being shunned by society. In the modern perspective, it might mean that, but it is more likely to mean a change in the way the house operates. Now there are two houses instead of one and laws would require that some amount of spousal support would be required. Let's also consider the emotional aspect of 'being sent away.' This is rejection at its most profound; it is a rending of union and confers to the person "I don't want you" and certainly fits the definition of the word 'unfaithful.' Being unwanted is a terrible feeling and wreaks havoc on a person's perspective of themselves and their God. A figurative look at that word could come across as apathy or dismissal. It might not be as intentional as divorce (the spoken "go away") but it would feel the same (or worse). To the one being "sent away," this is experienced as "I am present but unseen". Being ignored or dismissed while cohabitating may not seem like an overt act of treachery, but to the receiver, it feels the same.

When the verse is read in context, it doesn't lend itself as a defense (or weapon) against a wife's desire to exit the relationship. This is a passage about treating one another as brothers and sisters who are all made in the image of the same God. And that behavior should continue into the marriage relationship. Jesus echoed Malachi's sentiment in Matthew 19:4-9 (above), stating that divorce was granted because of a hardness of heart. Jesus is also addressing the men, and this multilayered topic is the same: divorce (and how they treat their wives) and a hard heart. It is the man's *heart* Jesus is first and foremost concerned with because he knows that a heart that is right with Him will have a greater chance of being right with those around him.

The soundbite mentality in today's world is widespread. The tendency to use these soundbites as a hammer of shame is forever tempting, though never right. We should ensure we are considering *people* first. A remark, if any, should be reflective of that. Then, if scripture is invoked, it needs to be used rightly to build the other person up, and, as Paul says, in love. Building up your spouse is a gain for both of you. Being *one* means when one of you is stronger, you are, as a sum, stronger. The opposite is also true. What you tear down and demean, it weakens you both.

If scripture is invoked, it needs to be used rightly to build the other person up.

Returning to our narrative, my behavior could be considered 'unfaithful' (treacherous or untrustworthy, or unreliable). Again, this wasn't intentional nor overt, but that's how it was felt by Stephanie. She didn't trust me with her heart and feelings. My ability to hold a job and be faithful in that regard didn't bring solace to her neglected heart. I was not operating in the spirit of the teachings in Malachi 2.

As we close this chapter, the next chapter indicates what abuse can occur when religion and scripture are misused within the context of the ND Christian marriage. While I did not use the above verses against my wife, my own black-and-white interpretation of other scripture was harmful to my wife and damaging to our relationship. We are thankful to the women who wanted to share their stories, and who desired reconciliation with their husbands, but due to the husbands' unfaithfulness (treachery and unintentional, yet unrepented abuse), they had to make the painful decision to separate or divorce.

Chapter Thirteen
Trapped in the Maze and Confusion of Abuse

BY REV. IRIS KNAPP &
REV. DR. STEPHANIE C. HOLMES

Any Christian counselor will tell you that abuse within marriage is very common, and there are a huge number of people who live in fear in their own homes. The husband or wife who is the victim of physical or emotional torture by their partner lives as if they are imprisoned in a double cell with their worst enemy. As much as we would like to believe otherwise, it happens within Christian marriages as well, although it is difficult to tell exactly how frequently because those involved are too ashamed or embarrassed to admit it, even to a friend.
—Rev. David Instone-Brewer, *Divorce and Remarriage in the Church*29

ow many times have you mentioned to someone that your loved one or friend is on the autism spectrum and been met with an excited response of, "Oh yeah–I know someone with autism!" You could already see the gears moving to form an opinion about your unique situation. A notable and recitable quote by Dr. Stephen Shore is often used in the world of neurodiversity: "If you've met one person with autism, you've met *one* person with autism."

This, of course, applies to any individual who belongs to a bigger group, whether it's race, religion, or country of origin—you fill in the blank. This chapter is about the complications of abuse that may arise in a neurodiverse Christian marriage. The abuse may be intentional or unintentional because of the complex dynamics that are unique to a neurodiverse/ neurotypical (ND/NT) relationship. Of course, just because someone is neurodiverse does not mean that they will be an abuser, but this chapter will share the stories of those relationships where abuse was present and often the diagnosis of autism was unknown for years, even decades into the marriage.

In some churches and Christian communities, women are stigmatized by being asked about their role in the abuse, which assumes they share in the blame. Misguided Christian teaching may contribute to a woman being told to submit to behavior that is unhealthy, or to refrain from arguing and giving an opinion. These women are made to feel they should have more sex and stay in a potentially dangerous relationship. These are not solutions and can be a form of spiritual abuse. (See the previous chapter for a list of Bible verses that are commonly twisted and incorrectly applied.) The situation becomes even harder when the husband has a role in church or ministry leadership, which includes pastors, worship leaders, deacons, elders, missionaries, small group leadership, and Sunday school teachers!

I am an ordained minister and have done full and part-time church, community, and para-church ministry for more than 40 years. This includes 10 years of starting and directing a Christian women's drug and alcohol rehabilitation program, and 24 years leading women's support, coaching, and small groups. I am a certified Christian life discernment coach. This simply means that I help people look at options and prayerfully consider their next steps and then walk with them through transitions. I am twice divorced and have personal experience with autism as the grandmother of a teenager who is on the spectrum along with other family members. These experiences have uniquely equipped me with great understanding and compassion for the women I am called to help. We have an amazing God who redeems our life experiences if we allow Him to.

Tragically, in many of the marriages I see that are struggling or don't make it, there has been some type of abuse, trauma or neglect. Some of it is unintentional, because the AS/ND person may struggle with Theory of Mind (ToM) or mind blindness, combined with black-and-white/rigid thinking and/or problems with executive functioning. These challenges complicate marriage at an entirely different level. Communication skills can be lacking or ineffective, as previously stated in the book: it's as if the spouses are speaking two different languages. If the proper skills and tools are not learned by both individuals, the resulting confusion and frustration can devolve into abuse. When narcissism is in combination with autism spectrum disorder, the challenges faced are even more serious.

This chapter contains narratives from a number of the women Dr. Stephanie Holmes, and I have worked with. We want to give them a platform to share their stories and to provide more clarity to pastors, counselors, and marriage helpers about what the presentation of abuse (intentional and unintentional) can look in a neurodiverse Christian couple (NDCC). Christian women do not get married with divorce in mind or even entertain it as an option. When a husband is unable to see a wife's point of view or doesn't care about her emotions, various patterns of abuse can begin to creep in. These personal stories have a common theme of the neurotypical / non-autistic (NT/NA) spouses slowly beginning to lose themselves, all the while trying to save the marriage at any cost, even to the detriment of their identity and health. Over time, and with much prayer and discernment, some of them realized that divorce was the only option for spiritual, mental, and physical health for them and their family. Of course, not all NDCC marriages end this way, but when they do, it's an earthquake event. As difficult as this outcome can be, clergy, counselors, and clients alike should know there is hope for the future.

Throughout this section, women will share some of their personal experiences from their hearts. These are real women. These are their words.

Personal Story

I feel I was let down when I went to my pastors for help. My faith was questioned, and that was a hard hit to take. My pastors just basically said I wasn't faithful enough, or I wasn't praying enough, or I just didn't believe enough. They told me that my expectations were too high and that I needed to be more submissive, and that really hurt because that wasn't it at all. I've gotten to the point where I'm wary of Christians. And I found that there's a lot of religion rather than a lot of Jesus, and that's very hard to take.

People were willing to allow me to be sacrificed for the marriage, really. The covenant of marriage became the more important thing, and that really hurt. People were willing to allow me to just wither away, as long as I remain married. I found a lot of people within the church lose sight of the individuals within the marriage.

Personal Story

When I shared details of the abuse in confidence with female Bible study leaders and a licensed church counselor, I was encouraged to stay in the situation, because the utmost concern of the church was saving the view of marriage. I was told I would "receive many crowns at the Bema seat of Christ" for all that I endured. The children and I were being offered up on the altar of marriage because there was such a focus on saving marriages at all costs, even if women and children were the casualties.

I was so desperate to honor God and my marriage, but applying the practical knowledge I was given only increased the abusiveness. The few Christian men in my husband's life did not understand neurodiversity and used extremely critical remarks to cause change instead of speaking with grace and truth. This made home life for myself and the kids even harder.

The church often propagates the idea that living in the same house, in an abusive situation, causing trauma to the wife and the children with long-term consequences is preferable to living in two separate homes. Through a series of extremely difficult events for both of us, we've lived in two separate homes over the last few years. This has allowed space for myself and the kids to heal and place boundaries on how we will be treated.

My husband does love me and our kids and as he now receives counsel with experts in the field of neurodiversity, he continues to grow in understanding how his actions have impacted us. He has learned that anger, rage, and abusive words are never appropriate or godly responses to his sensory challenges. He realizes he did not have any respect for me and is working to change that view. I look for ideas on how we can interact in ways that honor his needs without traumatizing the children. Also, I see how staying in a scared state in order to be a "good and submissive wife" prolonged the trauma and damage.

Personal Story

Not all ASD marriage stories involve outright or obvious abuse. So many things were explained by autism in our marriage that I marveled to learn there was one reason, one thing, behind a lot of the pain, difficulty, and confusion we experienced over the course of our 25 years of marriage. We saw many marriage counselors and would describe our marriage as "death by a thousand paper cuts." We both felt this, not just me. Most of the counselors didn't really seem to understand (apparent by the blank look on their faces), but it was the best way we knew how to speak about what our dynamics were really like. I believe that our story likely reflects many other ASD marriages where there is no huge betrayal or abuse, but many small things that add up over time, culminating in a breaking point where divorce has to be threatened in order to be the catalyst for change. As the non-ASD partner, I felt a myriad of emotions, including feeling neglected, gaslit, manipulated, betrayed, and incredibly lonely. When I would speak about these things, it came out as complaining because the nature of them was often subtle.

What Does Abuse Look Like?

There are five broad categories of the abuse seen most often in marriages.

- Spiritual/Religious
- Emotional/Verbal
- Sexual
- Neglect (Financial)
- Physical/Domestic

Spiritual Abuse

In their well-researched and biblical overview of abuse, Celestia and Steven Tracy note that spiritual abuse is an "inappropriate use of spiritual authority," such as the Bible or church tradition, to "force a person to do that which is unhealthy."[1] Spiritual abuse typically involves a "forceful or manipulative denial of that person's feelings and convictions" for the self-advancement of the abusive spiritual leader. Jesus explicitly condemns this in Matthew 21, when He indicts the Pharisees for the hypocritical misuse of their authority. In addition to power posturing, spiritual abuse involves performance preoccupation, unspoken rules, layers of legalism (seeking to earn God's favor and forgiveness based on rigid rule-keeping), and inflexible fundamentalism (harsh and unfair scrutiny of others in light of a strict standard that the one judging does not live up to).

> **Spiritual abuse is typically experienced with other forms of abuse and often produces the highest levels of toxic shame[1].**

Karla Downing states that a man who loves his wife as Christ loved the Church will find his wife has no difficulty respecting him and submitting to his spiritual leadership because he can be trusted. Downing continues to explain that placing yourself under the authority of someone who doesn't love you or care for you can be unwise and dangerous.[2] Colossians 3:19 (NIV) says, "Husbands, love your wives and do not be harsh with them." 1 Peter 3:7 (NIV) says, "Husbands, in the same way, be considerate as you live with your wives, and treat them with respect as the weaker partner and as heirs with you of the gracious gift of life, so that nothing will hinder your prayers." This tells the husband to consider his wife's needs, to adapt to her, and to treat her with respect. Women generally respond positively to husbands who treat them this way. But women have great difficulty being vulnerable with men who do not act lovingly toward them or who neglect their needs and dismiss their lived experiences. (Karla

Downing shared suggestions for Christian women navigating the complexities of difficult marriage in a podcast interview with Dr. Holmes on the Neurodiverse Christian Couples podcast.[3])

Many Evangelical Christian teaching instructs women to "submit [them]selves to [their] own husbands as [they] do to the Lord" (Ephesians 5:22, NIV). This teaching tends to position husbands as the spiritual head of the home, but when a husband operates in a way that is harming the family, as in the case of abuse, he forfeits the right to leadership and loses his functional position, even though he may still occupy the financial position of "head of the house."

Insight From Dr. Stephanie Holmes

As previously stated, Christian couples tend to reach out to pastors, lay leaders in the church, or their priest before reaching out to a professional secular counselor. Never in my 25-plus years of counseling (and now coaching) has a couple reached out for pastoral or professional counseling because their marriage was in good shape, and they simply wanted to go from good to great. This is usually what marriage small groups are for in the local church. When a couple comes to a Christian marriage helper and the wife has indicated she is being abused in any way, it is crucial that the helper does not add secondary spiritual abuse or religious trauma to an already complicated situation. It is also critical to look past the obvious and inquire about neurodiversity or possible mental health issues. Unless a helper is autism-trained, it is both ethical and moral for them to refer the couple to a counselor or coach who is so equipped. It cannot be expected of any pastor or Christian counselor to be trained in all forms of psychological counseling and/or neurodiversity. However, it can be expected that they will stay in their lanes and humbly admit if they are not adequately equipped. Recognizing neurodiversity takes skill – suspecting it may exist takes discernment and humility to ask for help.

If a Christian helper realizes they are unprepared to help, they can still offer spiritual or prayer support and check in on the couple, especially on the spouse who is saying she is being neglected or abused. Many AS/ND Christian men see their pastor, elders, or priest as a spiritual authority, and as such, these leaders likely have influence that no one else has with this man; they can ask the man for accountability – and get it. Referring the couple does not mean washing one's hands of them. Check in. If the wife feels unsafe and decides to move to another bedroom or needs the husband to leave the home, support safety. Instead of insisting they need to be under the same roof in order to work on their marriage, help them navigate their in-house (or out-of-house) separation. Offer protection and prioritize a standard of safety over any beliefs that marriage work must happen in a certain way. Instead of fearing offending the head of household, who more than likely the tithe or financial giver, check-in and hold the abuser accountable.

Emotional and Verbal Abuse

Emotional and verbal abuse is defined by the Tracys[1] as made up of a series of incidents that occur over time. Emotional abuse is much more than just verbal insults. Instead, it's characterized by repeated incidents (whether intentional or not) where a person is insulted, degraded, humiliated, threatened, or controlled. Verbal abuse is "a form of emotional maltreatment in which words are systematically used to belittle, undermine, scapegoat, or maliciously manipulate another person."[1] Proverbs 18:21 (NASB) tells us that our words are extremely powerful and can give life or tear down. In a figurative sense, verbal/emotional abuse is a distortion of the command in Genesis 1:28 (NAS) to "be fruitful," for our words are to give *life*. Emotional abusers systematically weaken their victims to gain control and strengthen themselves. They seek to destroy what matters most to their victim (a pet, work, appearance, family, friend, etc.). In summary, relational pain is created when one person seeks to gain power through posturing, verbal attacks, deceit, over-dependency, abandonment, or threats of abandonment.[1]

Tracy & Tracy[1,4] and Leslie Vernick[5] believe that emotional and verbal abuse can be among the more damaging forms of abuse because of their subjective nature and often occurs behind closed doors. Words can strike with force at the very core of who we are, for either good or evil. Just as with God's words, by which the heavens and the earth were made, our words carry great power. They can be wielded destructively, causing feelings of worthlessness, isolation, and hatred in others. The temptation is to downplay verbal abuse because it creates no physical pain and leaves no visible scars.[1,4] The thought is, "If there are no bruises, it wasn't abuse." However, nothing could be further from the truth. Therefore, the first step in dealing with verbal abuse is to recognize it for what it is. Listen and learn from women with lived experience:

Personal Story

In the early years of our marriage, navigating our challenges was akin to driving on an unlit, unfamiliar road. We lacked the tools and understanding to navigate the complex pathways of each other's minds. Our conversations often ended in confusion and frustration, leaving us to ponder what went wrong and why.

One example stands out. Preparing for a road trip, my husband suggested getting the car's oil changed. I attempted to use reflective listening, but each effort was met with criticism. My attempts to paraphrase his words were seen as altering his meaning, leading to accusations of manipulation or laziness. This interaction was a clear illustration of the challenges we faced in our communication—the struggle to find common ground in our perspectives.

    As years passed, we became all too familiar with these patterns. We would establish understanding, only to have it shattered in the heat of an argument. I was forced to confront the impact these experiences had on me. The diagnosis of PTSD was a reminder of the toll that these repeated conflicts had taken. I found myself questioning my own perception and struggling to find a sense of self amidst the chaos. The challenge was not just about finding the right words but also about understanding the underlying emotions and perspectives that shaped our interactions. It became clear that true understanding required more than just listening; it required empathy and a willingness to see beyond our perspectives.

A letter from an NT/NA spouse to her ND/AS Husband (Used with Permission)

From the very beginning, I sensed that something was off in how you could argue a point without me ever knowing what you really thought. I didn't understand how you could be so good at arguing, justifying, rationalizing, and excusing bad behavior or wrong actions—even bragging about those skills. I wondered why you accused me of not trusting you if I asked a question about something you did or said or wanted. You were always right, which made me always wrong. I didn't know why we couldn't have a spiritual life together without you putting me down, arguing a point, or dismissing my thoughts. When you were away in ministry, I felt lonely knowing I wasn't missed at all. It was awful to know that you didn't like the sound of my voice saying your name.

Personal Story

Abuse is a new term for what I lived in for 49 1/2 years before my husband told me one day, "I have decided I no longer love you and don't think I ever have." Abuse means to be treated with cruelty or violence on a regular basis. That sums up my life for so many years, but I never even thought that's what was happening.

    During those years, there were good and bad times. We worked with and were team leaders for Marriage Encounter in the Southeast area for seven years. He was a choir director and a music leader in churches we were members of over the years. The abuse was quiet and subtle, with me being told a lot, "We have talked about this already and don't need to discuss it anymore. You agreed with me and now you are causing an argument for nothing. We are doing it the way we discussed." This happened during all large decisions: car buying, camper buying. It was his way or nothing. Many times, he would convince me this WAS what WE had decided. I could never express anger at him, or it would amount to an awful time, and it just didn't seem worth the effort. Many times, he made me question my sanity—Did I really say okay? Is that what I said? However, he would be the one who would shut down and pout if he did not get his way. In these times of betrayal, I would withdraw, many times crying only in the shower, thinking of things I would say to stand up for myself. But I never did stand up for what I believed I had said. I just kept the peace and went along. I never shared these moments with even my best friends.

Personal Story

The man could argue in circles, gaslight, etc. better than anybody I've ever met. An argument with him would go like this:

Him: What a beautiful blue sky!
Me: Yes, it is a beautiful blue sky.
Him: What?!?! That's not blue; that's cerulean.
I was wrong even when I agreed with him.

Insight from Dr. Stephanie Holmes

Many pastors or spiritual leaders and Christian counselors do not view emotional or verbal abuse as "real abuse." Women have told me that their pastor or spiritual leader suggested the issue was their lack of resilience or failure to take things in stride and see what a good man their AS/ND husband truly was. This is because, very often, a different version of the AS/ND spouse is viewed at church than is experienced at home. Recent research conducted by Dye reported the effects of abuse on the developing brains of children.[6] Results showed that the impact of emotional or verbal abuse on these children was greater than that of physical or sexual abuse. The research found that when children grow up in a home with a verbally or emotionally abusive parent, the abuse negatively impacts mental health and can alter healthy brain development. Among the children studied, researchers found higher indexes for depression, anxiety, stress (which affected the immune system), and suicidal thoughts. Over the years I have worked with many children who grew up with an emotionally or verbally abusive Christian AS/ND or NT/NA father, and sadly, I have often heard that their mother's choice to *stay in the marriage* is a key factor in their distrust of the Church, or their decision to leave the faith entirely. The mother's decision to stay is frequently influenced by religious convictions (based on scripture taken out of context) or the direction of church leadership. These children did not see saving the marriage "at any cost" was a positive witness of their mother or of the faith. They felt unprotected by their Church and mother, who believed she was staying for the good of the marriage and the children.

Recalling the definitions Dr. Jim Wilder[15] gave us in a previous chapter, when there is Trauma A or B, this can affect the person's orbitofrontal cortex (OFC) or "joy center" and lead to loss of identity and ability to build love bonds; then fear bonds abound which will impact attachment.

When most people think of post-traumatic stress disorder (PTSD) or now complex PTSD (C-PTSD), many in spiritual leadership believe that something as catastrophic as war or witnessing a tragedy is the cause for PTSD. Researchers Hyland[28] and colleagues through the study of brain science found that continuing, unrelenting bullying or verbal or emotional abuse can lead to PTSD or C-PTSD. Many NT/NA women in ND relationships have been suffering from emotional and verbal abuse for years before having the courage to reach out for help.

Finally, while autism explains why someone may behave in a certain way or become more easily overwhelmed or dysregulated, it is not an excuse to yell names, profanity, or verbal vitriol when dysregulated (by the NT/NA spouse either). Mentioned both in Proverbs 8:13 and Matthew 12:34, scripture tells us that out of the abundance or overflow of the heart, the mouth speaks. What spews from one's mouth comes from what lies in the heart. This means that, while we can coach the NT/NA wife on how to approach various situations differently, neither she nor her approach should be blamed for how her AS/ND husband responds to her. Learning self-control, regulation, and how to take a pause or break when dysregulated or overwhelmed is work the AS/ND spouse should undertake, with spiritual leadership holding him accountable to this work. *(The authors of the book understand verbal, emotional, physical and spiritual abuse can also be inflicted by the NT/NA spouse).* When I begin work with a couple, I start with each partner individually, because each has different work to do before counseling/coaching is safe (See Appendix). If there is verbal abuse and dysregulation, this must be addressed before marriage can continue. In a professional workshop I attended led by Leslie Vernick at the AACC, she stated, "Not all work is marital work. If one spouse is abusive or contributing to an emotionally destructive marriage, that is that spouse's work to do." She reminded the audience of counselors that whether a person has a diagnosis or disability, there is also temperament and character to consider, which need to be separated from the diagnosis or mental or physical health issue.

Sexual Abuse

One of the most powerful and beautiful aspects of being made in the image of God is the possession of healthy sexuality, but the inherent power of sex can produce just as much destruction and pain as it does pleasure and life.[1] Sexual abuse is never minor—it's always very serious. Even when sexual abuse doesn't involve intercourse, force, or physical violence, it's still very serious and harmful. According to the Tracys,[1,4] sexual interaction is abusive when at least one of the following factors below are present:

1. Power differential

This exists when the abuser controls the victim, and the sexual encounter isn't mutually conceived or desired. Relational power can derive from the role relationship between abuser and victim, for example, when the offender is a teacher, parent, minister, or coach. Power can derive from the larger physical size or more advanced skill capability of the offender, in which case the victim may be manipulated, physically intimidated, or required to comply with the sexual activity. Power can also arise out of the abuser's capability to psychologically manipulate the victim (which, in turn, may be related to the offender's role or superior size). The offender may bribe, cajole, shame, or use scripture to manipulate the victim into cooperating.[1,4]

2. Knowledge differential

This occurs when the offender has a more sophisticated understanding of the significance and implications of the sexual encounter. Knowledge differential implies that the offender is older, more developmentally advanced, or more intelligent than the victim.[1,4]

3. Gratification differential

This refers to a situation in which the abuser is solely attempting to gain sexual gratification for him or herself. The goal of the encounter is not mutual sexual gratification, although perpetrators may become aroused by attempting to arouse their victims. Alternatively, the abuser may delude him or herself into believing that the goal is to sexually satisfy the victims. Nevertheless, the primary purpose of sexual activity is for the offender to obtain gratification at any cost.[1,4]

NT/NA Wives Share Sexual Abuse Stories

Personal Story

I had no idea the cost on my inner self after years and years of sexual relationship without connection or real intimacy in the midst of negative behaviors, words, and neglect. The pressure to have sex was always present. It didn't matter if I'd just had a baby ("The doctors don't really mean six weeks— there are other ways") or if I was sick or if we were traveling with the girls in the room with us. You expected sex as much and as often as possible. You have felt entitled because I am your wife, that is my duty, and it was essentially taught that it was [my duty]. And you hold on to this belief that no matter the status of the relationship, sex is owed to you.

Personal Story

My husband has Asperger's. He agrees that he has it. This summer he watched a person on YouTube who promoted polygamy and the husband being the man/leader of the house/marriage. My husband is all wrapped up in this, and I have prayed and prayed. And fasted. He wants me to study this with him and also live it. He also believes that porn, prostitution, and adultery are not sins ... if the husband does it. Nobody can reason with him. I think I still love him. We've been married over 30 years! What do I do as a Christian wife?

Personal Story

After we were married, my dream partner became critical, haughty, and withdrawn. There was a relentless demand for admiration and sex. My needs for affection and attention were only used as a precursor to sex. He would often goad me without mercy.

He told me while dating that he'd struggled with porn, but that all men did and that it was over. It resurfaced in the first months of our marriage and was a continuous pattern through our decades-long marriage. We sought the help of an elder. I was told that "God forgave [spouse's name], so couldn't I forgive this?" There was no mention of the sin of porn or the need for relational repair. As we raised our children, he often shared stories which portrayed him as the perfect father and were twisted to make me look bad. I would question the untruths and would be told that's how he remembered it. I began to notice patterns of him not doing what he said he would. I was told he either didn't say that or he no longer agreed.

Personal Story

We sought counseling in the church. When I would say, "He seems to only think of himself," I received the reply, "We're all selfish." When I asked how to respect him as a leader if he didn't lead, I was told to change my heart, forgive, submit, be "more available," etc. Again, porn seemed acceptable and almost expected. I was told that it "always takes two" to have problems in a marriage. I "learned" [was taught the false ideas] that if I constantly forgave, sought my joy in the Lord, and was respectful to my husband that it would all work out.

He set the narrative that he was "working so hard and I just couldn't forgive him." He would set up situations to ask the elders to pray for our marriage. If I said no, it played into his plan. When I got angry and lost it, that also helped to portray me as the crazy or wrong one. I couldn't figure out why we couldn't make progress in our relationship—we still had the same conflicts and conversations that we'd had for decades. When I would go to him and say something hurt me, he'd flip the conversation to say that I was too critical and mean to him. I would walk away thinking how I'd hurt him. I very slowly began to see the pattern of him not taking responsibility or changing behaviors but being the victim of our relationship. When I withdrew from our relationship due to all of the unresolved hurts and continuing harmful patterns, he would tell me, "Men's number one need is respect and sex—why are you withholding that from me?"

Neurodivergence became a tool for him to wield—either I should accept him, as he had autism, or he didn't have it and I was too critical. I was told that I should trust and forgive him, even if the behaviors continued. All of this was so incredibly confusing and disorienting. I didn't allow myself to ever use the "D" word. I thought that the only biblical reason for divorce was an actual affair.

Personal Story

When we first started dating, I was more than halfway through a weight loss program. I remember him being impressed with my discipline and focus. As our relationship became more serious, he said, "When you get to 125 pounds, I will marry you." I didn't think much about it at the time, except I thought he was just trying to keep me motivated.

I lost 80 pounds, and we did eventually get married after a tummy tuck, breast implants, and learning how to straighten my curly hair. I did want the tummy tuck because of the weight loss, but the rest was for him. At one point, he wanted me to dye my hair black because he liked "that look." When I refused, he then wanted me to wear a black wig. It was sexier for him.

Not long into our marriage, he wanted me to do things sexually that I wasn't comfortable with, though honestly, I did try because I believed I was supposed to in order to keep him satisfied sexually so he wouldn't turn back to porn. This had been a problem for him prior to our marriage. He had me watch a porn video to "teach me how." I'd never watched anything like that in my life, and he couldn't understand why it didn't "turn me on." I did say NEVER AGAIN after that.

He micromanaged my weight. If I gained a pound, he would notice and want me to restrict my eating. After surgery, when I gained some weight, he would look at me naked and tell me I was the fattest b–tch he had ever been with. At one point, he told me he had to be married so he could have sex and still be a Christian. He believed that was my main purpose in his life. It didn't make any difference if I was recovering from surgery or was in pain or just didn't want to—he was not to be denied. It was scripturally my place to submit!

He filed for divorced after I set a boundary of no sex until we started to go for help. I really didn't understand the level of abuse and control I had been under until the divorce was final. At that moment it felt like a physical weight had been lifted off of me.

Insight from Dr. Stephanie Holmes

While I am not a licensed sex therapist, in my early years as a licensed professional counselor (and before my focus changed to neurodiverse marriage) I worked with Christian
women who had experienced rape or marital sexual assault/rape or women who lived with
a spouse who had a porn addiction or sex addiction. I have seen a correlation between
wives who are in marriages where the husband has porn or sexual addiction, in that these
wives are more likely to be objectified and experience sexual, verbal, or psychological abuse.
More can be learned in listening to my discussion with Dr. Andrew Bauman.[7] whose
dissertation study concerned sexism and abuse of women in the Protestant church. The
intersection of sexual addiction and autism is discussed more thoroughly in the book
Determined for More by Shawna Meek.[8]

In my podcast interview with Pastor Jamal Baker[12] (a former licensed sex therapist and
Christian counselor who trained under the late Dr. Doug Rosenau[13] and the Penners[14]), he
stated that sexual intimacy is a result or fruit of a healthy relationship and should never be
demanded or entitled. We explored the misuse and twisting of 1 Corinthians 7:4 (NIV)
in our discussion, "The wife does not have authority over her own body but yields it to
her husband. In the same way, the husband does not have authority over his own body
but yields it to his wife." Sometimes an AS/ND husband or spiritual leaders will use this
scripture to coerce women to perform sex out of obligation or duty (sexual and spiritual abuse). The women are instructed that they will be guilty of the sin of withholding
unless both husband and wife have agreed to abstain from sex. This can have a catastrophic
impact, producing deep trauma. In this, limited writing space we cannot fully explore how
deeply harmed Christian women have been from pressures to provide "duty" sex[9] or by the
disclaimer that "every man has a battle" with porn or lust.[10] These ideas, combined with
black-and-white thinking, are harmful to the wife and often unintentionally supported (in
the husband's mind) by Christian leadership and Christian self-help books.[9,11] (I challenge
church leaders to read *The Great Sex Rescue* and give consideration to the research of 20,000
women on the impact and harm caused them by duty sex teachings).[9]

Neglect (Health/Financial Abuse)

Much of what is written about neglect as a form of abuse concerns children. It's spoken
of in terms of being left unattended or having inadequate food, clothing, medical care,
emotional support, or protection, or things that children are unable to do or provide on
their own. But what does neglect look like in a marriage with two capable adults? The
most common scenario I see is the neglect that comes in the form of financial domination
and control. Dr. Jim Wilder[15] outlines t neglect in his description of *Trauma A* (previously

discussed in Chapter 5), which is caused by the absence of necessary and good things in a person's life.

Financial abuse in marriage is when one partner exerts financial control over the other. It may involve fostering financial dependence by limiting the other spouse's ability to work or have access to money. According to Marter,[16] financial abuse in marriage is a form of domestic violence that can have harmful and lasting consequences and can take the form of one spouse maintaining full control over any funds, withholding it from the other or hiding information regarding finances. This kind of abuse typically doesn't start at the beginning of a new relationship; it often begins when two people form a more shared financial life, i.e., when they get married.

According to Marter,[16] like most forms of abuse, it doesn't go from zero to ten right away, or it would be easier to recognize or readily address. Financial bullying tends to be covert, starting with a few smaller behaviors, like commenting on the high grocery bill or asking how much your shoes cost. As the relationship progresses, it escalates into more serious behaviors, such as limiting your spending or giving you an allowance as if you were a child.

An NT/ND wife's letter to her AS/ND husband (Used with Permission)

It is a fact that all relationships require certain elements to be successful regardless of whether AS/ASD is present or not. Safety is at the top of that list. However, every form of these [safety and security] was violated in a catastrophic way for me last week. Your actions showed me that you are willing to go to frightening and ungodly lengths in your anger to try and force me to comply with your demands by threatening my safety and security (e.g., cutting off my access to funds and threatening to move my things out without my consent). It has also shown me that you will protect yourself at all costs (e.g., taking me off the bank account, which you did) before you will protect me—even from a wrongly perceived threat. How are these things possible if you say you know and love God? Is strong-arming anyone, especially your wife, something God condones? You've told me that none of the things in our life matter to you (e.g., house, possessions, business, etc.) if we aren't together and that you would just walk away from it all. And yet, you have trampled me in order to protect your money and yourself.

Personal Story

One Saturday evening, I had an accident that ended with a dead tree branch fell out of a tree and hit me in the head. I ended up with a trip to the trauma center at a nearby hospital. By Tuesday, he was tired of taking care of me and wanted to get out of the house. He insisted that we all go out for dinner. My face was swollen, I had two *black eyes, and I had bright blue sutures in the middle of my forehead. I didn't want to leave the house. But he insisted. He wouldn't order dinner in, and he wouldn't go without me. So, I covered up the stitches with bandages, pulled my son's baseball cap low over my forehead so nobody could see, and we went to dinner.*

It was my job to manage the cash flow. It was his job to decide how we spent our money. When I started counseling, he asked why I was wasting money on that. He was unemployed (again) at the time. He spent whatever he wanted whenever he felt like it. It was my job to make ends meet. He was unemployed 20-25% of our married life. When I expressed concern about spending, he would state—loudly, in front of the kids—"I make the God-d**ned f**king money, and we'll do what I say."

Twice when he lost a job, we ended up taking a vacation, which we clearly couldn't afford. He was clearly in charge, and I was powerless to argue. When I wanted to get long-term care insurance, he said flat out no—we can't afford it. At the same time, he was getting weekly massages, 90 minutes in length, to help him with his stress.

Insight from Dr. Stephanie Holmes

Financial abuse or neglect is one of the most common forms of abuse I have seen in NDCCs. Why? For those who believe that being the "head" means final authority, the area of finances is one of the main places to exert control. Most often, I do not think this is intentional, but AS/ND Christian men may take concepts from Christian financial programs (such as Dave Ramsey's financial peace teaching or Crown Financial) and apply what they see as black-and-white rules without nuance or context. Often, I have observed the husband applies these financial rules to the wife and not to himself. If he breaks the budget for one of his special interests or passions, or decides therapy, medical co-pays or vacation is not a necessary expenditure, then his decision becomes the way. The opposite can also be true with financial neglect: the AS/ND husband may not believe he needs to have a job, or he pursues many unsuccessful "entrepreneurial" or academic degree endeavors around his special interest and seems to have no problem laying the financial burden on his wife and demands support of his pursuits.

In another of our past podcasts, *When Helpers Caused Harm,*[17] an NT/NA wife, "Isabel," explained that her husband moved them from one country to another on an entrepreneurial adventure (telling her he had sought the Lord and received direction, when he had not.) This move ended up not only bankrupting them but led to her holding multiple jobs to provide for the family while caring (alone) for a child with special needs. He did not lift a finger to help in the home or with children and insisted that she just needed to wait for his business to be profitable.

Numbers and finances can be a strength for many on the spectrum, but if their knowledge or expertise leads them to believe they do not need to partner with their spouse about financial and budgetary decisions, the wife will end up in a situation without financial agency or input. This is often the reason many women married to men on the spectrum cannot leave or separate. Then when a divorce happens with an AS/ND man, I have witnessed countless times that because the husband was the primary breadwinner (and she stayed at home raising the kids), he believes the money and assets are *his* and will fight tooth and nail, running up the combined lawyer bills for both parties in excess of $50,000. If the wife leaves, he may hide accounts and assets in incredibly unethical ways. This is why an NT/NA wife may want to consult a certified divorce financial analyst (CDFA) prior to deciding to separate or leave her husband. CDFA Rhonda Nordyk, of Women's Financial Wellness Center addressed this topic on another of our recent podcasts.[18] State laws vary greatly, and many women do not know how to navigate these difficulties or understand what their state law says they are entitled to. Online resources such as the Institute for Divorce Financial Analyst's *Find a CDFA® professional,*[19] or FindLaw. com's *Divorce Information by State*[20] can be helpful starting points to find professional and understand local divorce and separation laws.

Physical Abuse/Domestic Violence

Physical abuse can take the form of child or spousal abuse (a.k.a., *intimate partner violence*), and is the injury or destruction of what should have been nurtured and enhanced.[1,4] God has created us with longings for love, nurture, and protection, so physical abuse is especially damaging. Love and affection are given and received through relational vulnerability, thus making the betrayal by a family member who harms instead of helping that much more destructive.[13] As a result of such betrayal, survivors often commit to never being vulnerable to anyone again, closing themselves off from love and intimacy.

Physical abuse is called domestic violence when someone causes or attempts to cause bodily injury to a family member or someone else who lives in the household. It's also considered domestic violence when the abuser doesn't physically injure his or her victims but instead asserts control with threats of imminent physical harm.[1,4] The Tracys document that domestic abuse can involve any of the following:

- Causing or attempting to cause physical or mental harm to a family or household member.
- Causing a family or household member to feel fear of physical or mental harm.

- Causing or attempting to cause a family or household member to engage in involuntary sexual activity by force, threat of force, or duress.

- Engaging in an activity toward a family or household member that would cause a reasonable person to feel terrorized, frightened, intimidated, threatened, harassed, or molested.

Most common instances of physical abuse/domestic violence are sexual assault, assault or battery, physical harm or serious injury, threats of harm, harassment, stalking, trespassing, damage to property, kidnapping, intimidation and unlawful restraint. These definitions are much broader than most people realize, because they involve the act of violence and the psychological torture involved in threats of harm.[1,4] Physical abuse perverts the God-ordained responsibility for humans to care for God's creation (Genesis 1:26-28, NASB). It also perverts God's mandate for parents and spouses to nurture, protect, and love vulnerable family members (Ephesians 5:22–30; 6:1–4: Colossians 3:18–21, NASB).

Narcissism

Individuals with ASD are not inherently violent or destructive, whereas those with certain personality disorders can be. Jodi Carlton, an experienced neurodiverse coach, shared on a past podcast[21] that people who truly have a combination of narcissism and autism can be dangerous, fully capable of harming someone and putting their life at risk.

Narcissistic personality disorder (NPD) is diagnostically defined in the *DSM-5*[22] as follows: "1. Has a grandiose sense of self-importance (e.g., exaggerates achievements and talents, expects to be recognized as superior without commensurate achievements). 2. Is preoccupied with fantasies of unlimited success, power, brilliance, beauty, or ideal love. 3. Believes that he or she is "special" and unique and can only be understood by, or should associate with, other special or high-status people (or institutions). 4. Requires excessive admiration. 5. Has a sense of entitlement (i.e., unreasonable expectations of especially favorable treatment or automatic compliance with his or her expectations). Is interpersonally exploitative (i.e., takes advantage of others to achieve his or her own ends). 7. Lacks empathy: is unwilling to recognize or identify with the feelings and needs of others. 8. Is often envious of others or believes that others are envious of him or her. 9. Shows arrogant, haughty behaviors or attitudes" (*DSM-5*, pp. 669-672). A person is not necessarily a narcissist just because they some they have some of these traits. The diagnosis is much more involved.[21,23]

Some NDCCs might wonder what the difference is between narcissism rage and dysregulation. Carlton says "narc rage" is about control. The victimized spouse gets sucked in by this, and the harder they try to get out of it, the more they are drawn in. People using this type of rage to control are dysregulated on purpose and will create chaos in order to throw their spouse off; Carlton says they can switch it on and off and walk out of the room—and they're fine.[21] ASD dysregulation has to do with the neurodiverse person's internal storm, and their spouse is not automatically in it. The AS/ND dysregulated person is likely trying to control their own world and/or their world seems to them to be out of control. Hurtful words and behavior can take place during a meltdown, but it's not the same as *narc rage*.[21]

Insight from Dr. Stephanie Holmes

Through my years of working with NDCCs, the least common form of abuse I have observed is physical violence or assault. But it can happen. I most often see this if the AS/ND husband has come from a family of origin where physical abuse occurred, or when they have ASD combined with a personality disorder or other untreated mental health issue. As previously noted, those on the spectrum are not inherently physically violent. What I most commonly hear about is the is overwhelmed and angry AS/ND Christian who uses corporal punishment or spanking (when disciplining children) in ways that are excessive and without relational empathy, which can lead to abuse of their children. Anecdotally, I have heard from NT/NA women that their AS/ND spouse uses physical intimidation or may break or throw items when in a dysregulated state. This, too, can be terrifying or traumatic to them and/or the children. My advice to pastors and spiritual leaders is that if such an occurrence is reported to you, *do something*. Churches are notorious for not reporting child abuse (despite mandated-reporting laws), and for not believing wives. If you are a wife who needs help out of domestic violence, contact your local women's shelter or contact The Psalm 82 Initiative.

Next Steps: Escaping the Maze

People will ask, "Weren't there warning signs when you were dating?" Most of the time, there weren't or the things that might have been a warning seemingly had an explanation. For example, if there was quirkiness, it must be his personality; the attention to detail was refreshing; the management of money made us feel secure; the compliments made us feel special; the church involvement and Bible knowledge showed we had the same values; and the success at work showed responsibility.

I've often compared these relationships to the story of the frog in hot water. The frog starts off in tepid water and just goes along while the water slowly heats up, and before long … they are boiled alive. Dating and sometimes early marriage is like tepid water, with the changes slowly taking place. Over time we get used to them, and before long … !

Maybe NT/NAs haven't noticed this because their spouse had been "masking" but can no longer maintain that effort in a long-term, close relationship. Along with that, these wives are "good Christian women" who won't divorce. They want to be faithful, and they don't leave because they feel they/we can't. Or they're told by Christian leaders that leaving is wrong, even if the marriage is soul-crushing or dangerous.

Becoming aware that you are in the boiling pot of water is frightening. Accepting the temperature of the water can be hard. We often lie to ourselves and will try to convince ourselves and others that "it's not really that hot in here"—once you have acquired a working and accurate thermometer and really see the temperature—now it is time to take ACTION! Action to move you towards the good and perfect plans the Lord has for his children. We can be encouraged by the reassurance God gave to his people through Jeremiah 29:11-13 (NIV), which says, "For I know the plans I have for you," declares the LORD, "plans to prosper you and not to harm you, plans to give you hope and a future. Then you will call on me and come and pray to me, and I will listen to you. You will seek me and find me when you seek me with all your heart." What that action is may be different from situation to situation. Please seek help and discernment in what action steps could be next, but no one can make that choice but you. No one will have to live with the decision you may make but you. Find support and community.

Personal Story

I began this journey as the perfect target. God provided a path for me to over-come and heal. I was led to experts who understood and offered education. I had to learn what had truly happened to me in order to heal. God provided specific answers and provisions for me at every step. I was led to a community who were committed to the Lord and each other. I now can walk in clarity and am empowered with hope and choice. I've seen some beauty from my ashes and know that my children can witness a healthier mom who has learned to walk closely with her God, trust Him, and experience His goodness and faithfulness. I hope they understand what true love is and to learn the difference between actions vs. words. I want them to understand that true love never expects the other to accept harmful behavior patterns. I hope that my experiences can bridge the gap for others in the church. Education is desperately needed for leaders, counselors, and those in similar relationships. Those who haven't ever experienced these issues have no way of understanding or being sensitive. Study of the Bible and God's heart, context, and intentions of passages about divorce is needed. I hope for others to understand that God does not value marriage more than the people in them and that a healthy marriage does indeed "take two."

Personal Story

All of the effects of my needs being ignored systematically and my requests (and cries) for help resulted in me experiencing emotional abandonment. I would try to talk to friends or counselors about this and it would just seem like I was complaining because I did not have words or vocabulary to explain what I was experiencing. It was not until I found a biblical counselor who helped me find my voice and pointed out that the things, I was experiencing were violations in our marriage that we began to make progress. I started prioritizing myself and making rules for him that protected me and others in our house. Interestingly, he was able to change immediately when a rule was made, coupled with the underlying threat of separation. This was painful for me because all my previous pleas fell on deaf ears because he simply did not care enough to make changes. If I had threatened divorce earlier, I would have gotten some of my needs met. That doesn't seem like how a Christian marriage should work.

Autism is still present in our marriage, but I am working hard to keep my autonomy and invest in myself, as I am a beloved daughter of Christ. For many years this felt unbiblical to me, that somehow autonomy was a form of separation from my spouse, but now I see that it is necessary. I am learning more about the limits of his braining wiring vs. character issues that can be addressed by Christian discipleship from other men and professional counseling. I am grateful for the resources that we have found, even though it took some time to find them. It seems that the marriages that end are the ones where the ASD partner is unwilling to try to change at all. I am grateful that my husband has taken this diagnosis seriously and is open to hearing about the times that he hurts people. He is doing deep work within himself to grow, and it is not easy for him. But he keeps at it and I am grateful.

Personal Story

I sought help alone. I found a counselor who understood autism and validated my experiences. We worked on healing me. I learned that I wasn't a failure as a Christian if my marriage was failing. I learned that I could walk with God outside of the conflict of my marriage. I learned that not everything was my fault as I'd believed and that his patterns of behavior were harmful. I wasn't crazy!! I learned the difference between a disappointing marriage and a destructive marriage. I learned that God cared deeply for me and that He felt very strongly about abuse in marriage—both physical and emotional.

While followers of Christ are called to enter suffering as He did, the call is to engage in *redemptive* suffering to reflect God's glory and accomplish His mission on earth.[25] We are not called to endure abuse in marriage as part of this suffering; marriage is meant to reflect the relationship of Jesus, the bridegroom, with us in marriage.[26] Abuse in any form is *not* a reflection of God's love for us; yet many women think they are doing God's will by staying in an abusive marriage, or that they are called to be submissive to an abusive husband. I know I believed that for many years that adultery was the only biblical reason for separation or divorce. I somehow felt I was I was not "released" from this marriage.

Many resources available to women and churches through the Psalm 82 Initiative discuss how suffering domestic abuse or any form of abuse in marriage is not in the interests of justice, righteousness, or goodness, and that churches should come alongside to support the abused and 'do no harm'. Christian leaders who encourage women to remain in abusive marriages are complicit in ongoing domestic violence and abuse and should be held to account for this complicit behavior.[26] Reflect on this quote from the Psalm 82 Initiative on submission: " 'Submission' is more closely understood under a rubric of cooperation rather than power. As we are taught elsewhere, each is expected to treat the others as better than themselves. It should be obvious that this does not mean that everyone is allowed to insist that they be treated as better than the others! The same principle is true in the home. Concluding that the wife should be cooperating with her Christlike husband does not allow the husband to *insist* on the wife's cooperation. The reason for this is, as we have seen, that 'power over' one another is forbidden. This is the biggest problem with the common view of authority in the home. To say that the husband is head of the wife says nothing about the husband having power, since a power-based relationship pattern is forbidden by Jesus. Rather, headship refers to the husband's responsibility to be the first to serve, first to love, and first to sacrifice – just like Jesus."[27] You can listen to an interview Dr. Holmes did with Thomas Pryde of the Psalm 82 Initiative as he shares how many of the women he helps to rescue from abusive situations are in a neurodiverse Christian marriage.[28]

As we close this chapter, we understand this information may be confusing or overwhelming. Many wives have endured trauma and abuse and did not have a word to describe their experience. Remember, no partner can make their spouse change or desire to work on the marriage, and Scripture tells us that "hope deferred makes the heart sick" (Proverbs 13:12, NIV). Hope is not a strategy. The information below can help you determine if you are in a destructive or abusive marriage. Whether or not your spouse is on the autism spectrum does not mean you must endure neglect, trauma or abuse.

Signs That You Are in an Emotionally Destructive Marriage

(Modified and used with permission from "*The Emotionally Destructive Marriage*," by Leslie Vernick, pages 18-37)[5]

Answer each question: Often——Sometimes——Seldom——Never

1. My spouse calls me names, such as *stupid* or *worthless*, or uses sexually degrading terms.
2. My spouse pressures me to do things I do not want to do.
3. My spouse uses the Bible to criticize me or to get me to do something he wants me to do.
4. My spouse dictates how often I can see/talk with my family of origin or who I may have as friends.
5. My spouse undermines me with our children.
6. My spouse speaks poorly about me to others (his family, friends, neighbors, church people).
7. I don't feel free to challenge my husband or disagree with him.
8. My spouse breaks things around the house when he's angry/upset and/or screams and curses at me.
9. When I tell my husband my deepest feelings, he laughs at me, ignores me, or uses them against me.
10. My spouse disregards my needs or badgers me till I give in to his demands.
11. My spouse calls or texts me often, wanting to know where I am, what I'm doing, and who I'm with.
12. My spouse monitors my emails, social media, and Internet use.
13. My spouse accuses me of things I did not do.
14. My spouse demands my attention when I'm busy with something or someone else.
15. My spouse does not like it when I get positive attention or affirmation from other people.
16. My spouse tells me I cannot tell anyone what happens between us.
17. My spouse uses sarcasm and ridicule to get me to stop talking or to change my mind.
18. My spouse refuses to listen to my point of view.
19. My spouse blows up when I ask questions about why he did something.
20. My spouse has threatened to harm me.

21. My spouse uses physical force to get me to do something he wants or something he doesn't want.
22. My spouse uses physical force to coerce me sexually.
23. My spouse withdraws from me if I don't do what he wants.
24. My spouse refuses to respond when I ask him questions—or ignores me for long periods of time.
25. My spouse changes the subject when I try to bring up something that's bothering me.
26. My spouse refuses to engage or participate in everyday family life.
27. My spouse plays mind games with me or tells me that he's the one who is being mistreated by me.
28. My spouse says the problems in our marriage are all my fault.
29. My spouse acts one way in public and another way at home.
30. There's a double standard with what's acceptable behavior. He has more leeway than I do.
31. I have no voice regarding how our finances are saved or spent.
32. I have no idea what my husband does with our money, even though I've asked.
33. My spouse omits information, which keeps me from knowing the whole story about things.
34. I feel trapped and/or crazy in my marriage.
35. I don't feel I can be myself and feel trapped in my marriage.
36. I feel like his mother in my marriage.
37. I feel tense and/or angry around my spouse.
38. My children are afraid of my spouse.

What's next? Buy yourself a journal and begin to process what you see about your marriage from taking the above test. Be as honest with yourself as you know how. This is essential if you want to know where you are. If you are worried that your husband might read your journal, you can write in a password-protected file on your computer. If you answered "often" on many of the questions, it's important that you start to document what's going on, for your own protection.

A Poem from an NT/NA Wife in Recovery from An Abusive Neurodiverse Marriage (used with permission)

Psalm 27, Personalized

The Lord is my light, and my salvation,
but it is difficult to see Him and to find Him,
in the midst of the blinding pain, the overwhelming oppression.
But yet,
I know He is there.

Whom should I fear? I should fear no one,
but it seems impossible not to be afraid of the one who hates me,
the one who crushes me to the ground with his unfair accusations and judgments,
full of offense and lies,
baring his teeth
like a lion ready to tear me apart,
puffing with his mouth
to ridicule and scorn,
shooting balls of fire from his mouth
while his hateful eyes fill me with fear and terror,
the finger jabbing, jabbing, jabbing
until something dies within me,
too afraid to move,
shaking in distress.

The Lord is the stronghold of my life -
whom should I dread?
No one, I know.
But oh, it is so hard not to dread,
not to dread the lion's eyes, the lion's presence near me,
seeing the mouth that jeers and pours out violence,
seeing the teeth that bare themselves in hatred against me.
Oh, it is so hard not to dread.

I confess my weakness,
that I tremble when in this presence of the lion
who has torn me from limb to limb,
crushing me with his whole being
over and over,
for as long as I can remember.
I confess that I shake,
and my stomach turns in knots,
and I cannot swallow.
Even when the lion is quiet next to me.
There is no telling when he will wake,
or what will wake him.

When the lion comes against me to devour my flesh,
as an enemy deployed to destroy me,
arrayed against me in battle,
with swords too numerous to count,
all pointing, all jabbing, all jeering, all roaring,
with the din so loud that I can no longer hear my thoughts,
or hear the One who loves me,
my rescuer, my helper.

I will remember.
I will remember that in the midst of the fierce battle,
in the midst of my enemy's searing hatred,
in the midst of the alarm,
that I will dwell in the house of the Lord.
He alone is my hiding place,
my high tower,
my secret refuge.
He alone is beautiful,
in the midst of the terror and violence.

I want to flee,

but I can flee <u>to Him</u>,

to the place He has for me,

where He will shield me from the one who hates me,

the one who seeks to destroy my life with his violence.

He is waiting for me there.

And He will let me in the door, and close it behind Him,

where the other cannot enter,

where he cannot follow,

where I can hide myself from him.

My Rescuer, the One who loves me,

the One who cares for my soul,

<u>He</u> will hide me under the cover of His tent.

He will set me high upon a rock,

where I can look down and see my adversary,

gnashing his teeth, seeking to devour me,

but he cannot reach me.

And I thank the One who saved me,

the One who delivered me from the mouth of the lion,

from the teeth of the one who sought to destroy me.

Though my heart still beats as though my chest would burst,

My rescuer begins to soothe my heart.

He strokes my hair on my head.

He covers my eyes from the sight of the lion, jumping at the door,

his teeth bared, shining in the darkness.

He covers my ears with His hands,

so that I do not have to hear the ear-splitting, heart-splitting roars,

aimed at my soul to destroy me.

I can almost sleep now.

Almost.

I slip my hand into the hand of my Rescuer.

I can trust Him.

<u>He</u> will not hurt me.

I close my eyes.

My dreams are filled with teeth …. Why are there so many teeth? And why so sharp?

Like daggers they are.

I wake in fear, shaking.

But He is still there.

<u>He</u>,

my Rescuer, my Rock,

and my Redeemer.

I look.

<u>He</u> is not angry.

His eyes are kind, and not full of swords.

They are full of love.

He speaks,

His voice is gentle,

so that I do not have to fear.

He will not abandon me to the lion.

He will not give me over to the will of my enemy,

to the false witnesses that rise up against me, breathing violence.

He will <u>value</u> my life,

instead of destroy it.

I can wait for Him.

Someday I will not fear.

Someday I will not dread.

Someday He will restore my soul.

I will wait for Him.

I will wait for Him in hope.

Suggested Resources for Your Next Steps (by Rev. Iris Knapp)

Called To Peace: Offering Hope and Healing for Victims of Domestic Abuse www.calledtopeace.org

Hawkins, D. (2017). *When Loving Him Is Hurting You: Hope and Help for Women Dealing with Narcissism and Emotional Abuse.* Harvest House Publishers.

Hunt, J. (2013). *Anger: Facing the Fire Within* Aspire Press.

Hunt, J. (2013). *Self-Worth: Discover Your God-Given Worth.* Aspire Press.

Hunt, J. (2023). *Verbal and Emotional Abuse.* Hope International Publishing.

Scazzero, P. (2017). *Emotionally Healthy Spiritually.* Zondervan.

Scazzero, G. (2013). *The Emotionally Healthy Woman.* Zondervan

Terkeurst, L. (2022). *Good Boundaries and Goodbyes.* Thomas Nelson.

Conclusion

8 Themes: What Neurodiverse Christian Couples Want You to Know

BY REV. DR. STEPHANIE C. HOLMES WITH RESEARCH ASSISTANCE FROM REV. DAN HOLMES, MS & BARBARA GRANT, MMFT, CAS, NCC

The number of Christian couples identifying as neurodiverse (ND) is on the rise, while the number of marriage helpers who are adequately trained to support neurodiverse couples work is limited and not yet keeping up with demand. In 2023 we decided to do a qualitative research study to learn more about the experience neurodiverse Christian couples (NDCCs) are having in their marriages. Out of the 318 respondents who answered our research survey, 286 replied to the open-ended question, ***"What would you want professionals or clergy or religious leaders helping neurodiverse couples to know?"*** We took their 286 responses and put them before three raters: I (Dr. Stephanie) was Rater 1, Dan, my husband, was Rater 2 (he represented the ND perspective), and Rater 3 was Barbara Grant, a neurodiverse couples coach and contributing author to this book. We wanted to identify themes found in these responses and to pull out specific quotes that represented these themes. We worked independently of each other and had the following results: I found 32 recurring themes, Dan found 22 and Barbara identified 20 major themes and 15 lesser ones. From this, we looked to see what common themes we all had consistently identified. When the themes were laid out on a grid, we identified 8 major categories that seemed to represent the overarching themes. (To read more about our process of qualitative exploratory research, you can refer to our published study: *Neurodiverse Christian Couples: Autism. Religion. Marriage: An Exploratory Qualitative Study.*[1]) The table below shows the themes (or codes) and the prevalence ranking each rater determined from the research data:

Rater 1 Code Ranking	Rater 2 Code Ranking	Rater 3 Code Ranking	Range of Responses Found
1	1	1	185–281
4	4	4	156–171
2	2	2	105–151
3	8	3	Code 3: 53–91
8	3	8	Code 8: 65–101
5	5	5	31–54
6	6	7	Code 6: 10–21
7	7	6	Code 7: 18–32

*Reprinted from published study[1]

Code 1: Uneducated or untrained therapists who are not neurodiverse couples- or autism-aware

Code 2: The marriage helper caused more harm or was not helpful

Code 3: Hyper-spiritual approach

Code 4: How challenging, complex, or traumatizing the relationship is

Code 5: Lack of emotional intimacy/connection

Code 6: Stigma of autism (neurodiverse) label

Code 7: Need for acceptance of neurodiversity by both partners

Code 8: Prevalence of autism being ignored

The theme that all three raters found to be most prevalent was: **Code 1: *"Uneducated or untrained therapists who are not neurodiverse couple or autism aware."*** The reviewed responses consistently stated that both secular and spiritual marriage helpers: failed to recognize or diagnose autism in adults; failed to understand the differences and complexities in neurodiverse relationships; lacked specific training in autism or neurodiverse relationships; and failed to acknowledge that neurodiverse relationships required different techniques and interventions than those used for neurotypical (NT) relationships. Overall, there was a consistent call to action for any marriage helpers (pastors, coaches, or counselors) to become autism-aware, informed and trained.

All three raters independently agreed that 185 of the 286 respondents indicated this singular issue or theme was the most important to communicate with anyone who wants to do neurodiverse couples' work. Raters 1 and 3 independently determined that over 250 respondents said that uneducated and untrained marriage helpers were the biggest challenge for a neurodiverse couple seeking help. These findings support previous research which noted the current lack of available ND-trained marriage helpers. Additionally, all three raters (who work as neurodiverse couple coaches) have heard this anecdotally from clients talking about their past experiences with providers who did not understand neurodiversity or mixed-neurotype relationships.

There is a deficit of ND-trained marriage helpers compared to the number of neurodiverse couples who are seeking help.[2,3,4] Another question on the survey asked the respondents how many marriage helpers of any kind they had seen in their marriage. The average response ranged from 5 to 7, with at least 5 respondents answering they had seen 10 or more counselors or pastors combined. For the second part of the research, 20 couples were interviewed for more in-depth information. They spoke candidly of the pain and frustration of having to change therapists, of feeling misunderstood and blamed for their failure to make progress, and of investing tens of thousands of dollars into therapy without a satisfactory return on their investment. In the open-ended responses to the survey, most respondents said that the untrained therapist or pastor did more harm than good and that some were "detrimental" to their marriage. Some neurotypical (NT, or non-autistic) spouses shared that when they went to their pastor or priest, they were encouraged to suffer in their marriage for the cause of Christ, or to submit or please their husband more so that he would change and become the man of God he needed to be. In many cases when pastors were involved as marriage counselors, the NT women experienced frustration and sometimes abuse because of the pastor quoting Scripture and implying that the marriage difficulties arose from the woman's lack of submission or obedience to her husband. The following are quotes from the survey responses, which illustrate the frustration and pain felt as a result of working with uneducated and untrained marriage helpers:

"Without specialized training they are unlikely to be helpful to a couple, and much more likely to do harm or at best, delay the beginning of helpful treatment."

"It feels incredible to me that clinicians are not considering autism and ADHD as a first line of questioning when a couple comes in with issues."

"So many more individuals are silently suffering and going undetected. Please become neurodiverse-aware as a baseline requirement to work with ND couples."

Another major theme (found as the third most prevalent by all three raters) was **Code 2: "The marriage helper caused more harm or was not helpful."** This theme represented responses that consistently stated that: the therapist or pastor did not validate the couple's experience of trauma; the therapist did not know about or understand *Ongoing Traumatic Relationship Syndrome* (which is also known as *Cassandra Syndrome*); the approach applied traditional marriage strategies which were not helpful, and even harmful; the helper failed to address autism or neurodiversity; there was a failure to address emotional abuse, neglect, indifference and apathy and its impact on the suffering spouse or the relationship. All three raters agreed that at least 105 or 36.7% of the respondents expressed a grievance or complaint about marriage help they had received. Raters 1 and 2 found that 150 believed this to be true, which indicates over 50% of the respondents found this to be an issue. A review of current research literature did not uncover any studies that specifically researched harm caused by untrained providers working with neurodiverse couples, but a study from 2012[5] reported that the majority of information available about neurodiverse couples stemmed from therapists or counselors writing books or blogs and that these were already reporting a rise in mixed-neurotype relationships and a need for more trained therapists to serve this need. The following responses from the survey illustrate **Code 2**:

"Both spouses are at risk of remaining unheard, uncoached and unhealthy – hopeless!"

"The typical counseling model can be harmful in some ways because it does not take into consideration the challenges of neurodiversity [in marriage]."

"[Helpers should] understand how differences in neurology can impact EVERY aspect of an intimate partner relationship and that there can be so much unintentional pain, hurt and trauma, because no professional or clergy has ever recognized the autistic traits in one or both partners."

While the idea of the *double-empathy problem*[6] was not explicitly stated by responders, many of the quotes indicated that neither neurotype felt understood or that the complexity of their relationship was understood by the professional or pastoral counselor.

Code 3 tied for the fourth most predominant theme and criticized marriage helpers for taking a *"hyper-spiritual approach"* or that they *"focused on the Christian marriage doctrine that the provider believed"*. Statements in this category mostly came from responders who identified as being of the Christian faith: 258 indicated Christian *Protestant*, 8 indicated Christian *other*, and 18 indicated they were Christian *Catholic*. This theme was based on 53-91 responses about harm, with Raters 2 and 3 observing higher responses to this code. Respondents' answers represented observations about helpers, such as: provider gave Sunday school advice (pray more, submit more, have more sex); focused on stereotypical gender roles and the lack of role-following as the issue in the marriage; blamed or pressured the woman to stay in the abusive marriage, as there was not adultery; the Bible and Scripture were used in a biased way towards the woman (both ND and NT respondents indicated this); the provider was judgmental or uninformed; the marriage problems were seen as spiritually-based or as spiritual warfare coming against the marriage; the provider said they do not believe in labels or diagnoses, or that a label or diagnosis was disrespectful to the man (ND); the man (ND) was the head of household and should be submitted to. As previously stated, people of faith who want marriage counseling tend to go to their pastor, priest, or spiritual leader first, and may only seek pastoral care instead of trained or licensed counselors.[7] (Note: Our study did not explore the qualifications or impact of marriage helpers from other faith backgrounds than Christian.)

The Rev. H.B. London (a former Focus on the Family vice president, now deceased) was quoted as saying that clergy in general are not trained in the basics of psychology or how to help those in complex situations, crises, or complex relationships.[7] In our (Dan and Stephanie) past experiences of church, pastors would state from the pulpit that no form of counseling was needed. We also heard pastors tell people not to seek counseling or take any form of psychotropic medication; they taught that all issues in this world are sin issues or obedience issues and that with proper church attendance or prayer and fasting, these could be resolved. John MacArthur, a well-known southern California pastor who is a proponent of conservative biblical counseling and teaches in the Reformed theology, Calvinist tradition, stated in 1993 (and continues to state) that, "Scripture does, after all, claim to be the only reliable resource to which we can turn to solve our spiritual problems" and "the word psychology means the 'study of the soul' and the soul cannot be studied by unbelievers."[8]

Many women respondents (both ND or NT) said that, in addition to the "spiritu-alization of marriage problems," they were reminded of their biblical role or place as a woman as a submissive helpmate. In the in-depth interviews, participants mentioned a harmful book that helpers sometimes referred to: *Recovering Biblical Manhood and Wom-anhood: A Response to Evangelical Feminism*.[9] Dan and I found an online copy of the book, which has been updated but lays out the principles of biblical *complementarianism*. It continues to hold to the premise that the husband is the spiritual leader and the ultimate *authority* in the home. The book has many pages detailing the roles of men and women in the local church as well as in Christian marriage. Additionally, several clients and inter-view respondents indicated their church or pastor were following several of the teachings of Bill Gothard and the Institute of Basic Life Principles (IBLP), which were exposed in a recent docuseries, *Shiny Happy People* (co-produced by Amazon Studios). Gothard, who (though single), held wide influence for decades and taught that all Christians were to marry. His teachings were based on men having "God-given authority," and that to disre-spect the husband was the same as disrespecting Jesus.

Many of the best-selling Christian marriage books from the last 20 years and the gender-role teachings of many evangelical churches, webcasts and podcasts have been reviewed and found to be harmful not only to women,[10,11,12] but to neurotypical and neurodiverse couples as well.[12,13,14] Harm can be magnified when someone in spiritual authority or a bestselling Christian author gives "spiritual" advice to spouses who may be "black-and-white," rigid thinkers, encouraging them to act as the final authority in the home. Some Christian wives in the study reported being told that even if their husband did have "a diagnosis" or "condition" (or if he disallowed medical care or made "reckless financial decisions"), he should still be *obeyed* and *respected* as the final authority even if the decision was not the best decision.

In one coaching situation I (Dr. Stephanie) worked on, the ND Christian husband treated his wife as a child when it came to finances. She was not able to have accounts or debit or credit cards in her name and was only added as an authorized user on his cards or accounts. He was given a substantial work bonus, and in one of our coaching sessions they had agreed that the money would be put into savings and not be used frivolously. Some-how, the wife found a statement that indicated a large portion of the savings was gone. She inquired about the missing money. He told her that as the head of the household, he did not need to check in with her, and that most of the money had been spent on breakfast or lunch out for himself since he chose not to pack a lunch. He stated, "If you wanted me to eat breakfast at home or not eat out, you should get up before me and make my breakfast and pack my lunch for me." When I asked him in a session about breaking his agreement (which he had made in front of me for accountability), he said, "As a *complementarian* (as opposed to *egalitarian* roles in Christian marriage), I hold 51% of the vote in this marriage and she has 49% of the vote. I decided as the one with the winning vote, it is inefficient to discuss things with her or get her opinion, when in the end, we will end up doing what I have decided is the best way forward or most efficient."

When well-intentioned spiritual counsel is given based on perceived gender roles instead of on each person's capabilities or capacities, or when marriage guidance is given without understanding the ND tendency towards literal, rigid thinking or the possibility of misapplication by the husband, both relational and personal harm can occur, especially for the wife. Many Christian women stated that this felt like wife-blaming and shaming by the spiritual authority, who seemed to dismiss these women's concerns and needs. Responses that made up the basis for Code 3 and indicated a participant received guidance that was skewed towards hyper-spiritualization included the following:

> *"I do believe the Christian community is saturated with 'just forgive and let the past go' mentality."*

> *"Both parties are stressed and hurting. Applying traditional 'Love and Respect' speak or just 'love her more with her love language' will not help and makes it worse."*

> *"Telling the woman to submit more just perpetuates the destructive cycle without making both members equally responsible for bridging the gap and rebuilding the relationship.*

> *Listen to me. Reach out and check in on us when I say we are in crisis. Stop staying if I trust God more everything will get better."*

The second most reported theme was **Code 4: *"How challenging, complex or traumatizing the relationship truly is."*** Responses that formed this major theme consistently cited: chronic communication problems; daily struggles which compound without resolution; sexless marriage or duty/obligation sex; high conflict; lack of conflict resolution; longevity of undiagnosed neurodiversity in the relationship; dual and co-occurring mental health issues; negative impact of dysregulation (shutdown or meltdowns); complex family dynamics; impulsivity; masking and camouflaging in sessions (or at church); executive function issues that impact daily life and dependability; ND partner may agree to a solution in front of therapist, then does not follow through, and the NT spouse carries the mental load.

Again, though this theme is listed as **Code 4**, it was the second most reported code in our study. The three raters agreed that at least 54% of the respondents indicated that the neurodiverse marriage dynamic is not only *challenging* and *complex*, but can be *traumatizing* for one or both parties, with a higher response about trauma from the NT spouse. While it is possible for the ND spouse to be on the receiving end of abusive behavior, research indicates a pattern of unintentional abuse or neglect is often reported by NT wives[15] as well as some NT wives reporting perpetual abuse.[16] At the time of this publication, published journal articles about abuse experienced by the ND spouse were not found, except in individual stories and blogs. Responses that typify the frustration and struggles described in **Code 4** are illustrated by these statements:

> *"My husband thought he was [autistic] from reading something; we both knew something was off and this made sense. His therapist said, 'No way!' And we went through years struggling, whereas an earlier diagnosis would have made a difference."*

> *"Neurodiverse relationships are really hard! We need concrete helpful tools, not just 'go on more dates and spend time together doing something fun, growing intimacy.'"*

> *"The challenges FAR exceed the typical challenges inherent in marriages and amount to differences in brain wiring akin to different languages and cultures, leading to incredible isolation and miscommunication."*

Studies[15,16] indicate that not only do NT spouses report various types of abuse and neglect, but they each report overly harsh discipline and complexities in co-parenting with their ND spouse. The spouses in these studies indicated that the ND spouse did not always understand or accept the ND diagnosis their child may have, nor did they understand appropriate expectations of neurotypically or atypically developing children. NT spouses felt that excessive demands or expectations were placed on the children by their ND spouse. This can become especially problematic if corporal punishment is practiced (and even encouraged) because of a singular scripture reference (Proverbs 13:24) that, taken out of context, seems to suggest that to "spare the rod" is to "spoil the child." A rules-based, black and white thinking parent may not be able to discern what is appropriate with small children, especially when they – and their child – are dysregulated. In my counseling and coaching practice, I have witnessed ND Christian men having high expectations of children for "first-time obedience and respect" without understanding the child's capability at their given biological or developmental age. If their spouse stepped in as a buffer to stop a harsh punishment, dysregulation by the ND would often ensue, and the NT was told they were undermining the ND's "God given authority as a parent."

The above case illustrates the type of complaint an NT Christian spouse may have when they go to their spiritual leader for help. Both Rater 1 and 3 have had clients where the ND Christian spouse may even appear to a quiet, meek person, masking their ND behaviors in sessions or at church and often volunteering and leading Bible studies. They may behave in the complete opposite way at home. Church leadership appreciates and praises behaviors like social masking and dutiful service, so convincing a church helper that the negative ND behaviors are really happening is very challenging. If the NT wife feels she is not getting help from church leadership or decides to stop going to that church, she is often seen as the one with the problem, or that she is not committed to her marriage or is not willing to submit to her ND husband's leadership. Meanwhile, the ND spouse is validated in their thinking and the abusive behaviors go unchecked.

Code 5 is the ***"lack of emotional intimacy or connection"*** in the marriage. This was most often reported by the NT spouse or was described by the ND spouse as "my spouse says we do not have a connection." This theme encompassed observations such as: no intimacy; lack of connection; unmet needs and longevity of unmet needs; emotional neglect; mocking or dismissing needs; stoicism; and the belief that logic and not having emotions is the superior way to be a human. While this made the list of 8 major themes, the raters were surprised that **Code 5** did not rate higher as a reported issue, since this is a common concern in all three raters' coaching practices. When respondents were given a list of several issues to check that applied to their marriage, the lack of connection was in the top five of most-checked issues. Over the past 10 years when I have asked my clients to rate their top 2 issues, nearly every NT spouse says *communication* and *connection* (i.e., a lack of emotional intimacy). The raters did note that **Code 4** issues (about complexity and trauma) outweighed the desire for intimacy and connection. Responses that illustrate the **Code 5** struggle are expressed by the frustrations of these respondents:

> *"Is there a tool(s) to make that better connection from this temporal location? I feel so alone, despite probably not very emotional connected enough for others. That makes me feel guilty. I really want to connect with others more."*

> *"Being in an ND relationship is very hard. A wife needs and expects certain things (like touch, affection, comfort and sex) that other people don't need or expect from the ND person. Just because he is a nice guy doesn't make him automatically a good spouse."*

Communication is the fuel for building connections, and communication is often compromised and complex in neurodiverse relationships. In working with neurodiverse Christian couples, I (Dr. Stephanie) have used an article called "The Five Levels of Intimacy."[17] To help concrete thinkers understand the levels of communication and how they lead to connection, the article[17] outlines these levels below:

Level 1: Safe Communication. This level of communication is seen as the most basic level of communication, without any degree of intimacy. This level conveys no feelings or vulnerability but is a simple transaction of information: an exchange of facts, data or basic observations.

Level 2: Others' Opinions and Beliefs. This level of communication is sharing about people in our shared circles or about what authors or podcasters have said. It tests the reactions of others without vulnerability or emotions. It included sharing plans or logistics about the kids or extended family, or about what others have said, but it is not personal or intimate.

Level 3: Personal Opinions and Beliefs. This level of communication starts to take a small risk of vulnerability by sharing a belief or opinion, but stays cognitive, fact-based, logical and left-brained.

Often when I talk to couples, they would state their communication rarely goes beyond Level 3, and that having a differing belief or opinion might cause conflict, which ND couples tend to avoid. Before sharing about these levels with couples, I have asked if the couple thought they had deep conversations, and both would say they might have them about special interests or political, religious, or spiritual matters, but not really about personal matters. The ND partner might say they thought they spoke at deep levels and that they enjoyed their intellectual discussions. However, when all the levels of communication were described, it became apparent that Level 3 often went deep enough for an ND spouse, and that this level of connection was perhaps all they needed.

Level Four: Feelings and Experiences. This level opens the door to vulnerability and intimacy by sharing joy, pain, failures, goals, and preferences: information about what makes us unique and who we are and what we value.

This does not include having meltdowns and shouting obscenities when angry, in place of the healthy and constructive sharing of feelings. When evaluating Level 4, the NT spouse would often say, "I do not feel I can share at this level with my ND spouse safely. I do not feel validated or understood and am even mocked or criticized." At the base of intimacy is being known and being seen. Many ND spouses felt they were being disallowed to share their feelings if they could not share their dysregulated feelings and outbursts.

> *Level Five: Needs, Emotions and Desires.* The author[17] states that sharing at this level is sharing at the deepest core of who we are. It requires safety, trust, and the ability to make requests and needs known and listened to without diminishing, dismissing, mocking or rejecting the other.

With the second most reported theme being **Code 4** (regarding the pain and rejection that stem from the challenges, complexities, and trauma), it is possible that the **Code 4** experience is connected to the lack of intimacy reported in **Code 5**. Many couples indicated they rarely make it past Level 2 communication without triggering a conflict. Level 3 is where my clients report that most conflict begins, and most NDCCs do not have the skill or tools to regulate and resolve conflict, so issues remain unresolved and the disconnect becomes wider. Challenges, complexities and trauma are rarely discussed and hardly ever resolved. In looking at the issues represented by **Codes 4** and **5**, it is important to restate the urgency of getting out of *Enemy Mode* with each other (see previous chapter), and of rebuilding *joy*, *hesed*, and group identity in order to develop a more connected and healthy marriage relationship. While taking individual responsibility is important, and assessing what contributes to the conflict cycle, some ND clients get lost in wanting to make the conflict equal or 50-50 shared responsibility and this is seldom the case.

Code 6 was one of the least brought up in the 8 major codes, but it reflects what was discussed in the first two chapters of this book concerning the "stigma of autism." **Code 6** observations made by ND respondents consistently included: stop trying to fix me or cure me; autism is not a sin or demon; autism is not a disease; autism is not all about deficits; and autism is seen negatively in society. The three raters believe that some of this stigma stems from personal shame, and we have had clients who do not want to be assessed or who refuse to believe their diagnosis based on their own negative bias about what being on the autism spectrum means. According to recent research,[18] negative stigma is partly due to a lack of understanding of autism, and that autistic traits are generally viewed negatively by society at large. While media and entertainment are beginning to broaden the cultural view of autism, most respondents still believe there is a negative bias or stigma associated with being neurodiverse or carrying that label, especially in the wider Christian community. More than half of my (Stephanie's) clients indicate a negative response to the diagnosis and cite stigma. The three of us agreed only 3.49% of the respondents specifically indicated a negative stigma, but we do not believe this is fully representative of the population. The ratio of NDs to NTs who answered the survey was 1:2, and the ND respondent was more likely to skip the open-ended questions (which featured this issue about stigma and labels). Participant statements that reflect this theme include:

> *"I would like them to know that people on the spectrum don't need to be fixed but to respect how they see the world differently and meet them where they are in terms of readiness to address challenges that need support."*

> *"Diverse is not a disease. It's a lot of work for both people. Calm communication and timeouts are allowed and helpful. Both people have to be accepting of the differences.*

> *The ND spouse may have viewpoints and attitudes that are quite atypical. However, this doesn't mean they are incorrect."*

Code 7 reflects, ***"A need for acceptance of neurodiversity by both partners."*** Statements and reflections that encompass this coded theme included: both partners need to adjust expectations; both partners must not compare their relationship to an NT-NT relationship; the provider (helper) should not place NT-NT standard(s) on the couple; both partners need to see the other's perspective; and sometimes alternative living situations are required to stay together. This theme came up between 18-32 times but tended to be stated more by an ND partner. All three raters believe providing psychoeducation about neurodiversity for the couple – and anyone who works with neurodiverse couples – should be a high priority. This code also reflects the *double empathy problem,*[6] in that neither spouse is able to be fully empathetic to the neurotype of the other or to the other's lived experience in the marriage relationship.

Each person in an ND marriage would do well to stop comparing themselves and their marriages to any NT-NT marriage that they know. Marriage helpers, especially clergy, may incorrectly encourage goals that one spouse may not be capable of reaching. Expectations should be based on what is possible and realistic for an ND couple, not on what perceived "normal" Christian marriage is supposed to be, especially if goals are set according to that helper's personal beliefs.

Many ND couples are trying creative living solutions to stay together which include varying degrees of joint or separate dwellings. Only 56% of the survey respondents reported living in the same house and sharing a bedroom. Only 5.5% of the respondents indicated they were divorced, and under 2% said they were legally separated or only together for financial reasons. Therefore, a large portion live in separate rooms, in separate parts of the house, or separate spaces, but come together on weekends. Some have an in-home, separated and celibate relationship in order to stay married and keep their covenantal vows. Reasons given for creative living solutions centered on protection from meltdowns (dysregulation), sensory profiles of the spouse and/or children, different preferences on house décor or cleanliness, and long-term unresolved conflict or trouble communicating without conflict. Of those who completed our survey, 38.23% of couples said they have at least one child with ADHD, and 52.6% said they have a child suspected or diagnosed as being on the autism spectrum. All three raters have seen that families with multiple neurodiverse family members have more challenges, complexities and possibilities of trauma occurring. Due to complex developmental, emotional and sensory issues within neurodiverse family systems, alternative spousal living arrangements (while remaining faithful to each other) can sometimes provide "grace and space" and optimize healing and growth for all family members.

For ND couples who are trying to stay together, we in the Christian helping field need to normalize these options if they are working for safety and peace in the home, especially if the couple does not feel they can biblically divorce or remarry. Many couples are trying to keep their marriage together, but they may not do so in a conventional way. The authors of this book are not supporters of adultery or open marriage, but sometimes creative living arrangements are necessary (much like an accommodation or modification is needed at school or work for children and adults on the spectrum), and an alternate living arrangement is often a needed modification for the family when more than one person in the home have differences, delays, diagnosis, or diversities.

Finally, **Code 8**, *"the prevalence of autism is being ignored,"* centered on the issues resulting from a failure of professionals and clergy to acknowledge the increased prevalence of autism in marriage. At least 22% of respondents indicated that they feel adult autism is being ignored or dismissed. Responses reflecting this theme include the individuality and different expressions of autism from person to person, and that a neurodiverse experience is an acceptable way to live. Included in this code was a call for action to research later-in-life autism diagnosis, and for professionals to understand masking and camouflaging and how these can keep someone from getting a proper diagnosis or identification. This is reflected and supported by research as well.[1,2,4,19,20,21,22,23,24] Participant responses included:

"Masking can make one appear fine when that is not the case and often the (NT) spouse appears needy or controlling when the opposite is true; they are not validated which perpetuate a negative cycle for seeking help from professionals or clergy."

"ND relationships are much more common than is commonly accepted/acknowledged and should be considered as a high possibility when marriage counseling is sought."

Both NDCs and NDCCs are seeking support from trained professionals to help them navigate their complex marriages. Those who are of the Christian faith are looking for pastors or professionals who can not only support their faith in a mutually edifying way, but who can understand and accommodate autism in marriage counseling. Christian marriage helpers can promote positive change in this direction, but they must learn to discern when religion or inflexible beliefs about faith are complicating an already challenging neurodiverse Christian marriage. Since an ND spouse may not yet have identified that they are on the spectrum, a lack of discernment on the part of a helper can further exacerbate the *double empathy* problem: when a couple and their helper are all not aware there is neurodiversity, the ND marriage issues can be thought to stem from past neglect, abuse, or trauma for one or both spouses. Traditional marriage counseling approaches will not help. Better diagnostic training for identifying adults on the spectrum is needed, since prevalence rates of ASD in children continue to increase worldwide. Neurodiverse hereditary rates increase the possibility that today's ASD adults have been missed: they are a "lost generation" of autistics who have not yet been identified. Many who are on the spectrum may resist evaluation or diagnosis due to negative stigmas. Faith-based communities can add further stigma, especially if being a-typical or having a diagnostic label is perceived as unbiblical or coming from a lack of faith, or worse, is a result of sin.

At this point if you are trying to determine which marital theology is subscribed to by Rev. Dr. Stephanie Holmes and Rev. Dan Holmes, authoritarianism, complementarianism, or egalitarianism, the answer is none of the above. We would say there are biblical issues with all three approaches as a stand-alone approach. We highly recommend the work of Dr. Joy and Bruce C.E. Fleming[25], based on the dissertation research of Dr. Joy Fleming. You can find more of their resources at TRU316[25], the Eden Podcast, and The Eden Book Series based on Genesis 3:16. Bruce Fleming has been a repeated and listener-requested guest on our NeuroDiverse Christian Couples podcast. Many of the texts cited in Chapter 12 as weaponized Scripture are re-examined in The Eden Series.

NDCCs are more likely to reach out first to their pastor or church staff for marriage help, and the Christian helping field is further behind the non-faith helping fields in addressing the needs of autism in marriage. Further research into NDCC marriages is needed to better understand how religious views may contribute to potential abuse or neglect, specifically if the ND husband adheres to a rigid interpretation of complementarian roles and disciplinary rules in marriage. Not only is being uninformed not helpful, but it can also be very harmful to one or both partners and the relationship. More research is required on many aspects of the NDCs and NDCCs.

If you are working with a couple that identifies as a Neurodiverse Christian Couple, seek training and understanding. We can help train you at the *International Association of Neurodiverse Christian Marriage (www.christianneurodiversemarriage.com)*. At our website you will find free and paid courses, a podcast link to our full episode catalog and weekly blogs. You can find YouTube videos at *Dr. Stephanie C. Holmes*. If you want to support and serve NDCCs, reading this book is your first step. Take the next step to be trained in either ND marriage support, marriage therapy or coaching. If you want to know more about the marriage and family experience of a neurodiverse family system, our first book *Embracing the Autism Spectrum: Finding Hope & Joy Navigating the Neurodiverse Family Journey* is available on our HolmesASR website listed in the resources section.

Appendix A
Are you ready for marriage work? 10 Questions to Consider

REV. DR. STEPHANIE C. HOLMES & BARBARA GRANT, MMFT, CAS, NCC

After a spouse(s) is found to be neurodivergent, most couples want to start marriage work, but they may not *both* be ready to work together in joint sessions. Depending on what help a couple seeks, doing joint work at the start may be traumatizing for one or both. Identifying *all* the issues at play (in addition to neurodiversity) is critical to making progress. Here are some questions to consider:

Question 1: Is there an addiction of any kind in either spouse? This includes substances of any kind (alcohol drugs, prescription medications etc.), pornography, sex or fetishes, food, gambling, technology or gaming. If there is an addiction or abuse of the above, these things are individual issues to be worked on. These problems are likely contributing to the couple's marital problems, but they are issues that can and should be worked on individually, first. Marriage coaching and counseling are not the appropriate context for an individual to address these challenges, as substance abuse and other addictions are separate diagnoses that require specialized care.

Question 2: Is there active abuse that makes it unsafe to work on the marriage in the same home? If there is domestic violence or any form of active abuse, it may not be safe to work on the marriage under the same roof. *Safety is paramount.* If one or both spouses are abusive, this should be worked on prior to doing joint marriage work. Abuse is an individual character issue that impacts marriage, but it is not something that marital work can address. The one who is abusive needs to do substantial personal work before joint marital work is safe. Specialized help is required for issues of abuse.

Question 3: Is there significant depression, anxiety, or another mental health issue that may be causing suicidal ideation or other patterns of dysfunction or self-harm? Like addictions or abuse, these are special psychiatric challenges that may require a spouse to seek psychiatric care and possible medication. Some level of emotional and mental stability is needed for successful joint marriage work to address a neurodiverse couple's issues.

Question 4: Are there childhood traumas or adverse events that have not been acknowledged or worked through and healed by either spouse? This work also needs to be done individually. Sometimes it can be worked on simultaneously while joint marriage work is being done, but working through childhood trauma and abuse is individual work that will impact marital work. We recommend that each person do their own work with someone different than the marriage coach or counselor.

Question 5: Is there trauma right now in the relationship? Depending on the type of trauma (A or B) joint marital work may be able to start, but your coach or counselor may need to work with each of you separately before working together. Safety and self-regulation are essential to cultivate before starting joint marital work. Your neurodiverse-trained coach or counselor should also be *trauma-informed.*

Question 6: Are there any BEEPS? "BEEPS" is defined by Dr. Jim Wilder and others (in *Joy Starts Here*) as: Behaviors, Events, Experiences, People, or Substances that we form dysfunctional attachments to *instead* of attaching to God and people in *joy*.[1] These are patterns of thinking and behavior that each person should examine individually, as there may be *fear* bonds, which can become significant obstacles to developing healthy *joy* or *love* bonds.

Question 7: Does each spouse acknowledge and accept the neurodiversity in the marriage? While a formal diagnosis may not be necessary, true change in a marriage is difficult if *both* spouses do not acknowledge and accept neurodiversity and begin to adjust their relationship expectations accordingly. Each partner is responsible for learning about autism, ADHD, and neurodiversity and its impact on marriage. If both partners accept the reality of neurodiversity, marital work with a neurodiverse-trained coach or counselor can be very productive.

Question 8: Is each partner willing to look at their contribution to the marriage dynamic and be coachable and teachable, with humility and openness? Never should a spouse blame 100% of the marriage issues on neurodiversity. Are both willing to look at how they contribute to the negative or traumatizing relational cycles? Are both committed to doing their individual and joint work? If so, working with a neurodiverse-trained coach or counselor can be fruitful.

Question 9: Is either partner angry and defensive about the neurodiversity in the marriage? Denial or defensiveness can indicate there are issues of unresolved personal shame. These can run very deep and be difficult to identify and eradicate. Similarly, a tendency to blame shift may be motivated by a sense of shame. Some individual work to identify and remediate denial, defensiveness or shame may be needed in addition to marriage work.

Question 10: Are there struggles and challenges in co-parenting children with neurodivergence? Additional care or support may be needed to understand the needs of neurodivergent and/or special needs kids. Co-parenting is often difficult for NDCCs to traverse together (for both NT or ND children) and will need additional parenting support. Many communities have family support resources for how to parent neurodivergent children, and such support is separate from marriage work.

The contributing authors of this book also believe in the transformative power of support groups. Group work facilitated by qualified and trained coaches or counselors can be a great way to get started in doing individual or marital work. Faith-based support groups are available for NT/NA spouses, NA/ND spouses, or couples,[2] and there are also online courses for neurodiverse Christian couples.[3]

Appendix B
Resources to Gracefully Navigate Your Neurodiverse Marriage

REV. DR. STEPHANIE C. HOLMES, REV. DAN HOLMES NEURODIVERSE CHRISTIAN COUPLE (NDCC) COACHES & COACHING COACHES OF NDCCS

Stephanie and Dan Holmes write from lived experience as a NeuroDiverse Christian Couple (NDCC) as well as professional experience working with NDCCs. Their first book, written with their adult children, *Embracing the Autism Spectrum: Finding Hope & Joy Navigating the NeuroDiverse Family Journey* focuses on their parenting journey of neurodivergent children and discovering their own neurodiversity in marriage.

Dr. Stephanie C. Holmes was formerly a licensed professional counselor (LPC) in the state of North Carolina. She received her bachelor's degree in psychology from Campbell University, her master's in counseling from Liberty University, and her doctorate in education from Abilene Christian University. She is an ordained minister, author, autism researcher, speaker, and certified autism specialist. When her daughter Sydney was diagnosed with Asperger's Syndrome, her world and focus changed from a thriving marriage and family therapy practice to a world of Individualized Education Programs, 504 educational plans, and understanding how to help students and individuals with challenges and needs in the classroom and the church setting. Today, she pulls from personal as well as professional experience to focus on neurodiverse marriages and family systems. She is the owner and founder of Autism Spectrum Resources for Marriage & Family, LLC, and she and Dan are co-founders of The International Association of NeuroDiverse Christian Marriage, LLC, and the podcast NeuroDiverse Christian Couples. Dr. Holmes and her family, Dan, Sydney & Erica, share their different perspectives and insights as a neurodiverse family!

Dan Holmes is a seasoned leader with a rich background in systems architecture, design, and consulting. He received his bachelor's degree in management information systems from The University of Charlotte (UNCC at the time), and his master's in computer science through The Georgia Institute of Technology (GT). In addition to his technical roles, he is a professional coach who guides Neurodivergent men, helping them harness their unique potential in personal and professional spheres. These dual roles allow him to integrate innovative thinking with empathy, fostering a culture of understanding and driving holistic growth. Dan is an ordained minister, Master Life Coach, and has served in church ministry through band ministry, small group leadership and board leadership. He received his own identification on the spectrum in 2019 and is a co-founder with Stephanie of The International Association of NeuroDiverse Christian Marriage, LLC and their podcast, NeuroDiverse Christian Couples.

Holmes & Holmes Coaching Services are found at:
www.HolmesASR.com
www.christianneurodiversemarriage,com

One on One Coaching
Couples' Coaching
Group Coaching
Online Courses for Couples, Professionals and Parents
Blogs
Podcast: NeuroDiverse Christian Couples Found at: https://www.spreaker.com/podcast/neurodiverse-christian-couples--4992356
Stephanie and Dan share their personal and professional experience as well as interviews with researchers and coaches and fellow neurodiverse couples.

Workbook For Groups Found at www.christianneurodiversemarriage.com
QR Codes For Resources

Charity Rochford TI-CLC & Jeremy Rochford TI-CLC, C-MHC, C-YMHC NDCC Neurodiverse Family, Parent & Marriage Coaches

Jeremy and Charity, Team Rochford, as they are affectionately known, are an ND/NT couple who have been happily married for over 20 years. They have two Neurodivergent children, both of whom are on the Autism spectrum and most likely they inherited those genes from Jeremy, who himself, received an Autism/ADHD diagnosis later in life.

Both are Trauma Informed (TI) Certified Life Coaches (CLC) who specialize in helping Neurodivergent and Neurodiverse Families understand communication, culture, and their own unique family dynamic. Together, as a Neurodiverse couple and family, they've founded NeuroFam to support other ND/NT families through the intricacies of navigating life in a world that (far too often) doesn't understand their struggles.

Jeremy, with his BA in Communication (California University of Pa), and Charity, with her BA in Psychology (California University of Pa), live in a small town outside of Pittsburgh, PA with their two awesomely neurodivergent children, an overused coffee maker, and multiple emotional support stuffed animals.

Offers One on One Coaching, Couples' Coaching and Groups

Find Out More At: www.OurNeuroFam.com
Podcast: NeuroFM found on Mental Health News Radio

Robin Tate, MA, MS, BCC, CAS
Autism/ADHD Life & Neurodiverse Couples Coach

Robin is a professionally trained coach with ten years of teaching experience; she owns her own coaching and education practice (Robin Tate LLC). As a Neurodivergent (ADHD) woman, Robin has a lifetime of personal and professional experiences with Autistic/ADHD adults. Robin holds a Master of Science in Reading and a Master of Arts in Counseling. She is credentialed as a Board-Certified Coach (BCC), Associate Certified Coach (ACC), and Certified Autism Specialist (CAS). With a focus on Autistic individuals as well as their relationships, she trained with The Association for Autism & Neurodiversity (AANE). She holds AANE certifications as an "AsperCoach" and a Neurodiverse Couples Coach. Robin is a UCLA PEERS "Certified Young Adult Provider". She has also trained with JST Coaching Training, The Professional Christian Coaching Institute (PCCI), and The International Association of Neurodiverse Christian Couples. Robin has completed Gottman Level 1 and 2 training. Her coaching approach is trauma-informed, strength-based, and client-centered. Robin is passionate about helping couples build safe, inclusive, homes where each person can be authentic and grow to reach their unique life and couples' goals.

Offers One on One and Couples' Coaching

Find Out More At: https://www.robintatellc.com/

Barbara Grant, MA MFT, CAS
Neurodiverse Couples Coach

Barbara Grant, MA MFT, CAS, NCC, has a master's in Marriage & Family Therapy, is a Certified Autism Specialist (IBCCES), and is a certified Neurodiverse Couples Coach (AANE). She has also been trained by the International Association of ND Christian Marriage and is a contributing author to their blogs.

She has been coaching and offering Biblical counseling since 2005, working with individuals, couples, and groups. Her current coaching practice focuses on neurodiverse couples, individuals, and families and offers support groups for neurotypicals. Barbara enjoys people! She is neurotypical; her first marriage (of 20 years) was to a neurodiverse partner and has a neurodiverse adult child from that marriage. She brings a lifetime of experience, compassion, and understanding to all her clients and is becoming a significant voice in the growing dialog about how to best support and strengthen neurodiverse relationships.

Offers One on One Coaching, Couples' Coaching and Groups for NT/NA Spouses

Find Out More At: https://bg-hc.com/

Rev. Iris Knapp
Women's Life & Discernment Coach

Iris has over 50 years of ministry experience, now ministering as a Life Coach. She was raised Jewish and came to know Jesus as Messiah in 1969 during the "Jesus Freak" revival.

She is certified with Light University, AIFC Australian Institute of Family Counseling, Ministerial Licensed with IAOG International Assemblies of God Fellowship, and ND Training with the International Association of ND Christian Couples. She has personal family ties to the autism spectrum. Her passion is to see women fulfill their potential in their God-given calling and her heart is to lead women through restoration, growth, and purpose so that they can be all that God has created them to be.

Offers One on One Coaching for Women and Groups for Women

Find Out More At: www.coachingwithiris.com

Mary H. Jones, MD, FAAP
ASD Clinical Specialist & Life Coach

Dr. Mary Jones is a physician, Autism Spectrum Clinical Disorder Specialist, and Professional Christian Coaching Institute-trained life and leadership coach. As a devoted mother of a child on the autism spectrum as well as a neurodiverse Christian marriage, Dr. Jones brings a unique blend of personal experience and professional expertise to her work.

Her unwavering passion lies in advocating for individuals on the spectrum within the Black community, as well as for their families, caregivers, and service providers. Dr. Jones firmly believes that education and the dismantling of cultural taboos are pivotal in fostering a deeper understanding of autism and neurodiversity within Black culture. By addressing these issues head-on, she endeavors to empower her community to embrace autism from their own cultural perspective.

Dr. Jones is committed to breaking down barriers to diagnosis and early intervention within the Black community. By promoting awareness and cultural sensitivity, she aims to expedite the diagnosis process, ensuring timely access to crucial services. Her ultimate goal is to facilitate equitable opportunities for individuals with autism in the Black community, enabling them to achieve the same quality of life as their counterparts in other communities.

Offers One on One Coaching and Groups

Find Out More At: https://drmarycoaches.com/
Podcast: Dr. Mary Podcast
https://www.mentalhealthnewsradionetwork.com/the-dr-mary-podcast/

Rev. Jenilee Rachel Goodwin
Certified Christian Life Coach, NeuroDiverse Trained Coach

As a certified professional life coach (ICCI), a certified autism coach (NCDD) and an ordained minister (AG), Jenilee has over 20 years of career ministry experience. Serving in stateside churches and overseas missions, Jenilee brings lived experience, problem solving skills, compassionate support and creativity into each coaching session. Jenilee asks the hard questions while listening, guiding and coaching clients in their unique life situation. Jenilee is trained in the Equipping Profile, a personal development coaching tool that helps discover growth points and possible barriers to growth. Through one-on-one coaching and group coaching, Jenilee uses the Equipping Profile, book studies, and even some homework to establish personal development plans, helping clients move forward in healthy ways.

With many in her immediate family on the autism spectrum, Jenilee has a special call and place in her heart for moms of kids on the spectrum and for NT wives going through the difficulties of ND marriages. Even more specifically, a passion for these women who are also in full time ministry or missions. There are very few places to share the full story. In coaching with Jenilee, you can share every single page of the story.

Offers One on One Coaching and Groups for Women

Specializes in Women in Ministry/Mission and Parents of Neurodivergent Teens/YoungAdults
Find Out More At: https://jenileerachel.com/

Appendix C
Navigating Your Neurodiverse Family Journey

Want to hear the rest of the story? Rev. Dr. Stephanie C. Holmes with her husband Rev. Dan Holmes and daughters Sydney & Erica write about their family's neurodiverse journey! Who was the first identified neurodivergent family member? When did Stephanie & Dan discover they were a NeuroDiverse Christian Couple? Find out more about the book, workbook, and courses for parents and family at www.HolmesASR.com and www.christianneurodiversefamilies.com. Embracing the Autism Spectrum includes hindsight learning, devotions, and additional blogs and articles!

About the Authors

Rev. Dr. Stephanie C. Holmes was formerly a licensed professional counselor (LPC) in the state of North Carolina. She received her bachelor's degree in psychology from Campbell University, her master's in counseling from Liberty University, and her doctorate in education from Abilene Christian University. She is an ordained minister (IAOG), author, autism researcher, speaker, Master Life Coach (ICCI), and certified autism specialist (CAS). When her daughter Sydney was diagnosed with Asperger's Syndrome, her world and focus changed from a thriving marriage and family counseling practice to a world of Individualized Education Programs, 504 educational plans, and understanding how to help schools and churches properly include and support individuals with challenges and needs. Today, she pulls from personal as well as professional experience to focus on neurodiverse marriage and family systems. She is the owner and founder of Autism Spectrum Resources for Marriage & Family, LLC, and she and Dan are co-founders of The International Association of NeuroDiverse Christian Marriage, LLC (IANDCM) and their podcast NeuroDiverse Christian Couples (NDCC).

Rev. Dan Holmes is a seasoned leader with a rich background in systems architecture, design, and consulting. He received his bachelor's degree in management information systems from the University of North Carolina at Charlotte (UNCC), and his master's in computer science through the Georgia Institute of Technology (GT). In addition to his technical roles, he is a professional coach who guides neurodivergent men, helping them harness their unique potential in personal and professional spheres. These dual roles allow him to integrate innovative thinking with empathy, fostering a culture of understanding and driving holistic growth. Dan is an ordained minister (IAOG), and Master Life Coach (ICCI). He received his own identification on the autism spectrum in 2019.

Stephanie and Dan Holmes, married in 1994, write from lived experience as a Neuro-Diverse Christian Couple (NDCC) as well as professional experience working with other NDCCs. Their first book, written with their adult children, *Embracing the Autism Spectrum: Finding Hope & Joy Navigating the NeuroDiverse Family Journey* focuses on their parenting journey of neurodivergent children and discovering neurodiversity in their marriage. Stephanie and Dan reside in GA, although Stephanie remains a Carolina girl at heart.

Jeremy & Charity Rochford (Team Rochford) are a NeuroDiverse Christian Couple happily married for over 20 years. They have two neurodivergent children both of whom are on the autism spectrum, who most likely inherited those genes from Jeremy, who himself, received an autism/ADHD (AuDHD) diagnosis later in life. Both are trauma-informed certified life coaches who specialize in helping neurodivergent and neurodiverse families (IANDCM trained) understand communication, culture, and their own unique family dynamics. Together, they founded OurNeuroFam. Jeremy, with his bachelor's in communication (California University of PA), and Charity with her bachelor's in psychology (California University of PA), live in PA with their two awesomely neurodivergent children, an overused coffee maker, and multiple emotional support stuffed animals.

Robin Tate, MA, MS, BCC, and CAS is an autism/ADHD/AuDHD life and neuro-diverse couple's coach. Robin is a professionally trained coach with 10 years of teaching experience; she owns her own coaching and education practice (Robin Tate LLC). As a neurodivergent (ADHD) woman, Robin has a lifetime of personal and professional experiences with AS/ADHD/AuDHD adults. She holds a master's degree in reading and a master's degree in counseling. She holds several certifications with additional training (AANE & IANDCM). Her coaching approach is trauma-informed, strength-based, and client-centered. She works with individuals and couples.

Barbara Grant, MA MFT, CAS is a neurodiverse couples coach. She holds her master's in marriage and family therapy and is a certified autism specialist (IBCCES) and certified neurodiverse couples coach (AANE & IANDCM). She has been coaching and offering biblical counseling since 2005, working with individuals, couples, and groups. Her current coaching practice focuses on neurodiverse couples, individuals, and families and offers support groups for neurotypicals. Barbara enjoys people! She is neurotypical and her first marriage of 20 years was to a neurodiverse partner and has a neurodiverse adult child from that marriage.

Rev. Iris Knapp is a life and discernment coach for women. Iris has over 50 years of ministry experience, now ministering as a Life Coach. She was raised Jewish and came to know Jesus as Messiah in 1969 during the "Jesus Freak" revival. She is certified with ICCI and the Australian Institute of Family Counseling (AIFC), and ministerial licensed with the International Assemblies of God Fellowship (IAOG). She has personal family ties to autism and is a neurodiverse relationship-aware coach (IANDCM). Her passion is to see women fulfill their potential in their God-given calling so that they can be all that God created them to be. She is the founder of Coaching with Iris.

Mary H. Jones, MD, FAAP is a physician and professional Christian coach as well as an ASD clinical specialist. As a devoted mother of a child on the spectrum as well as a wife in a neurodiverse Christian marriage, Dr. Jones brings a unique blend of personal experience and professional expertise to her work. Her unwavering passion lies in advocating for individuals on the spectrum within the Black community as well as for their families, caregivers, and service providers. Dr. Jones firmly believes that education and the dismantling of cultural taboos are pivotal in fostering a deeper understanding of autism and neurodiversity within Black culture. Dr. Jones is committed to breaking down barriers to diagnosis and early intervention within the Black community. She is the founder of Dr. Mary Coaches and has a podcast, The Dr. Mary Podcast. She has received additional training under IANDCM.

Carol Reller, MS is a retired speech-language pathologist (SLP) who has her master's in speech-language pathology as well as a clinical rehabilitative services credential. She retired after working in the field of speech and language. In her last 21 years, she worked with preschool through high school students as an itinerant therapist with a focus on articulation, language, and communication. She has been married to Greg for over 30 years and they have three adult children. Greg was identified with what was then known as Asperger's after 25 years of marriage. She and Greg benefit from coaching, books and podcasts on autism, and group work to continue to learn and grow, and navigate their marriage. She enjoys scrapbooking, hiking, reading, and tending to their 5 acres of land which includes a garden, orchard, and animals.

References

Scripture Use

King James Bible (2008). Oxford University Press. (Original work published in 1769).

New International Version (1984). International Bible Society. (Original work published in 1973).

The ESV Study Bible: English Standard Version (2008). Crossway Bibles; Wheaton, IL.

The Holy Bible: New American Standard Bible. 1995, 2020. LaHabra, CA: The Lockman Foundation

The Holy Bible: New King James Version (1982). Thomas Nelson; Nashville, TN.

The Holy Bible: New Living Translation (1996). *Gift and Award Edition.* Tyndale Publishers: Carol Stream, IL

The Holy Bible: KJV, NKJV, ESV, NIV. Bible Gateway, www.biblegateway.com

Dr. Stephanie Holmes' Research Articles

Holmes, S. (2020). Creating an inclusive climate for students on the autism spectrum. School of Education Leadership. https://digitalcommons.acu.edu/school_ed_leadership/5/

Holmes, S. (2023a). Exploring a later in life diagnosis and its impact on marital satisfaction in the lost generation of autistic adults: An exploratory phenomenological qualitative study. *Global Journal of Intellectual & Developmental Disabilities, 12*(1), 001-0010

Holmes, S. (2023b). Neurodiverse Christian couples: Autism. Religion. Marriage an exploratory qualitative study. *International Journal of Psychiatry, 8*(5), 106-116.

Holmes, S. (2024). NeuroDiverse Relationships: Neuroplasticity and Hope for Building the Autistic Brain's "Joy Center." *Global Journal of Intellectual & Developmental Disabilities, 13*(1), 001-003.

Introduction

1. American Psychiatric Association. (2013). *Diagnostic and statistical manual of mental disorders (5th ed.).* Arlington, VA: American Psychiatric Publishing.

2. Baumer, N. & Frueh, J. (2021, November). *What is neurodiversity?* Harvard Health Publishing. https://www.health.harvard.edu/blog/what-is-neurodiversity-202111232645

3. American Psychiatric Association. (1994). *Diagnostic and statistical manual of mental disorders (4th ed.).* Arlington, VA: American Psychiatric Publishing.

4. American Psychiatric Association. (2000). *Diagnostic and statistical manual of mental disorders (4th ed., text rev.).* Arlington, VA: American Psychiatric Publishing.

5. Holmes, S. (2020). Creating an inclusive climate for students on the autism spectrum. School of Education Leadership. https://digitalcommons.acu.edu/school_ed_leadership/5/

6. Murphy, C. (2011). An Interview with Emily Rubin. *The ASHA Leader, 16*(1) https://leader.pubs.asha.org/doi/10.1044/leader.FTR5.16012011.np

7. Stitcher, J., Herzog, M., Visovsky, K., Schmidt, C., Randolph, J., Schultz, T., & Gage, N. (2010, September). Social competence intervention for youth and Asperger syndrome and high functioning autism: An initial investigation. *Journal of Autism and Developmental Disorders*, 40(9), 1067-1079. doi:10.1007/s10803-010-0959-1

8. Hoffman, M. (2023, September 12). *Pastor resigns from Stoutland School Board amidst backlash from autism comments during sermon.* K8News. Gray Television, Inc. https://www.kait8.com/2023/09/13/pastor-resigns-stoutland-school-board-amidst-backlash-autism-comments-during-sermon/

Chapter 1

1. Holmes, S. (2023a). Exploring a later in life diagnosis and its impact on marital satisfaction in the lost generation of autistic adults: An exploratory phenomenological qualitative study. *Global Journal of Intellectual & Developmental Disabilities, 12*(1), 001-0010.

2.   Attwood, T. (1998). *Asperger's syndrome: A guide for parents and professionals.* UK: Jessica Kingsley Press.

3.   Attwood, T. (2006). *The complete guide to Asperger's Syndrome.* UK: Jessica Kingsley Press.

4.   Helps, S. (2016). Systemic psychotherapy with families where someone has an autism spectrum condition. *NeuroRehabilitation, 38,* 2230-230.

5.   Holmes, S. (2023b). Neurodiverse Christian couples: Autism. Religion. Marriage an exploratory qualitative study. *International Journal of Psychiatry, 8*(5), 106-116.

6.   Volkmar, F., & Klin, A. (2000). Diagnostic issues in Asperger Syndrome. In A. Klin, F. Volkmar & S. Sparrow (Eds.). *Asperger Syndrome* (pp. 25-71). The Guildford Press.

7.   Scalise, E., & Holmes, S. (2015). Light it up blue: Understanding autism spectrum disorder. *Christian Counseling Today, 20*(2), 11–16.

8.   Bai, D., Yip, B. H. K., Windham, G. C., Sourander, A., Francis, R., Yoffe, R., Glasson, E., Mahjani, B., Suominen, A., Leonard, H., Gissler, M., Buxbaum, J. D., Wong, K., Schendel, D., Kodesh, A., Breshnahan, M., Levine, S. Z., Parner, E. T., Hansen, S. N., Hultman, C., Reichenberg, A., & Sandin, S. (2019). Association of genetic and environmental factors with autism in a 5-country cohort. JAMA Psychiatry, 76(10), 1035–1043. https://doi.org/10.1001/jamapsychiatry.2019.1411. PMID: 31314057; PMCID: PMC6646998.

9.   Center for Disease Control. (2023). Data & statistics on autism spectrum disorder. https://www.cdc.gov/ncbddd/autism/data.html

10. World Health Organization (2023). *Autism.* https://www.who.int/news-room/fact-sheets/detail/autism-spectrum-disorders

11. Lai, M., & Baron-Cohen, S. (2015). Identifying the lost generation of adults with autism spectrum conditions. *Psychiatry, 2*(11), 1013–1027.

12. Stoddart, K. P., Burke, L. & King, R. (2012). *Asperger's Syndrome in adulthood: A comprehensive guide for clinicians.* Norton Publishers.

13. Mitran, C. (2022a). Challenges of licensed counselors and other licensed mental health providers working with neurodiverse adults: An instrumental case study. *The Family Journal.* https://doi.org/10.1177/10664807221123553

14. Parker, M. & Mosley, M. (2021). Therapy outcomes for neurodiverse couples: Exploring a solution-focused approach. *Journal of Marital and Family Journal,* 1-20.

15. Smith, R., Netto, J., Gribble, N., & Falkner, M. (2020). 'At the End of the Day, It's Love': An Exploration of Relationships in Neurodiverse Couples. *Journal of Autism and Developmental Disorders, 51*(9), 3311–3321. https://doi.org/10.1007/s10803-020-04790-z

16. Strunz, S., Schermuck, C., Roepke, S., Ballerstein,S., Ahlers, C., & Dziobek, I. (2016). Romantic relationships and relationship satisfaction among adults with Asperger Syndrome and High-Functioning Autism. *Journal of Clinical Psychology,* 1-13.

17. Heasman, B., & Gillespie, A. (2018). Perspective-taking is two-sided: Misunderstanding between people with Asperger's Syndrome and their family members. *Autism, 22*(6), 740-750.

18. Ingersoll, B., & Wainer, A. (2014). The broader autism phenotype. In F. R. Volkmar, S. J. Rogers, R. Paul, & K. A. Pelphrey (Eds.), *Handbook of autism and pervasive developmental disorders* (4th ed., pp. 28–56). Wiley.

19. Rosen, N., Lord, C., Volkmar, F. (2021 January). The diagnosis of autism: From Kanner to DSM-III to DSM-5 and Beyond. *Journal of Autism and Developmental Disorders, 51,* 4253-4270.

20. Silverman, C. (2015). NeuroTribes: The legacy of autism and the future of neurodiversity by Steve Silberman. *Anthropological Quarterly, 88*(4), 1111–1121.

21. Klin, A.,Volkmar, F., & Sparrow, S. (2000). *Asperger Syndrome.* The Guilford Press.

22. Klin, A., & Volkmar, F. R. (1997). Asperger syndrome. In D. J. Cohen & F. R. Volkmar (Eds.), *Handbook of autism and pervasive developmental disorders* (pp. 94-122). Wiley.

23. Brown, C., & Dunn, W. (2022). *Adolescent/adult sensory profile users' manual.* Psychological Corporation.

24. Mitran, C. (2022b). A new framework for examining impact of neurodiversity in couples in intimate relationships. *The Family Journal, 30*(3), 437–443. https://doi.org/10.1177/10664807211063194

25. Parker, M., Diamond, R., & Auwood, L. (2020). Exploring exceptions and discovering solutions: A care presentation of autism and the family. *Family Process, 59*(4), 1891–1902. https://doi.org/10.111/famp.12500

26. Arad, P., Shechtman, Z., & Attwood, T. (2021). Physical and mental well-being of women in neurodiverse relationships: A comparative study. *Journal of Psychology & Psychotherapy, 12*(1), 1–22. https://doi.org/10.21203/rs.3.rs-955119/v1.

27. Baron-Cohen, S., Wheelright, S., Skinner, R., Martin, J., & Clubley, E. (2001). The autism-spectrum quotient (AQ): Evidence from Asperger syndrome/high-functioning autism, males and females, scientists and mathematicians. *Journal of Autism and Developmental Disorders, 31*(1), 5-17.

28. Holmes, S. (Host). (2021c, October 22). *Psychopharmacology and autism with Dr. Matthew Fisher* [Audio podcast]. https://podtail.com/en/podcast/springbrook-s-converge-autism-radio/talking-autism-with-dr-stephanie-holmes/

29. Milton, D. (2012). On the ontological status of autism: the 'double empathy problem'. *Disability & Society 27*(6), 883-887.

30. Crompton, C., Ropar, D., Evans-Williams, C., Flynn, E., Fletcher-Watson, S. (2022). Autistic peer-to peer information transfer is highly effective. *Autism 24*(7), 1704-1712.

31. Carpenter, P., & Roer, K. (2022). *The security culture playbook: An executive guide to reducing risk and developing your human defense layer.* Wiley.

32. Carpenter, P. (2019). *Transformational security awareness.* Wiley

33. Carpenter, P. (n.d.) Podcasts: 8ᵗʰ Layer Insights & Digital Folklore

34. Westbrook, C. (2020). *Best places to work: An autistic adventure in corporate America.* KDP.

35. Westbrook, C. (2016). *Debt and circuses: Protecting business owners from their enemies, their allies, and themselves.* KDP

Chapter 2

1. Holmes, S. (2023a). Exploring a later in life diagnosis and its impact on marital satisfaction in the lost generation of Autistic adults: An exploratory phenomenological qualitative study. *Global Journal of Intellectual & Developmental Disabilities 12*(1), 1-10.

2. Arad, P., Shechtman, Z., & Attwood, T. (2021). Physical and mental well-being of women in neurodiverse relationships: A comparative study. *Journal of Psychology & Psychotherapy, 12*(1), 1–22. https://doi.org/10.21203/rs.3.rs-955119/v1.

3. Aston, M. (2014). *The other half of Asperger Syndrome (Autism Spectrum Disorder): A guide to living in an intimate relationship with a partner who is on the Autism Spectrum,* 2ⁿᵈ ed. Jessica Kingsley Publishers.

4. Bostick-Ling, J., Cumming, S., & Bundy A. (2012). Life satisfaction of neurotypical women in intimate relationship with an Asperger's partner: A systematic review of the literature. *Journal of Relationships Research,* 1-11. https://doi.org/10.1017/jrr.2012.9

5. Holmes, S. (2023b). Neurodiverse Christian couples: Autism. Religion. Marriage an exploratory qualitative study. *International Journal of Psychiatry, 8*(5), 106-116.

6. Rench, C. (2014). *When Eros meets Autos: Marriage to someone with autism spectrum disorder* (Doctoral dissertation, Capella University).

7. Chapman, G. (2010). *The five love languages; The secret to love that lasts.* Chicago: Northfield Publishing

8. Garrett, M. & Garrett. R. (2019). *Love needs: Discover your top 10 languages of loving.* Kindle Direct Publishing.

9. Stone, D., & Heen, S. (2014). *Thanks for the feedback: The science and art of receiving feedback well.* New York; The Penguin Group.

10. Holy Bible, New International Version (NIV). (2011). Biblica, Inc.

Chapter 3

1. Vermeulen, P. (2023). *Autism and the Predictive Brain: Absolute Thinking in a Relative World.* Routledge Taylor & Francis Group.

2. World Health Organization. (2019). 6B41 Complex post-traumatic stress disorder. In *International statistical classification of diseases and related health problems* (11th ed.). https://icd.who.int/browse/2024-01/mms/en#585833559

3. Harbuz, M. S., Richards, L. J., Chover-Gonzalez, A. J., Marti-Sistac, O., & Jessop, D. S. (2006). Stress in autoimmune disease models. *Annals of the New York Academy of Sciences, 1069*(1), 51-61.

4. Porcelli, B., Pozza, A., Bizzaro, N., Fagiolini, A., Costantini, M., Terzuoli, L., Ferretti, F. (2016). Association between stressful life events and autoimmune diseases; A systematic review and meta-analysis of retrospective case-control studies. *Autoimmunity Reviews, 15*(4), 325-334.

5. Song, H., Fang, F., Tomasson, G.(2018). Association of stress-related disorders with subsequent autoimmune disease. *JAMA, 319*(23), 2388-2400.

6. Whitacre, C., Cummings, S., & Griffin, A. (1994). 4- the effect of stress on autoimmune disease. *Handbook of Human Stress and Immunity, 77-100.*

7. Stojanovich, L., & Marisavljevich, D. (2008). Stress is a trigger of autoimmune disease. *Autoimmunity Reviews, 7* (3), 209-213.

8. Attwood, T., & Garnett, M. (2023). What exactly is camouflaging? Found at attwoodandgarnettevents.com

9. Lai, M., Lai, M-C., Lombardo, M.V., Ruigrok, A.N.V., et al. (2017) 'Quantifying and exploring camouflaging in men and women with autism.' *Autism* 21(6), 690-702.

10. American Psychiatric Association (2013). *Diagnostic and statistical manual of mental disorders* (5th ed.).

11. Holmes, S. (2016). Marriage on the Autism Spectrum: He said/She said. American Association of Christian Counselors. Found at https://aacc.net/2017/03/14/marriage-on-the-autism-spectrumaspie-nt-marriage-he-said-she-said/

12. Deci, E., & Ryan, R. (2002*). Handbook of self-determination research*. Rochester, NY: The University of Rochester Press.

13. Holmes, S. (2020). Creating an inclusive climate for students on the autism spectrum [Dissertation]. School of Educational Leadership. Retrieved from https://digitalcommons.acu.edu/school_ed_leadership/5/

14. Ryan, R., & Deci, E. (2000). Self-determination theory and the facility of intrinsic motivation, social development, and well-being. *American Psychologist, 55*(1), 68-78. doi:10.103/0003-066X.55.1.68

15. Wehmeyer, M., Abery, B., Mithaug, D., & Stancliffe, R. (2003). *Theory in self-determination: Foundations for educational practice*. Springfield, IL: Charles C Thomas.

16. Olson, A. (2013). The theory of self-actualization. Psychology Today. Retrieved from https://www.psychologytoday.com/us/blog/theory-and-psychopathology/201308/thetheory-self-actualization

17. PDA Society (n.d). Pathological Demand Avoidance: Part of the Autism Spectrum. "What is demand avoidance." Retrieved from https://www.pdasociety.org.uk/what-is-pda-menu/what-is-demand-avoidance/

18. Holmes, S., Holmes, D., Holmes S., & Holmes, E. (2023). *Embracing the Autism Spectrum: Finding Hope & Joy Navigating the NeuroDivese Family Journey*

Chapter 4

1. Engelbrecht, N. (2023). The autism sex ratio. Paper retrieved at https://embrace-autism.com/the-autism-sex-ratio/

2. Asperger, H. (1944). Die, "Autistischen Psychopathen" im kindesalter. *Archiv f. Psychiatrie 177,*76-136

3. Kanner, L. (1943). Autistic disturbances of affective contact. Retrieved from https://autismtruths.org/pdf/Autistic%20Disturbances%20of%20Affective%20Contact%20-%20Leo%20Kanner.pdf

4. Loomes, R., Hull, L., Mandy, W. (2017). What is the male-to-female ratio in autism spectrum disorder? A systematic review and meta-analysis. *Journal of American Academy of Child and Adolescent Psychiatry, 56*(6), 466-474

5. McCrossin, R. (2022). Finding the true number of females with autistic spectrum disorder by estimating the biases in initial recognition and clinical diagnosis. *Children, 9*(2), 272.

6. Attwood, T. (2007). *Complete guide to Asperger's syndrome*. Jessica Kingsley Publishers.

7. Gillberg, C., & Coleman, M. (2000). *The biology of the autistic syndromes*. Cambridge University Press.

8. Gillberg, C. (2002). *A guide to Asperger Syndrome*. Cambridge University Press.

9. Bargiela, S., Steward, R., & Mandy W. (2016). The experiences of late-diagnosed women with autism spectrum conditions: An investigation of the female autism phenotype. *Journal of Autism and Developmental Disorders, 46,* 3281-3294.

10. Head., A.M., McGillivray, J.A., & Stokes, M.A. (2014). Gender differences in emotionality and sociability in children with autism spectrum disorders. *Molecular Autism 5*(1), 19.

11. Sedgewick, F., Hill, V., Yates, R., Pickering, L., & Pellicano, E. (2015). Gender differences in the social motivation and friendship experiences of autistic and non-autistic adolescents. *Journal of Autism and Developmental Disorders, 46*(4), 1297-1306.

12. Carroll, W. (2021). Sister to sister: A phenomenological study of women's experiences of having a sister with autism spectrum disorder based on the female autism phenotype. [Dissertation Research].

13. Duvekot, J., van der Ende, J., Verhulst, F. C., Slappendel, G., van Daalen, E., Maras, A., & Greaves-Lord, K. (2017). Factors influencing the probability of a diagnosis of autism spectrum disorder in girls versus boys. Autism, 21(6), 646–658. https://doi.org/10.1177%2F1362361316672178

14. Lehnhardt, F. G., Falter, C. M., Gawronski, A., Pfeiffer, K., Tepest, R., Franklin, J., & Vogeley, K. (2016). Sex-related cognitive profile in autism spectrum disorders diagnosed late in life: Implications for the female autistic phenotype. Journal of Autism and Developmental Disorders, 46(1), 139–154. https://doi.org/10.1007/s10803-015-2558-7

15. Whyte, E. M., & Scherf, K. S. (2018). Gaze following is related to the broader autism phenotype in a sex-specific way: Building the case for distinct male and female autism phenotypes. Clinical Psychological Science, 6(2), 280–287. https://doi.org/10.1177%2F2167702617738380

16. Hull, L., Petrides, K.V., and Mandy, W. (2020). The female autism phenotype and camouflaging: A narrative review. *Review Journal of Autism and Developmental Disorders, 7,* 306-317.

17. Attwood, T., & Garnett, M. (n.d.). Autistic women in couple relationships. Retrieved from https://attwoodandgarnettevents.com/autistic-women-in-couple-relationships/

18. Crompton, C.J., Ropar, D., Evan-Williams, C.V., Flynn, E.G., Fletcher-Watson, S. (2020). Autistic peer-to-peer information transfer is highly effective. *Autism, 24*(7), 1704-1712.

19. Strunz, S., Schermuck, C., Roepke, S., Ballerstein,S., Ahlers, C., & Dziobek, I. (2016). Romantic relationships and relationship satisfaction among adults with Asperger Syndrome and High-Functioning Autism. *Journal of Clinical Psychology*, 1-13.

20. Ying Yew, R., Samuel, P., Hooley, M., Mesibov, G., Stokes, M. (2021). A systematic review of romantic relationship initiation and maintenance factors in autism. *Personal Relationships, 28*(4), 777-802

21. Stone, D., & Heen, S. (2015). *Thanks for the feedback: The science and art of receiving feedback well.* Penguin.

22. Scazzero, P., & Scazzero, G. (2022). *Emotionally Healthy Relationships Updated Edition Workbook plus Streaming Video: Discipleship that Deeply Changes Your Relationship with Others.* HarperChristian Resources.

23. Kranowitz, C., & Miller, L.J. (2016). *The Out of Sync grows up: Coping with sensory processing disorder in the adolescent and young adult years (The out-of-sync child series).* A TarcherPerigee Book.

24. Kranowitz, C. S. (2016). *The out-of-sync child grows up: Coping with sensory processing disorder in the adolescent and young adult years.* Penguin.

25. Brown, C., & Dunne, W. (2002). Adolescent/Adult Sensory Profile User's Manual. San Antonio, TX: Psychological Corporation.

26. Volkmar, F.R., Young, G.S., Stahmer, A.C., Griffith, E.M., & Rogers, S.J. (2009). *American Journal of Psychiatry, 157*(2), 262-267.

27. Chapman, G. (2009). *The five love languages: How to express heartfelt commitment to your mate.* Moody Publishers.

28. Kendrick, A., & Kendrick, S. (2013). *The love dare.* B&H publishing group.

29. Simone, R. (2012). *22 things a woman with Asperger's syndrome wants her partner to know.* Jessica Kingsley Publishers.

30. Holmes, S., Holmes, D., Holmes, S., & Homes, E. (2023). *Embracing the autism spectrum: Finding hope and joy navigating the neurodiverse family journey.* Book Baby.

31. Wiley, LH. (2011) *Safety Skills for Asperger Women: How to Save a Perfectly Good Female life.* Jessica Kingsley Publishers.

32. Autism Spectrum Resources for Marriage and Family Podcast (2023). Interviews with autistic women. Autism and the 3 Shoes Approach with Laura Nadine Dooley. Found at https://www.spreaker.com/episode/autism-the-3-shoes-approach-with-laura-nadine-dooley--52106145

33. Autism Spectrum Resources for Marriage and Family Podcast (2023). Interviews with autistic women. What you need to understand about women on the spectrum. Guest Dr. Natalie Engelbrecht. Found at https://www.spreaker.com/episode/what-you-need-to-understand-about-women-on-the-autism-spectrum-with-dr-natalie-engelbrecht--52524535

34. Autism Spectrum Resources for Marriage and Family Podcast (2023). Interviews with autistic women. Autism Translated with Guest Toni Boucher. Found at https://www.spreaker.com/episode/autism-translated-with-toni-boucher--52114776

35. Autism Spectrum Resources for Marriage and Family Podcast (2023). Interviews with autistic women. Autism in Heels with Guest Jennifer Cook. Found at https://www.spreaker.com/episode/autism-in-heels-with-jennifer-cook--52723303

36. Psalm 82 Initiative. Calling civil and religious leaders to recognize and respond to abuse more effectively. Found at https://www.psalm82initiative.org/

37. Neurodiverse Christian Couples Podcast (2023). Thomas Pryde. Does Malachi 2:16 say,"God hates divorce." Part 1 Found at https://www.spreaker.com/podcast/neurodiverse-christian-couples--4992356

38. Neurodiverse Christian Couples Podcast (2023). Thomas Pryde. Does Malachi 2:16 say,"God hates divorce." Part 2 Found at https://www.spreaker.com/episode/does-malachi-2-16-say-god-hates-divorce-with-thomas-pryde-part-2--50945840

Chapter 5

1. Wilder, E.J., & Hendricks, M. (2020). *The other half of church: Christian community, brain science, and overcoming spiritual stagnation.* Chicago: Moody Publishers.

2. Neurodiverse Christian Couples Podcast (2023 Jan). *Escaping enemy mode with Dr. Jim Wilder* [Audio podcast]. https://www.spreaker.com/episode/escaping-enemy-mode-with-dr-jim-wilder--52449734

3. Stone, D., & Heen, S. (2015). *Thanks for the feedback: The art and science of receiving feedback well.* Penguin Books

4. Wilder, E. J., Khouri, E., Coursey, C., & Sutton, S. (2013). *Joy starts here: The transformation zone.* Independently Published.

5. Brown, B. (2012). *Daring greatly: How the courage to be vulnerable transforms the way we live, love, parent, and lead.* Avery Publishing.

6. Rowland, D. (2020) Redefining autism. Journal of Neurology, Psychiatry, and Brain Research, 20 (2). https://kosmospublishers.com/wp-content/uploads/2020/08/Redefining-Autism.pdf

7. Harden, A., Girgis, R., Lacerda, A., Yorbik, O, Kilpatrick, M., Keshavan, M., & Minshew, N (2006 October). Magnetic resonance imaging study of the orbitofrontal cortex in autism. *Journal of Child Neurology, 21*(10). 866-871ro

8. Girgis, R., Minshew, N., Melhem, N., Nutche, J., Keshavan, M. & Hardan, A. (2007). Volumetric alterations of the orbitofrontal cortex in autism. *Progress in Neuro-Psychopharmacology and Biological Psychiatry, 31*(1), 41-45.r

9. Bachevalier, J., & Loveland, K. (2006). The orbitofrontal-amygdala circuit and self-regulation of social-emotional behavior in autism. *Neuroscience & Biobehavorial Reviews 30*(1), 97-117.

10. O'Doherty, J., Kringelbach, M., Rollis, E., Hornak, J., & Andrews, C. (2001 Jan.). Abstract reward and punishment representations in the human orbitofrontal cortex. *Nature Neurosciences, 4*, 95-102.

11. Völlm, B., Taylor, A., Richardson, P., Corcoran, R., Stirling, J., McKie, S., Deakin, J., & Elliott, R. (2006). Neuronal correlates of theory of mind and empathy: A functional magnetic resonance imaging study in nonverbal task. *NeuroImage, 1,* 90-98.

12. Coursey, C., Brown, A. (2020). *Relational skills in the Bible.* Deeper Walk International.

13. Coursey, C., & Warner, M. (2023). *4 Habits of joy-filled person.* Northfield Publishing.

14. Gill, W.J. (2015). *Face to Face: 7 Keys to Secure Marriage.* WestBow Publisher.

15. Neurodiverse Christian Couples Podcast (2022 May). *Introduction to attachment and relationships with Dr. Gill* [Audio podcast]. https://www.spreaker.com/episode/introduction-to-attachment-and-relationships--49696286Gill, W.J. (2015). *Face to Face: 7 Keys to Secure Marriage.* WestBow Publisher.

16. Wilder, E.J., Friesen, J., Bierling, A., Koepcke, R., & Poole, M. (2013). *Living from the heart Jesus gave you: 15th anniversary edition.* Chicago: Moody Publishers.

17. Chavous, E., Cummins, R., & Miller, L. (2021). *Emotional Intelligence in Christ.* Documeant Publishing.

18. Wilder E.J., & Woolridge, R. (2022). *Escaping enemy mode: How our brains unite or divide us.* Chicago: Moody Publishers.

19. Gottman, J., Gottman, J. M., & Silver, N. (1995). *Why marriages succeed or fail: And how you can make yours last.* Simon and Schuster.

20. Wilder, J., & Warner, M. (2018). *The Solution of Choice: Four good ideas that neutralized Western Christianity.* Deeper Walk International.

21. Clendenen, R. (2021). Hebrew word study: Hesed. https://csbible.com/hebrew-word-study-hesed/#:~:text=When%20someone%20went%20beyond%20what,than%20loyalty%20from%20a%20spouse.

22. Holmes, S., & Holmes, D., Holmes, S., & Holmes, E. (2023). *Embracing the Autism Spectrum: Finding Hope & Joy in the NeuroDiverse Family Journey.* Book Baby Publishers.

23. Metzger, B. (1951). *Jesus and Others and You (JOY).*

24. Scazzero. P. (2017). Emotionally healthy spirituality: It's impossible to be spiritually mature while remaining emotionally immature. Zondervan.

25. Scazzero, P., & Scazzero, G. (2023). Emotionally healthy relationships, expanded edition workbook, plus streaming video: Discipleship that deeply changes your relationship with others. Harper Christian Resources

26. Scazzero, P. (2017). Emotionally healthy relationships day by day: A 40-day journey to deeply change your relationships. Zondervan

27. Cameron, T. (2015). The forty-day word fast: A spiritual journey to eliminate toxic words from your life. Charisma House

28. Gregoire, S. W., Lindenbach, R. G., & Sawatsky, J. (2021). *The great sex rescue: The lies you've been taught and how to recover what God intended.* Baker Books.

29. Wilder, E.J., & Warner, M. (2016). *Rare leadership: 4 uncommon habits for the increasing of trust, joy, and engagement in the people you lead.* Chicago: Moody Publishers.

Chapter 6

1. De Groot, K., & Van Strien, J. W. (2017). Evidence for a broad autism phenotype. *Advances in Neurodevelopmental Disorders, 1,* 129-140.

2. Holmes, S. C. (2023). Neuro Diverse Christian Couples: Autism. Religion. Marriage an Exploratory Qualitative Study. *Int J Psychiatry, 8*(5), 106-116.

3. Raymaker, D. M., Teo, A. R., Steckler, N. A., Lentz, B., Scharer, M., Delos Santos, A., ... & Nicolaidis, C. (2020). "Having all of your internal resources exhausted beyond measure and being left with no clean-up crew": Defining autistic burnout. *Autism in adulthood, 2*(2), 132-143.

4. Miller, W. R., & Rollnick, S. (2012). *Motivational interviewing: Helping people change.* Guilford press.

5. Attwood, A. (2006). *The complete guide to Asperger's syndrome.* Jessica Kingsley Publishers.

6. Cloud, H., & Townsend, J. (2017). *Boundaries updated and expanded edition: When to say yes, how to say no to take control of your life.* Zondervan.

7. Wilkinson, M. (2017). A whole-person approach to dynamic psychotherapy. In M. F. Solomon & D. J. Siegel (Eds.). *How People Change: Relationships and Neuroplasticity in Psychotherapy* (pp. 77-103). WW Norton & Company. HOW DO PEOPLE change?

8. Solomon, M. (2017). How couple therapy can affect long-term relationships and change each of the partners. In M. F. Solomon & D. J. Siegel (Eds.). *How People Change: Relationships and Neuroplasticity in Psychotherapy* (pp. 270-300). WW Norton & Company.

9. Fletcher, T. (2023). *Understanding Trauma – Part 2/3 and 3/3 – Results of Shame* [Video]. YouTube. https://www.youtube.com/playlist?list=PLpvbEN3KkqoL81XgB4Pfl7pMhddi9nkXp

10. Andersen, R. (2023, September 27). *Rejection sensitive dysphoria and autism: Is there a link?* Autism Parenting Magazine. https://www.autismparentingmagazine.com/autism-dysphoria-link/

11. Dodson, W. (2018). How ADHD Ignites Rejection Sensitive Dysphoria. ADDitudeMag.com. https://www.additudemag.com/rejection-sensitive-dysphoria-and-adhd/

12. Fox, T. (2013, July 18). *Stephen M. R. Covey's guide to building trust.* The Washington Post. https://www.washingtonpost.com/news/on-leadership/wp/2013/07/18/stephen-m-r-coveys-guide-to-building-trust/

13. The Holy Bible, New International Version. (1984). International Bible Society. (Original work published 1973).

14. Anderson, N. T. (2000). *Victory Over the Darkness: Realize the Power of Your Identity in Christ.* Gospel Light Publications.

Chapter 7

1. Mehrabian, A. (1971). *Silent messages* (Vol. 8, No. 152, p. 30). Belmont, CA: Wadsworth.

2. American Psychiatric Association. (2013). *Diagnostic and statistical manual of mental disorders (5th ed.).* Arlington, VA: American Psychiatric Publishing.

3. Nason, B. (2014). The Autism Discussion Page on the core challenges of autism: A toolbox for helping children with autism feel safe, accepted, and competent. Jessica Kingsley Publishers.

Chapter 8

1. Moraine, P. (2016). *Autism and everyday executive function.* Jessica Kingsley Publishers.

2. Dawson, P., & Guare, R. (2016). *The smart but scattered guide to success: How to use your brain's executive skills to keep up, stay calm, and get organized at work and at home.* Guilford Publications.

3. Fiedler, M., Hofmann, C., Montag, C., & Kiefer, M. (2023). Factors related to the development of executive functions: A cumulative dopamine genetic score and environmental factors predict performance of kindergarten children in a go/nogo task. *Trends in Neuroscience and Education, 30,* 100200. doi:10.1016/j.tine.2023.100200

4. Hours, C., Recasens, C., & Baleyte, J. M. (2022). ASD and ADHD Comorbidity: What Are We Talking About? *Frontiers in psychiatry, 13*, 837424. doi:10.3389/fpsyt.2022.837424

5. Rodgers, A.L. (2024, April 19). *Hormonal changes & ADHD: A lifelong tug-of-war.* ADDitudeMag.com. https://www.additudemag.com/hormonal-changes-adhd-puberty-postpartum-menopause-andropause/

6. Zelazo P. D., and Carlson S.M., The Neurodevelopment of Executive Function Skills: Implications for Academic Achievement Gaps. Psychology & Neuroscience, 13(3), 273-298. Retrieved January 27, 2024, from https://psycnet.apa.org/fulltext/2020-75726-003.pdf.

7. Barkley, R. A. (2012). *Executive functions: What they are, how they work, and why they evolved.* Guilford Press.

8. Attwood, T. (2008). *The complete guide to Asperger's syndrome.* Jessica Kingsley Publishers. (Reprinted from *London*)

9. Myhill, G., & Jekyll, D. (2008, December). *Asperger Marriage; Partnership through a different lens.* Pathfinders for Autism. http://www.pathfindersforautism.org/wp-content/uploads/2017/01/Asperger-Marriage.pdf

10. Marmorstein, A. (2023, November 1). *AuDHD: When It's ADHD and Autism.* Spectroomz. Retrieved January 27, 2024, from https://www.spectroomz.com/blog/audhd-autism-and-adhd.

11. Craig, F., Margari, F., Legrottaglie, A. R., Palumbi, R., De Giambattista, C., & Margari, L. (2016). A review of executive function deficits in autism spectrum disorder and attention-deficit/hyperactivity disorder. *Neuropsychiatric disease and treatment*, 1191-1202. doi:10.2147/NDT.S104620. PMID: 27274255; PMCID: PMC4869784

12. Townes, P., Liu, C., Panesar, P., Devoe, D., Lee, S. Y., Taylor, G., Arnold, P. D., Crosbie, J., & Schachar, R. (2023). Do ASD and ADHD Have Distinct Executive Function Deficits? A Systematic Review and Meta-Analysis of Direct Comparison Studies. *Journal of attention disorders, 27*(14), 1571–1582. doi:10.1177/10870547231190494

13. American Psychiatric Association, D. S. M. T. F., & American Psychiatric Association. (2013). *Diagnostic and statistical manual of mental disorders: DSM-5* (Vol. 5, No. 5). Washington, DC: American Psychiatric Association.

14. Bölte, S., Neufeld, J., Marschik, P. B., Williams, Z. J., Gallagher, L., & Lai, M. C. (2023). Sex and gender in neurodevelopmental conditions. *Nature Reviews Neurology, 19*(3), 136-159.

15. Grissom, N. M., & Reyes, T. M. (2019). Let's call the whole thing off: Evaluating gender and sex differences in executive function. *Neuropsychopharmacology, 44*(1), 86–96. doi:10.1038/s41386-018-0179-5

16. Mcleod, S. (2023, December). *Carl Rogers Humanistic Theory and Contribution to Psychology.* Simply Psychology. http://www.simplypsychology.org/carl-rogers.html

17. McLeod. (2024, January 24). *Vygotsky's Theory of Cognitive Development.* Simply psychology.com. https://www.simplypsychology.org/vygotsky.html

18. Boston University Medical Center. (n.d.). *The Transtheoretical Model (Stages of Change).* sphweb.bumc.bu.edu. Retrieved January 27, 2024, from https://sphweb.bumc.bu.edu/otlt/MPH-Modules/SB/BehavioralChangeTheories/BehavioralChangeTheories6.html

19. Wilson, B. M., Main, S., O'Rourke, J., & Slater, E. (2023). Needing more, needing less: unravelling why a prompt dependency cycle forms in neurodiverse relationships. *Journal of Social and Personal Relationships, 40*(9), 2892-2917

20. Bercovici, D. (2022, September 21). *Executive challenges in autism & ADHD.* Embrace Autism. Retrieved January 27, 2024, from https://embrace-autism.com/executive-challenges-in-autism-and-adhd/

21. Wilder, E.J., Khouri, E.M., Coursey, C. M. & Sutton, S.D.. (2013) *Joy starts here:*

22. *The transformation zone.* LifeModelWorks.org.

23. Barkley, R. (n.d.). *The important role of executive function and self-regulation in ADHD.* russellbarkley.com. https://www.russellbarkley.org/factsheets/ADHD_EF_and_SR.pdf

24. Alexithymia. (2024, January 28). In *Wikipedia.* https://en.wikipedia.org/wiki/alexithymia

25. Bercovici. D., (2023, April 5). *Pathological demand avoidance, autism, & ADHD.* Embrace Autism. Retrieved January 27, 2024, from https://embrace-autism.com/?s=PDA

26. Bercovici. D., (2023, May 11). *Rejection Sensitive Dysphoria in ADHD & autism.* Embrace Autism. Retrieved January 27, 2024, from https://embrace-autism.com/?s=RSD

27. Frith, U., & Happé, F. (1994). Autism: Beyond "theory of mind". *Cognition, 50*(1-3), 115-132.

28. Kolbert, J., & Nadeau, K. (2002). *ADD-friendly ways to organize your life.* Brunner-Routledge.

29. Gant, V. (2021, August 14). *A new approach to the issue of diversity, equity and inclusion.* https: /www.iheart.com/podcast/256-mind-for-life-31115076/episode/61-

diversity-equity-and-inclusion-85842882/. Retrieved January 27, 2024, from http://www.mindforlife.org/061/

30. Vernick, L. (2013). *The emotionally destructive marriage: How to find your voice and reclaim your hope.* WaterBrook Press.

Chapter 10

1. Chavous, E., Cummins, R., & Miller, L. (2021). *Emotional intelligence in Christ.* Documeant Publishing.

Chapter 11

1. U.S. Center for Disease Control and Prevention. (2023) Community Report on Autism. Spotlight On: Racial and Ethnic Differences in Children Identified with Autism Spectrum Disorder (ASD). https://www.cdc.gov/ncbddd/autism/addm-community-report/spotlight-on-racial-ethnic-differences.html

2. Heasley, S. (2020). *Black children wait longer for autism diagnosis.* Disability-Scoop https://www.disabilityscoop.com/2020/08/25/black-children-wait-longer-autism-diagnosis/28811/

3. Medows-Fernandez, A (2022). *For black families, neurodivergence means challenges- and endless opportunities to redefine parenting.* Parents. https://www.parents.com/kindred/for-black-families-neurodivergence-means-challenges-and-endless-opportunities-to-redefine-parenting/

4. Constantino, J. N., Abbacchi, A. M., Saulnier, C., Klaiman, C., Mandell, D. S., Zhang, Y., ... & Geschwind, D. H. (2020). Timing of the diagnosis of autism in African American children. *Pediatrics, 146*(3). https://www.ncbi.nlm.nih.gov/pmc/articles/PMC7461218/

5. Brawley O. W. (1998). The study of untreated syphilis in the negro male. *International journal of radiation oncology, biology, physics, 40*(1), 5–8. https://doi.org/10.1016/s0360-3016(97)00835-3

6. Yu, Q., Li, E., Li, L., & Liang, W. (2020). Efficacy of interventions based on applied behavior analysis for autism spectrum disorder: A meta-analysis. *Psychiatry investigation, 17*(5), 432.

7. Bible, H. (1996). New living translation. *Gift and Award Edition.*

8. Mar, N. (June 11, 2023). *Unmasking racism in autism diagnosis.* The International Association of NeuroDiverse Christian Marriages. https://www.christianneurodiversemarriage.com/post/unmasking-racism-in-autism-diagnosis

Section 3 Introduction

1. Holmes, S. & Holmes, D. (2024, August). *Autism Q&A with ND clinician & Coach David Glick* [Audio podcast]. https://www.spreaker.com/podcast/neurodiverse
2. Holmes, S. & Holmes, D. (2022, October 24). *Key ingredients to God-honoring marriages- humility, acceptance, vulnerability, teachability & curiosity* [Audio podcast]. https://www.spreaker.com/episode/key-ingredients-to-god-honoring-nd-marriages-humility-acceptance-vulnerability-teachability-curiosity--51483697-christian-couples--4992356

Chapter 12

1. American Psychiatric Association. (2013). *Diagnostic and statistical manual of mental disorders* (5th ed.). American Psychiatric Publishing.
2. Hollander, E. & Ferretti, C. (2023 March). Psychiatric News: American Psychiatric Association. *Special Report: Autism Spectrum Disorder and inflexible thinking- affecting patients across the lifespan.* Retrieved from: https://psychnews.psychiatryonline.org/doi/10.1176/appi.pn.2023.04.4.34
3. Baron-Cohen, S., Leslie, A. M., & Frith, U. (1985). Does the autistic child have a 'theory of mind'? Cognition, 21, 37-46. doi:10.1016/0010-0277(85)90022-8
4. Holmes, S. (2020). Creating an inclusive climate for students on the autism spectrum. School of Education Leadership [Dissertation]. Retrieved from https://digitalcommons.acu.edu/school_ed_leadership/5/
5. Garnett, M. & Attwood, T. (2023). What is high functioning autism? An in-depth look by Dr. Michell Garnett & Professor Tony Attwood. Retrieved from: https://attwoodandgarnettevents.com/high-functioning-autism/
6. Vermeulen, P. (2023). *Autism and the predictive brain: Absolute thinking in a relative world.* London: Routledge.
7. Garnett, M. & Attwood, T. (2023). What is high functioning autism? An in-depth look by Dr. Michell Garnett & Professor Tony Attwood. Retrieved from: https://attwoodandgarnettevents.com/high-functioning-autism/
8. Petrolini, V., Jorba, M., & Vicente, A. (2023 February). Frontiers in Psychiatry. *What does it take to be rigid? Reflections on the notion of rigidity in autism.* Retrieved from https://www.frontiersin.org/articles/10.3389/fpsyt.2023.1072362/full
9. American Psychiatric Association. (1994). *Diagnostic and statistical manual of mental disorders* (4th ed.). American Psychiatric Publishing.

10. Arad, P., Shechtman, Z., & Attwood, T. (2021). Physical and mental well-being of women in neurodiverse relationships: A comparative study. *Journal of Psychology & Psychotherapy, 12*(1), 1–22. https://doi.org/10.21203/rs.3.rs-955119/v1

11. Aston, M. (2009). *The Asperger's couple's workbook: Practical advice and activities for couples and counsellors.* Jessica Kingsley Publishers.

12. Aston, M. (2012). *What men with Asperger Syndrome want to know about women, dating and relationships.* Jessica Kingsley Publishers.

13. Brown, C., & Dunn, W. (2002). *Adolescent/adult sensory profile users' manual.* Psychological Corporation.

14. Attwood, T. (2015). *The complete guide to Asperger's Syndrome.* Jessica Kingsley Publishers.

15. Bolling, K. L. (2015). *Asperger's Syndrome/Autism Spectrum Disorder and marital satisfaction: A quantitate study* (Doctoral dissertation, Antioch University). Available from ProQuest Dissertations.

16. Holmes, S. (2023). NeuroDiverse Christian couples: Autism. Religion. Marriage. An Exploratory qualitative study. *International Journal of Psychiatry, 8* (5),106-116.

17. Myhill, G., & Jekel, D. (2008). *Asperger marriage: Viewing partnership thru a different lens.* Asperger/Autism Network. https://www.aane.org/asperger-marriage-viewing-partnerships-thru-different-lens/

18. Stoddart, K. P., Burke, L., & King, R. (2012). *Asperger's Syndrome in adulthood: A comprehensive guide for clinicians.* Norton Publishers.

19. Crompton, C., Ropar, D., Evans-Williams, C., Flynn, E., Fletcher-Watson, S. (2022). Autistic peer-to peer information transfer is highly effective. *Autism 24*(7), 1704-1712.

20. Pappas, S. (2012, May 30). *Autism may diminish belief in God.* Live Science. https://www.livescience.com/20654-autism-belief-god.html

21. Liu, E., Carter, E., Boehm, T., Annandale, N., & Taylor, C. (2014). In their own words: The place of faith in the lives of young people with Autism and Intellectual Disability. *Intellectual and Developmental Disabilities 52*(5), 388-404.

22. Bustion, O. (2017). Autism and Christianity: An ethnographic intervention. *Journal of American Academcy of Religion, 85*(3), 653–681. https://doi.org/10.1093/jaarel/lfw075

23. Coker, A., Smith, P., Bethea, L., Kig, M., & McKeown, R. (2000). Physical health consequences of physical and psychological intimate partner violence. *Archives of Family Medicine 9*(5), 451–457. https://triggered.clockss.org/ServeContent?url=http://archfami.ama-assn.org/cgi/content/full/9/5/451

24. Lawrence, E., Orengo-Aguayo, R., Langer, A., & Brock R. L. (2012). The impact and consequences of partner abuse on partners. *Partner Abuse,3*(4), 406-428.

25. Vernick, L. (2009). *The emotionally destructive marriage.* WaterBrook Press.

26. Baskerville, G. (2020). *The life-saving divorce: Hope for people leaving Destructive relationships.* Life Saving Press.

27. Lewis, L. (2017). "We will never be normal": The experience of discovering a partner has autism spectrum disorder. *Journal of Marital and Family Therapy,* 1–13. https://doi.org/10.1111/jmft.12231

28. Mitran, C. (2022a). Challenges of licensed counselors and other licensed mental health providers working with neurodiverse adults: An instrumental case study. *The Family Journal.* https://doi.org/10.1177/10664807221123553

29. Tracy, S. & Tracy, C. (2023). *Mending the Soul: Understanding and healing abuse.* 2nd ed. Michigan: Zondervan Reflective.

30. Clinton, T., & Pingleton, J. (2017). *The struggle is real: How to care for mental health and relational needs in the church.* WestBow Publishers.

31. Lyles, M. (2017). How to understand basic bio-physiological issues in mental and relational health. In T. Clinton & J. Pingleton (Eds.), *The struggle is real: How to care for mental health and relational needs in the church* (pp. 45–58). WestBow Publishers.

32. Burns, R. (2017). How to develop an effective divorce recovery ministry. In T. Clinton & J. Pingleton (Eds.), *The struggle is real: How to care for mental health and relational needs in the church* (pp. 353–370). WestBow Publishers.

33. Gregoire, S., Lindenbach, R., & Sawatsky, J. (2023). *She deserves better.* Baker Books.

34. Holmes, S. (2017). How to develop an effective support ministry for parents of autistic and special needs children. In T. Clinton & J. Pingleton (Eds.), *The struggle is real: How to care for mental health and relational needs in the church* (pp. 401–418). WestBow Publishers.

35. Gregoire, S., Lindenbach, R., & Sawatsky, J. (2021). *Great sex rescue.* Baker Books.

36. Strunz, S., Schermuck, C., Roepke, S., Ballerstein,S., Ahlers, C., & Dziobek, I. (2016). Romantic relationships and relationship satisfaction among adults with Asperger Syndrome and High-Functioning Autism. *Journal of Clinical Psychology,* 1-13.

37. AANE (2018). Neurology Matters in Couples Therapy: Training 101 Materials. Fundamentals on Woking with Neurodiverse couples in therapy. Available for purchase at https://aane.thinkific.com/pages/buy

38. Emerson, E. (2004). *Love & Respect: The Love she desires; The respect he desperately needs.* Thomas Nelson Publishing.

39. Brown, F. (2000). Enhanced Brown-Driver-Briggs Hebrew and English Lexicon of the Old Testament. *Bellingham: Logos Research Systems, 296.*

40. Swanson, James. *Dictionary of Biblical Languages with Semantic Domains : Hebrew (Old Testament).* Oak Harbor: Logos Research Systems, Inc., 1997.

41. Sounds of Vision (Admin. By Integrity's Hosanna! Music) (1983). *Blow the Trumpet in Zion.*

Chapter 13

1. Tracy, S. R., & Tracy, C. G. (2023a). *Mending the soul: Understanding and healing abuse.* Zondervan.

2. Downing, Karla (2013). *10 Lifesaving Principles for Women in Difficult Marriages.* Beacon Hill Press of Kansas City; Revised

3. Holmes, S. & Holmes, D. (2022, January 3). *Help for women in complex marriages with Karla Downing* [Audio podcast]. https://www.spreaker.com/episode/help-for-women-in-complex-marriages-with-karla-downing--48129735

4. Tracy, C.G. (2023b). *Mending the soul: Workbook for men and women.* www.mendingthesoul.org

5. Vernick, L. *The emotionally destructive marriage.* Waterbrook, 2013

6. Dye H. L. (2019). Is emotional abuse as harmful as physical and/or sexual abuse? *Journal of child & adolescent trauma, 13*(4), 399–407. https://doi.org/10.1007/s40653-019-00292-y

7. Holmes, S. & Holmes, D. (2022, December 19). *Becoming an emotionally safe man with Andrew Bauman* [Audio podcast]. https://www.spreaker.com/episode/becoming-an-emotionally-safe-man-with-andrew-bauman--52061685

8. Meek, S. (2024). *Determined for More: A Story of Perseverance Through Divorce, Betrayal Trauma, Emotional Deprivation and Autism.* Living Stones Press.

9. Gregoire, S.W., Lindenbach, R.G., & Sawatsky, J. (2021). *The Great sex rescue: The lies you've been taught and how to recover what God intended.* Baker House Books.

10. Arterburn, S., & Stoeker, F. (2000). *Every man's battle: Winning the battle against temptation one victory at a time, first edition.* Waterbrook Press.

11. Gregoire, S.W., Lindenbach, R.G., & Sawatsky, J. (2023). *She deserves better.* Baker House Books.

12. Holmes, S. & Holmes, D. (2024, February 12). *Intimacy & sex: The designer is the definer with Pastor Jamal Baker* [Audio podcast]. https://www.spreaker.com/episode/intimacy-sex-the-designer-is-the-definer-with-pastor-jamal-baker--58421999

13. Rosenau, D. E. (2002). *A celebration of sex: a guide to enjoying God's gift of sexual intimacy.* Thomas Nelson.

14. Penner, C., & Penner, J. J. (2003). *The gift of sex: A guide to sexual fulfillment.* Thomas Nelson.

15. Wilder, E. J., Khouri, E., Coursey, C., & Sutton, S. (2013). *Joy starts here: The transformation zone.* Independently Published.

16. Marter, J. (2022) *Are you a victim of financial abuse or neglect?* PsychologyToday.com. https://www.psychologytoday.com/us/blog/mental-wealth/202209/are-you-victim-financial-abuse-or-neglect

17. Holmes, S. & Holmes, D. (2021). *When helpers cause harm* [Audio podcast]. https://www.audible.com/podcast/When-Helpers-Can-Cause-Harm/B09K5TZ9KW

18. Holmes, S. & Holmes, D. (2024, April 29). *Navigating a complex and adversarial divorce with CDFA Rhonda Nordyk* [Audio podcast]. https://www.spreaker.com/episode/navigating-a-complex-and-adversarial-neurodiverse-divorce-with-cdfa-rhonda-noordyk--59149234

19. Institute for Divorce Financial Analysts. (n.d.). *Find a CDFA® professional.* https://institutedfa.com/find-a-cdfa

20. FindLaw.com. (2023, June 8). *Divorce information by state.* https://www.findlaw.com/family/divorce/divorce-information-by-state.html

21. Holmes, S. (2024). *When autism and narcissism are combined with Jodi Carlton* [Video file]. YouTube. https://www.youtube.com/watch?v=_C7DgVzXs8g&t=10s

22. American Psychiatric Association (APA). (2013). *Diagnostic and statistical manual of mental disorders* (5th ed.). https://doi.org/10.1176/appi.books.9780890425596

23. Wilder, E. J. (2018). *The pandora problem: Facing narcissism in leaders & ourselves.* Deeper Walk International.

24. Water, L. (2018). *When suffering is redemptive: Stories of how anguish and pain accomplish god's mission.* Lexham Publishers.

25. Sweetman, E. (ed.) (2019). *Restored: Ending violence against women.* Restored UK.

26. Psalm 82 Imitative (n.d.). Power over others is anti-Christ. Psalm82initiative.wordpress.com. https://psalm82initiative.wordpress.com/2021/05/20/power-over-others-is-anti-christ/

27. Holmes, S. & Holmes, D. (2022, September 12). *Does Malachi 2:16 say, "God hates divorce?" with Thomas Pryde, part 2* [Audio podcast]. https://www.spreaker.com/episode/does-malachi-2-16-say-god-hates-divorce-with-thomas-pryde-part-2--50945840

28. Hyland P, et al. (2020). Does requiring trauma exposure affect rates of ICD-11 PTSD and complex PTSD? Implications for DSM-5.

29. Instone-Brewer, D. (2006). *Divorce and remarriage in the church: Biblical solutions for pastoral realities. IVP.*

Conclusion

1. Holmes, S. (2023b). Neurodiverse Christian couples: Autism. Religion. Marriage an exploratory qualitative study. *International Journal of Psychiatry, 8*(5), 106-116.

2. Arad, P., Shechtman, Z., & Attwood, T. (2021). Physical and mental well-being of women in neurodiverse relationships: A comparative study. *Journal of Psychology & Psychotherapy, 12*(1), 1–22. https://doi.org/10.21203/rs.3.rs-955119/v1

3. Mitran, C. (2022a). Challenges of licensed counselors and other licensed mental health providers working with neurodiverse adults: An instrumental case study. *The Family Journal.* https://doi.org/10.1177/10664807221123553

4. Myhill, G., & Jekel, D. (2008). *Asperger marriage: Viewing partnership thru a different lens.* Asperger/Autism Network. https://www.aane.org/asperger-marriage-viewing-partnerships-thru-different-lens/

5. Bostick-Ling, J., Cumming, S., & Bundy A. (2012). Life satisfaction of neurotypical women in intimate relationship with an Asperger's partner: A systematic review of the literature. *Journal of Relationships Research,* 1–11. https://doi.org/10.1017/jrr.2012.9

6. Milton, D. (2012). On the ontological status of autism: the 'double empathy problem'. *Disability & Society 27*(6), 883-887.

7. Clinton, T., & Pingleton, J. Eds. (2017). *The struggle is real: How to care for mental health and relational needs in the church.* WestBow Publishers.

8. MacArthur, J. (1993). Rediscovering Biblical counseling. Retrieved from http://articles.ochristian.com/article2279.shtml#:~:text=So%20the%20supreme%20qualification%20for,the%20shallows%20of%20behavior%20modification.

9. Piper, J. & Grudem, W., Eds. (1992). *Recovering Biblical manhood and womanhood: A response to evangelical feminism.* Wheaton: Crossway.

10. Gregoire, S. (2023). *Fixed it for you, Volume 1: Rescuing and Reframing common evangelical messages on sex and marriage.* Bare Marriage.

11. Gregoire, S., Lindenbach, R., & Sawatsky, J. (2021). *Great sex rescue.* Baker Books.

12. Gregoire, S., Lindenbach, R., & Sawatsky, J. (2023). *She deserves better.* Baker Books.

13. Baskerville, G. (2020). *The life-saving divorce.* Life Saving Press.

14. Vernick, L. (2009). *The emotionally destructive marriage.* WaterBrook Press

15. Lewis, L. (2017). "We will never be normal": The experience of discovering a partner has autism spectrum disorder. *Journal of Marital and Family Therapy*, 1–13. https://doi.org/10.1111/jmft.12231

16. Rench, C. (2023). *When eros meets autos: Marriage to someone with Asperger Syndrome.* Presses Universitaires.

17. Wilson, B. (2020 March). The five levels of intimacy. Family Life Canada. Retrieved fromhttps://www.familylifecanada.com/blog/the-five-levels-of-intimacy/

18. Turnock, A., Langley, K., & Jones, C. R. (2022). Understanding stigma in autism: A narrative review and theoretical model. *Autism in Adulthood*, 4(1), 76-91..

19. Brown, C., & Dunn, W. (2002). *Adolescent/adult sensory profile users' manual.* Psychological Corporation.

20. Fusar-Poli, L., Brondino, N., Politi, P., & Aguglia, E. (2022). Missed diagnoses and misdiagnoses of adults with autism spectrum disorder. *European Archives of Psychiatry and Clinical Neuroscience*, 272(2), 187–198. https://doi.org/10.1007/s00406-020-01189-w Epub 2020 Sep 6. PMID: 32892291; PMCID: PMC8866369.

21. Holmes, S. (2023a). Exploring a later in life diagnosis and its impact on marital satisfaction in the lost generation of Autistic adults: An exploratory phenomenological qualitative study. *Global Journal of Intellectual &Developmental Disabilities* 12(1), 1-10.

22. Lai, M., & Baron-Cohen, S. (2015). Identifying the lost generation of adults with autism spectrum conditions. *Psychiatry*, 2(11), 1013–1027.

23. Mitran, C. (2022b). A new framework for examining the impact of neurodiversity in couples in intimate relationships. *The Family Journal*, 30(3), 437–443. https://doi.org/10.1177/10664807211063194

24. Stagg, S., & Belcher, H. (2019). Living with autism without knowing: Receiving a diagnosis in later life. *Health Psychology and Behavioral Medicine*, 7(1), 348–361. https://doi.org/10.1080/21642850.2019.1684920

25. Fleming, J., & Fleming B. (n.d.). Resources found at https://tru316.com/the-eden-podcast/#

Appendix A

1. 1. Wilder, E. J., Khouri, E., Coursey, C., & Sutton, S. (2013). *Joy starts here: The transformation zone.* Independently Published.

2. 2. The International Association of Neurodiverse Christian Marriages. (n.d.). Group coaching. https://www.christianneurodiversemarriage.com/groupcoaching

3. 3. The International Association of Neurodiverse Christian Marriages. (n.d.). Courses. https://www.christianneurodiversemarriage.com/courses

Appendix B

1. 1. The International Association of Neurodiverse Christian Marriages. (n.d.). Courses. https://www.christianneurodiversemarriage.com/courses

Appendix C

1. 1. Autism Spectrum Resources for Marriage & Family, LLC. (n.d.). Courses. www.HolmesASR.com
2. 2. Holmes, S., Holmes D., Holmes S., Holmes, E. (2023). *Embracing the Autism Spectrum: Finding Hope & Joy in the NeuroDiverse Family Journey*. BookBaby.

A free ebook edition is available with the purchase of this book.

To claim your free ebook edition:

1. Visit MorganJamesBOGO.com
2. Sign your name CLEARLY in the space
3. Complete the form and submit a photo of the entire copyright page
4. You or your friend can download the ebook to your preferred device

Morgan James BOGO™

A **FREE** ebook edition is available for you or a friend with the purchase of this print book.

CLEARLY SIGN YOUR NAME ABOVE

Instructions to claim your free ebook edition:
1. Visit MorganJamesBOGO.com
2. Sign your name CLEARLY in the space above
3. Complete the form and submit a photo of this entire page
4. You or your friend can download the ebook to your preferred device

Print & Digital Together Forever.

Snap a photo

Free ebook

Read anywhere